Exploring Science

Exploring Science

The Cognition and Development of
Discovery Processes

David Klahr

*In collaboration with Kevin Dunbar, Anne L. Fay,
David Penner, and Christian D. Schunn*

Foreword by Herbert A. Simon

A Bradford Book

The MIT Press
Cambridge, Massachusetts
London, England

This book was set in Palatino by Graphic Composition, Inc. and was printed and bound in the United States of America.

Library of Congress Cataloging-in-Publication Data
Klahr, David.
    Exploring science: the cognition and development of discovery processes / David Klahr with Kevin Dunbar . . . [et al.]; foreword by Herbert A. Simon.
      p.   cm.
    "A Bradford book."
    Includes bibliographical references and indexes.
    ISBN 0-262-11248-5 (hc.: alk. paper)
    1. Discoveries in science.   I. Title.
Q180.55.D57K55   2000
509—dc21   99-31045
                                                              CIP

To my children
—Anna, Joshua, Sophia, and Benjamin—
for sharing their explorations with me
and to my wife
Pam
for helping each of us
to understand and appreciate
what we discovered.

Contents

Foreword

Some forty years ago came the beginnings of the so-called cognitive revolution, which gradually diverted psychology from the dominant behaviorist framework toward three new directions: a concern with a wider range of tasks than were then in common experimental use, an interest in the specific information processes within the human head that convert stimulus into response, and a tolerance for a wider range of methods of observation and experiment than were admitted by behaviorism.

To be sure, much of this same enrichment had been taking place for some time in German "thought psychology" and Gestalt psychology, but the new developments in cognition contributed a clarity and rigor that enabled both strands of thought, behaviorist and Gestalt, to join in a single powerful stream. Theoretical terms such as "goal," "means-ends analysis," "heuristic search," "understanding," and even "intuition" were given operational meaning, so that their presence or absence in thought processes could be assessed objectively and their interactions observed. Methods of obtaining thinking-aloud protocols from problem solvers and observing eye movements were improved, and the conditions for their validity determined. Symbolic languages for computer programming were developed for expressing psychological theories in rigorous form and testing them by comparison of computer simulations with human experimental data.

Of course, there is thinking and thinking. There is the "routine" thinking of everyday affairs and everyday problem solving that the Gestaltists labeled "nonproductive" to distinguish it from the more complex (and presumably admirable) "productive" thinking. Much of the early work of the cognitive revolution focused on thinking in relatively simple and humdrum tasks, although experimental analysis showed it to be far less "routine" than had been thought, and revealed a set of basic processes that appeared and reappeared in almost every task domain that was studied. Soon we had running models of these processes that could produce the human thought behavior that was observed in a wide range of such tasks.

Success whets ambition: in this instance, the ambition to extend the theories to thinking that was clearly productive, and even "creative." One area that attracted early attention was the process of musical composition; another was chess playing; a third, somewhat later, was the psychology of drawing and painting; a fourth, and the one that is most relevant to this book, was the psychology of scientific discovery. To cover the whole area of human creative activity we would have to add many more, for there is a potential for excellence and creativity in every domain of human endeavor. But all these theories must share many common elements, so that progress in any one casts a great deal of light on the others.

Following this path, psychology has been led to the study of scientific discovery: the processes of observing natural phenomena and designing experiments to elicit new phenomena, the processes of conceiving theories to explain the observed phenomena and testing these theories, the processes of inventing new instruments of observation and improving their power and accuracy. In carrying out this research on discovery, it did not escape notice that there is something childlike about scientific discovery: that the creative scientist nurtures a feeling of wonder about the world and a continual curiosity that is reminiscent of the wonder and curiosity so often displayed by children. Of course, this resemblance is not accidental. The child, too, is discovering a new world, and the processes and methods of the scientist are quite relevant, if in modified form, to the child's learning and exploring.

It is this hypothesized kinship between children (more generally, young people) and scientists that David Klahr and his colleagues have sought out in the innovative and exciting experiments described in this book. They find similarities between children and adults, but also clear differences, leading them to qualify and sharpen the hypothesis of "child as scientist" and its reciprocal of "scientist as child." We see them arriving at a theory of discovery that describes in closely similar terms much of the seeking and learning behavior of both youngsters and mature scientists, thereby enriching our understanding of both. We see them also illuminating the differences between child and adult that the education and experiences we provide to our children must aim at closing.

Wonder and curiosity are still in desperately short supply in a world filled with problems that call for a deep understanding of nature and ourselves. The research reported in this highly instructive book suggests new approaches to preserving the wonder and curiosity of our children as they grow to adulthood, and to enhancing their skills of satisfying that curiosity by exploration and inquiry. Those skills will be critical in permitting them to deal in productive and creative ways with the problems they will encounter in their professional and personal lives, and—perhaps most important of all—in enabling them to preserve a sense of wonder about their world.

Herbert A. Simon

Preface

Here was a first principle not formally recognized by scientific methodologists: When you run onto something interesting, drop everything else and study it. (B. F. Skinner, 1956, p. 223)

In the early 1980s I ran into something very interesting indeed. As Skinner recommended, for quite a while I dropped nearly everything else to study it. Actually, the thing of interest ran into me when one of my graduate students, Jeff Shrager, programmed a toy robotic tank called "Big-Trak" to travel down the corridors of Baker Hall, turn into my office, and startle me with several shots from its laser cannon. "Now *this*," I thought, "is *very* interesting!" I realized that Jeff had produced a solution to several problems that he and I had been struggling with.

One such problem was how to investigate they way in which people construct mental models of moderately complex devices that they encounter in their everyday lives, such as calculators, videocassette recorders, and automatic teller machines. We speculated that by observing people learning to use such devices—without instruction—we might gain some insight into aspects of both device design and complex problem solving. At the time, we were motivated by a mixture of interests in human-computer interaction and complex problem solving. In addition, we were influenced by the work of Herbert Simon and his colleagues on the modeling of the inductive processes underlying several important scientific discoveries (Simon, Langley, and Bradshaw, 1981). We believed that this work was relevant to our interests because we had a vague notion that what people do as they discover how such devices work is not so different from what scientists do when they attempt to discover how the world works. Our problem was to devise a paradigm with which to study these issues.

In addition, I was seeking a context in which to extend my research on how children solve formal problems, such as the Tower of Hanoi (Klahr and Robinson, 1981), to less well-structured domains. Thus, I wanted to include a developmental perspective in any study of learning to use complex devices, but I felt that calculators and automatic teller machines would be too difficult to use with young children. We were familiar with the "simulated research environments" used by Cliff Mynatt, Michael Doherty, and Ryan Tweney (1977) to study hypothesis-testing strategies in adults, and we had been considering the idea of creating our own computer games as a context, but we had not found a satisfactory solution. Then Jeff had the brilliant idea of using a toy he had acquired as an undergraduate: BigTrak. As soon as I saw it come lumbering into my office, I knew that BigTrak was indeed "something interesting" that would enable us to study the processes of scientific discovery in children and adults.

Having selected BigTrak as a suitable context for our work, we went on to use it to study complex cognition in adults. In the investigations of "instructionless learning," adult subjects were simply presented with the BigTrak, *with no instruction whatsoever*, and asked to figure out how it worked. Shrager (1985) argued that in this kind of situation initial hypotheses were generated through an analogy-like process he called "view application," in which previously stored knowledge structures are mapped to specific BigTrak elements. For example, if the "calculator view" is activated, then a mapping is made between BigTrak's keys and calculator keys, and the associated knowledge that calculators have memories is used to hypothesize that BigTrak has one also. Shrager's model focused almost entirely on this first phase of the discovery process (Shrager, 1987).

It soon became clear, however, that with a device as complex as Big-Trak, the instructionless learning approach was too open-ended to provide sufficiently tractable data to support the formulation of a clear theoretical account of the discovery process in adults (see Shrager and Klahr, 1986), and too difficult for children. At this point we made a small but important change in our paradigm. We decided that rather than give people *no* information about how BigTrak worked, we would provide instruction on its basic commands, and then ask people to discover only one additional complex function. We felt that by providing the initial training we would have a much stronger analogy to the real world of scientific discovery in which scientists are always working in a context of a body of knowledge that they then attempt to extend. Moreover, because this initial training was mastery-based, it allowed us to reduce some of the variance in the initial domain-specific knowledge with which our subjects started their discovery efforts.

From this evolved the program of research on the developmental psychology of scientific discovery described in this book. The nine studies described here include a description and theoretical analysis of children and adults attempting to make discoveries about a variety of systems, including BigTrak (chapters 4 and 5), its computer-based isomorphs (chapters 5 and 6), and an even more complex discovery microworld (chapter 7). After all these years, I still find people's behavior as they attempt to make discoveries in these microworlds extremely interesting and revealing about the psychology of the discovery process. Skinner's advice was, I believe, well taken.

Acknowledgments

Although this book focuses on the cognitive processes of the individual scientist, science is a highly social activity. In preparing this book I have benefited from the support of many colleagues and several institutions, and I extend my gratitude to each of them. First and foremost are the four people listed on the title page of this volume: Kevin Dunbar, Anne Fay, David Penner, and Chris Schunn. I have been fortunate to work with this set of creative and gifted colleagues, and the core empirical chapters of this book are based on research done in collaboration with them. Although I do not hold them responsible for the way our collaborative work was integrated into this book, they shared equally in the conception, execution, and writing of the initial reports upon which much of the work in this book is based. In Chris's case, even the writing of the chapter in this volume was done collaboratively.

Another set of colleagues provided me with various levels of feedback and commentary. Jennifer Schnakenberg meticulously read the first draft and provided a dauntingly long list of typos, inconsistencies, and other types of errors. Her keen eye continued to help improve the final product through the subsequent phases of copyediting, proofreading, and indexing—this time with the added assistance of Anne Siegel and Jolene Watson. Jen also assisted in the preparation of the reference list and the illustrations in this volume, as did my secretaries David Pickering and Virginia Fraser.

The participants in my seminar on scientific discovery read subsequent drafts of all the chapters and made many useful suggestions. This group included, at various times, Sharon Carver, Zhe Chen, Kevin Crowley, Nobuyuki Fujimura, Jeremy Gottlieb, Kevin Grobman, Heisawn Jeong, Oh-Seek Kwon, Bethany Rittle-Johnson, Sharon Roque, Christian Schunn, Toshiya Tanaka, Douglas Thompson, Eva Erdosne Toth, and Martha Ziegler. Finally, as the book neared completion, extremely valuable comments were provided by several of the MIT Press reviewers, especially Josh Klayman, and by two colleagues, Shari Ellis and Bob Siegler. Their comments made the book substantially better integrated than it would have been otherwise. The entire publication process was smoothly and effectively handled by editors Amy Brand and Deborah Cantor-Adams at MIT Press: their contributions make me feel both fortunate and wise about my choice of publisher.

The BT and Dancer microworlds were programmed by Philip Lee and Matthew Day and then substantially enhanced by Chris Schunn. David Andersen helped prepared them for distribution over the Internet. Special thanks to Margaret Kinsky, who played several different roles in this project including research assistant, secretary, artist, and even costume designer and seamstress (see figure 5.1).

Many people and institutions supported this work by allowing their students and children to participate in our various studies. I am indebted to the parents, administrators, and teachers at the Carnegie Mellon Children's School, the Ellis School, Community Day School, and the Community College of Allegheny County for their enthusiastic cooperation with this project. During the course of the studies reported here, financial support came from the National Institute of Child Health and Human Development, the A. W. Mellon Foundation, and the James S. McDonnell Foundation.

Three people—of startlingly different intellectual and personal styles—helped shape this project by profoundly influencing my personal values and scientific ideas over an extended period. It is clear that this book would not have existed without Herbert Simon's pioneering contributions to the psychology of scientific thinking. The influence of two other colleagues and friends may not be apparent to anyone but me: I sadly regret that neither Allen Newell nor Richard Schoenwald lived long enough for me to present them with a copy of this book as a token of my appreciation.

Finally, I thank my family for encouraging me to pursue this project while keeping me sufficiently engaged in their lives that I managed to enjoy the whole endeavor.

Chapter 1
Investigating Scientific Thinking: Why and How

The whole of science is nothing more than a refinement of everyday thinking. It is for this reason that the critical thinking of the physicist cannot possibly be restricted to the examination of concepts of his own specific field. He cannot proceed without considering critically a much more difficult problem, the problem of analyzing the nature of everyday thinking.
(Einstein, 1936, p. 59)

More than sixty years have passed since Albert Einstein made this remarkable statement. In that time there have been enormous advances in our understanding of the "difficult . . . problem of analyzing the nature of everyday thinking." Indeed, the fundamental premise of this book is that we now know enough about cognition that we can return to the first part of Einstein's statement and use what we know about everyday thinking to advance our understanding of scientific thinking.

What, then, is scientific thinking? How is it related to everyday thinking? What is its developmental course? In other words, what are the cognitive and developmental processes that have enabled scientists to make the discoveries that comprise the prodigious body of information we call "scientific knowledge"? The aim of this book is to provide some partial answers to these questions. The book describes a series of studies with children and adults conducted in my laboratory over the past decade. The purpose of these studies has been to investigate scientific discovery processes in the psychology laboratory by creating discovery contexts that evoke the kind of thinking characteristic of scientific discovery in the "real world." I will argue that when participants attempt to solve the problems posed by our discovery tasks, they invoke many of the same higher-order cognitive processes that scientists use as they practice their trade. By carefully analyzing the behavior of our participants as they solve the discovery problems we pose for them, we hope to shed some light on the psychology of scientific discovery.

Our approach is but one of several ways of understanding science, and in this chapter, I place our work in the larger context of what has come to be called "science studies." Before turning to that context, however, I offer a few justifications for the endeavor itself.

Why Study Science?

The doing of science has long attracted the attention of philosophers, historians, anthropologists, and sociologists. More recently, psychologists also have begun to turn their attention to the phenomenon of scientific thinking, and there is now a large and rapidly growing literature on the psychology of science. (A good description of the field in its infancy can be found in Tweney, Doherty, and Mynatt, 1981, and a recent summary of topics and findings from investigations of the developmental, personality, cognitive and social psychology of science can be found in Feist and Gorman, 1998.)

What accounts for the appeal of science as an object of study? The answer varies somewhat according to discipline. From my perspective as a cognitive scientist, I see five reasons for studying science: to appreciate its human and humane value, to understand its mythology, to study the processes of human thinking in some of its most creative and complex forms, to gain insight into the developmental course of scientific thinking, and to design artifacts—computer programs and associated instrumentation—that can carry out some of the discovery processes of science and aid human scientists in carrying out others. I will describe each of these later.

Value

The nature of human thinking is one of the "Big Questions," along with the nature of matter, the origin of the universe, and the nature of life. The kind of thinking we call "scientific" is of special interest, both for its apparent complexity and for its products. Scientific thinking has enhanced our ability to understand, predict, and control the natural forces that shape our world. As the myths of Prometheus and Pandora forewarned us, scientific discoveries have also provided foundations for a technical civilization fraught with opportunities, problems, and perils; and we call on science increasingly to help us solve some of the very problems it has inadvertently created. The processes that produced these outcomes are irresistible objects of study. Indeed, the same forces that motivate physicists, chemists, mathematicians, and biologists to understand the important phenomena in their domains drive historians, philosophers, sociologists, and psychologists to investigate science itself.

Mythology
There is a rich mythology about the ineffability of the scientific discovery process. This has produced a paradoxical view of science as magic, a view that has captured the romantic imagination. As Boden (1990, p. 288) puts it in her book on the psychology of creativity, "The matters of the mind have been insidiously downgraded in scientific circles for several centuries. It is hardly surprising then if the myths sung by inspirationalists and romantics have been music to our ears. While science kept silent about imagination, antiscientific songs naturally held the stage."

Moreover, in many cases, the mythology has been promulgated as much by scientists as by nonscientists. "I am not sure," says Albert Einstein in one of his discussions with Max Wertheimer, "whether there can be a way of really understanding the miracle of thinking" (p. 227). Although Einstein suggests that we may never "really understand" cognitive processes, it is clear from the quotation that opens this chapter that he does allow that the same processes that support everyday thought also support scientific thought. In another context, he reiterates the same point: "The scientific way of forming concepts differs from that which we use in our daily life, not basically, but merely in the more precise definition of concepts and conclusions; more painstaking and systematic choice of experimental material, and greater logical economy" (Einstein, 1950, p. 98).

I believe that Einstein was wrong about the first claim (that thinking is miraculous) and correct about the second (that scientific concept formation is not qualitatively different from the everyday variety). One of the goals of this book is to show how normal cognitive processes enable humans to generate the "precise definitions," "systematic choice of experimental material," and "logical economy" that Einstein identifies as the hallmarks of scientific thought. The hope is that intense investigation of the cognitive processes that support scientific thinking can contribute to the demystification of the discovery process.

Pressing the Limits
A common scientific strategy for understanding a complex system is to explore its behavior at the boundaries. "Pushing the envelope" allows us to test whether the same mechanisms that account for normal performance can account for extreme performance. For example, the same forces that account for lift in an airplane's airfoil also account for stalls, but the mechanisms of subsonic flight cannot fully account for the dynamics of supersonic flight. In human cognition, the *products* of scientific thinking lie at the boundaries of thought capabilities. They epitomize the systematic, and cumulative construction of our view of the world around

us (and in us). Scientific knowledge represents, as David Perkins (1981) puts it, "the mind's best work."

There are other manifestations of cognitive excellence, but science has an internal criterion of progress that sets scientific discovery somewhat apart from other complex human thought, such as the creation of new art or political institutions. This contrast between progress in science and in other endeavors is modestly argued in the following excerpt from a letter written in 1894 by Pierre Curie to Marie Sklodovska, soon to be Madame Curie:

> It would be a fine thing, just the same, in which I hardly dare believe, to pass our lives near each other, hypnotized by our dreams: your patriotic dream, our humanitarian dream, and our scientific dream.
>
> Of all those dreams the last is, I believe, the only legitimate one. I mean by that that we are powerless to change the social order and, even if we were not, we should not know what to do; in taking action, no matter in what direction, we should never be sure of not doing more harm than good, by retarding some inevitable evolution. From the scientific point of view, on the contrary, we may hope to do something; the ground is solider here, and any discovery that we may make, however small, will remain acquired knowledge. (Schuster, 1940, p. 422)

Although the products of science reach one of the limits of human thought, it remains an open question whether or not the processes that support creative scientific discovery are substantially different from those found in more commonplace thinking. The working hypothesis in this book is that they are not.[1] Sir Francis Crick's (1988) reflections on the processes leading to discovery of the structure of DNA concur with this view: "I think what needs to be emphasized about the discovery of the double helix is that the path to it was, scientifically speaking, fairly commonplace. What was important was *not the way it was discovered*, but the object discovered—the structure of DNA itself" (p. 67; emphasis added).

Although Crick views the thinking that led him and James Watson to make this remarkable discovery as "fairly commonplace" scientific thinking, he stops short of the additional claim—made by Einstein—that commonplace scientific thinking is not basically different from everyday thinking. Combined, the two claims support the view that one can study scientific thinking by, for example, examining the thought processes of participants in psychology experiments. Even if the discoveries that participants make in such experiments—the products of their inquiries—are of no scientific significance, the explication of the processes used to make those discoveries can add to our understanding of real-world scientific discovery.

Developmental Paradox
Psychological investigations have produced diametrically opposing views of the development of scientific reasoning skills with reasonable arguments and supporting evidence on both sides. On one side are those who view the child as a scientist, and on the other side are those who view scientific thinking as manifest only in those with extraordinary mental skills and extensive formal training. The positive view of the child-as-scientist issue is exemplified by the assertion that "the child can be thought of as a novice scientist, who adopts a rational approach to dealing with the physical world, but lacks the knowledge of the physical world and experimental methodology accumulated by the institution of science" (Brewer and Samarapungavan, 1991, p. 210). In a similar vein, Annette Karmiloff-Smith (1988) concludes from her studies, "Clearly, children go about their task as true scientists do, building theories about the physical, social and linguistic worlds, rather than reasoning as inductive logicians" (p. 193). Advocates of this view "talk about our everyday conceptions of the world as implicit or intuitive theories, and about changes in those conceptions as theory changes" (Gopnik, 1997). The argument is that children use the same cognitive processes as do scientists in making sense of the world and in generating new knowledge about it. In its most poetic form, this characterization of the child as scientist sometimes takes on an aura of lost innocence, as in the following claim from a dean of science at a major university: "Children are born scientists. From the first ball they send flying to the ant they watch carry a crumb, children use science's tools—enthusiasm, hypothesis, tests, conclusions—to uncover the world's mysteries. But somehow students seem to lose what once came naturally" (Elder, 1990).

However, not everyone is convinced by such claims. Deanna Kuhn (1989) concludes her extensive investigations of how adults and children understand the complementary roles of theory and evidence in scientific argumentation by asserting that: "the process in terms of which mental models, or theories, are coordinated with new evidence is significantly different in the child, the lay adult, and the scientist. In some very basic respects, children (and many adults) do not behave like scientists" (p. 687).

One can find empirical support for each of these incompatible positions. On the one hand, many investigators (e.g., Kuhn, Amsel, and O'Loughlin, 1988; Kern, Mirels, and Hinshaw, 1983; Siegler and Liebert, 1975) have demonstrated that trained scientists, and even untrained lay adults, commonly outperform children on a variety of scientific reasoning tasks. On the other hand, the developmental literature is replete with reports indicating that very young children demonstrate surprising competence at formulating theories (Brewer and Samarapungavan, 1991; Wellman and Gelman, 1992; Karmiloff-Smith, 1988), reasoning about critical experiments (Sodian, Zaitchik and Carey, 1991; Samarapungavan, 1992), and evaluating evidence (Fay and Klahr, 1996), whereas adults demonstrate systematic and serious flaws in their reasoning (Kuhn, Amsel, and O'Loughlin, 1988; Schauble and Glaser, 1990), even after years of formal scientific training (Mitroff, 1974).

The conflicting theoretical claims and empirical results emerging from the child-as-scientist debate have important implications for science education. Moreover, the debate raises some deep questions about how both scientists and children "really" think—questions that can only be approached through more precise formulation and study of the empirical and the theoretical aspects of scientific thinking and discovery. Indeed, that is one of the primary goals of this book.

Machines in the Scientific Process
The final reason for studying science is that such study may lead to better science. What we learn about the science of science leads into a kind of "engineering of science" in which—as in other areas—we use our knowledge of a natural process to create artifacts that accomplish the same ends by improved means.

This has already happened for scientific discovery, as computational models used as theories of discovery in specific domains have been transformed into computer programs that actually do some of the discovery in these domains. An early example of this transition from psychological model to expert system was the DENDRAL program, which taking mass spectrogram data as input, identified the molecules that had produced the spectra. Among the descendants of DENDRAL are programs that carry out automatically much of the analysis for genome sequencing in biology, and programs that, independently or in association with human scientists, discover plausible reaction paths for important chemical reactions.

Recent examples include Raul Valdés-Pérez's (1994a, 1994b, 1994c) systems for discoveries in chemistry and physics, Siemion Fajtlowicz's in mathematics (Erdos, Fajtlowicz, and Staton, 1991), James Hendrickson's program for the synthesis of organic compounds (Hendrickson and Sander, 1995), and Janice Callahan and Stephen Sorensen's (1992) systems for making discoveries in the social sciences (see Valdés-Pérez, 1995, and Darden, 1997, for brief reviews of recent work in the field). These systems will not be described in this book, but they are worthy of note because, in the long run, ideas from expert-systems research are likely to make further contributions to the theory of human scientific thinking; and vice versa, components of human discovery processes may be embedded in practical expert systems.

Why Study Scientific Discovery?
Scientific discovery is a highly attractive area for research because it possesses relevance to one of the great scientific questions, a mythology, a domain for testing theory at the limits, a developmental paradox, and direct applicability to expert system design. How does one go about doing such research? In the next section, I address this question.

How to Study Science

Empirical investigations of science can be organized into five partially overlapping categories: (1) historical approaches, (2) sociological approaches, (3) computational modeling, (4) on-line studies of real science, and (5) studies of "simulated science" in the psychology laboratory. All of the work described in this book falls into the last of these categories. However, in order to put our work in a broader context, I will briefly describe the other approaches.

Historical Approaches
Historical accounts of scientific discovery usually aim at describing the cognitive and motivational processes of persons who have made major contributions to scientific knowledge. To varying degrees, they examine both the processes germane to the scientific problems themselves ("internalist" accounts) and the interaction of these processes with the broader social environment ("externalist" accounts). The data for these analyses derive from diaries, scientific publications, autobiographies, lab notebooks, correspondence, interviews, grant proposals, and memos (Duncan and Tweney, 1997; Galison, 1987; Gooding, 1990; Gruber, 1974; Holmes, 1985; Ippolito and Tweney, 1995; John-Steiner, 1997; Nersessian, 1992; Thagard, 1992) as well as assessments of scientists' personalities (Feist, 1991, 1994; Terman, 1954). These sources are sometimes further enriched by retrospective interviews with the scientists—for example, Wertheimer's (1945) classic analysis of Einstein's development of special relativity, or Thagard's (1998) analysis of the recent discovery of the bacterial origin of stomach ulcers.

Historical studies have very high face validity because, by definition, they investigate the very phenomena that they seek to explain. Topic and scope are chosen after the fact, so there is no doubt that a real discovery by a real scientist is the focus of investigation. The temporal resolution of such investigations depends on the sources of data available. It is quite coarse when the primary sources are publications; but it can become much finer—on a scale of days, say—to the extent that laboratory notebooks and correspondence are available. However, historical studies seldom permit the study of anything approaching minute-by-minute, or even hour-by-hour sequences of the scientists' thoughts.

Given the unique and often idiosyncratic aspects of the interaction between a particular scientist, a particular state of scientific knowledge, and a particular discovery, historical studies are highly likely to generate new phenomena. The downside of this potential for novelty is low external validity. It is low because such investigations, for example, Gooding's analyses of Faraday's extensive and meticulous notebooks (Gooding, 1990), are limited to a single scientist. Nevertheless, as such studies accumulate they can be treated collectively as a sample of events that can be compared and contrasted to find the underlying general laws.

But from the perspective of a cognitive psychologist, historical approaches suffer from the subjective and unverifiable nature of much of the raw data. Even when based on daily lab notebooks, the data are subject to all of the self-reporting biases that make retrospective verbal reports less rigorous than concurrent verbal protocols (Ericsson and Simon, 1993). And when the accounts are based on the recollections and introspections provided in autobiographies of great scientists (e.g., Hadamard, 1945; Poincaré, 1929), or by systematic interviews with scientists about their work (e.g., Rowe, 1953) reliability is always in doubt: "But did they *really* think this way?" asks Nancy Nersessian (1992) of her own analysis of Maxwell's discovery of electromagnetic field theory. "In the end we all face the recorded data and know that every piece is in itself a reconstruction by its author" (p. 36). Simon (1986) makes the point even more colorfully:

> But there is something a little unseemly about depending wholly on the volunteered testimony of scientists for our understanding of the psychology of scientific research. It is a little like putting a Geiger Counter on the podium and asking it to deliver a lecture on physical theory. We do not ask the Geiger Counter for theory: we ask it for data so that *we* may construct a theory. By the same token, what scientists say about their discovery processes, however veridical it may turn out to be, has to be taken not as a theory of those processes, but as data from which such a theory may be constructed. (p. 159)

Sociological Approaches
These analyses attempt to account for the major discoveries in terms of political, anthropological, or social forces (Bloor, 1981; Pickering, 1992;

Sadish and Fuller, 1994). In these approaches, the mechanisms linking such forces to actual scientific practice are usually motivational, social-psychological, or psychodynamic, rather than cognitive processes (Bijker, Hughes, and Pinch, 1987). An interdisciplinary amalgam of such studies has developed under the rubric "social studies of science" (for examples, see Mahoney, 1979; Laudan, 1977). This orientation to the study of science has provided us with important accounts of the contexts in which scientists do their work. However, such accounts (e.g., Latour and Woolgar, 1986) are all at a large "grain size" with respect to the questions addressed in this book.

Some of this work has taken on a distinctly deconstructionist tone that serious scientists have justifiably denounced (Gross and Levitt, 1994) and even parodied (Sokal, 1996). From my perspective the deconstructionist path is unfortunate, because it has led some people in the physical and biological sciences to conclude mistakenly that all "social science approaches"—including cognitive psychology—have little to contribute to a better understanding of science. Fortunately, such criticism does not apply to the work presented in this book because the work conforms to the same canons of science as the fields it aims to better understand.

Computational Models of Discovery
The goal of work in this area is to formulate theories of different aspects of the scientific discovery process in sufficiently precise terms to be cast in the form of a computational model. In assessing such models, it is necessary to distinguish between different goals in the fields of artificial intelligence (AI) and cognitive psychology. The goal in artificial intelligence is to understand the abstract nature of intelligent computation as well as to create systems that exhibit intelligence, whereas the goal in cognitive psychology is to understand how intelligence is manifested in humans. Computational models of discovery differ in the extent to which they emphasize either AI or cognitive psychology goals—that is, whether they are intended either as systems to actually *do* science, or as cognitive theories, or as a bit of both. Thus, some models focus on artificial-intelligence goals without regard for psychological plausibility. "The goal [of such models] is not the simulation of human scientists, but the making of discoveries about the natural world, using methods that extend human cognitive capacities" (Darden, 1992, p. 252). Examples include Valdés-Pérez's (1994*a*, 1994*b*, 1994*c*) systems for discoveries in chemistry and physics, Fajtlowicz's in mathematics (Erdos, Fajtlowicz, and Staton, 1991), Hendrickson's program for the synthesis of organic compounds (Hendrickson and Sander, 1995), and Callahan and Sorensen's (1992) systems for making discoveries in the social sci-

ences (see Valdés-Pérez, 1995). (See Darden, 1997, for a brief review of recent work in the field.)

More relevant to our focus are models that try to replicate the cognitive processes of major scientists as they made important scientific discoveries. In this approach, one constructs computational models of key steps in the discovery process (see Shrager and Langley, 1990, for an introduction to this literature). The approach relies on the same types of information as the psychohistorical accounts, in that it also looks at the historical record. However, it goes well beyond the traditional psycho-historical accounts by proposing cognitive mechanisms sufficiently specific to be cast as computational models that can make the same discoveries as did the focal scientist. To the extent that any computational model of concept formation or rule induction has relevance for the scientific discovery process, this approach has a long history (Hovland and Hunt, 1960; Simon and Kotovsky, 1963). More recent (and much more complex) examples of the approach are epitomized by the pioneering work of Simon and his colleagues. They have formulated computational models of the cognitive processes used by Kepler, Glauber, Krebs, and others in making their discoveries (Cheng and Simon, 1992; Kulkarni and Simon, 1990; Simon, Langley, and Bradshaw, 1981; Langley et al., 1987).

On-line Studies of Real Science
The most direct way to study science is to study scientists as they ply their trade. The observer records the important activities of day-to-day lab meetings, presentations, and pre- and post-meeting interviews, lab notes and paper drafts. The raw data are then coded and interpreted within the framework of psychological constructs.

Both pragmatic and substantive factors make direct observation extraordinarily difficult, and therefore the least common approach to studying science. It requires the trust and permission of the scientists to allow an observer in their midst. The observer must be sufficiently well versed in the domain of investigation to understand deeply what is happening and what the fundamental issues, problems and solutions are.[2] Moreover, it is extremely time-consuming. One recent exemplary case of this approach can be found in Kevin Dunbar's studies of four different world-class labs for research in molecular genetics (Dunbar, 1994, 1997; Dunbar and Baker, 1994). Giere's (1988, chap. 5) account of how a high energy physics lab is organized provides a somewhat similar example of the *"in vivo"* approach, in contrast to the *"in vitro"* approach of laboratory experiments.

Simulated Science in the Psychology Laboratory
Research in this category includes psychological studies of participants' thinking processes in contexts designed to present several important

characteristics of scientific problems. The general paradigm is to present people with situations crafted to isolate one or more essential aspects of "real world" science and to carefully observe their problem-solving processes. As noted, Dunbar has called these types of studies *in vitro* investigations of scientific thinking. Because most of the work described in this book falls into this category, I am not unbiased in my assessment of its merits, of which I see several:

1. Such studies allow the researcher great latitude in selecting the type of subject under investigation. Participants can be selected from populations having interesting characteristics (e.g., scientists, college sophomores, math majors, schoolchildren, and so on).

2. The approach enables the researcher to exert substantial control over participants' prior knowledge, through the type of selection mentioned above, and through various levels of background training in the domain under investigation.

3. Laboratory studies facilitate the observation of the dynamic course of scientific discovery in great detail, and the corresponding use of a variety of assessment methodologies, such as rule analyses (Siegler, 1976), which focus on detailed characterizations of individual strategies, and microgenetic studies (Kuhn et al., 1995; Siegler and Jenkins, 1989), which focus on detained, finegrained analysis of the acquisition of new strategies.

4. These types of investigations enable one to control the "state of nature," that is, the thing to be discovered by the participants. Such studies have used a variety of things to be discovered, including (1) an arbitrary rule that the experimenter has in mind (Gorman, 1992; Wason, 1960); (2) a computer microworld that embodies some natural causal factors and some arbitrary ones such as the effect of engine size, wheel size, color, and body type on the speed of race cars (Schauble, 1990); (3) the causal factors in a real physical domain, such as the effects of various shapes, weights, and channel depths on the speed of model boats (Schauble et al., 1991) or the effects of size, shape, and material on the sinking rates of objects dropped in water (Penner and Klahr, 1996*a*); (4) the physics of a complex artificial universe (Krems and Johnson, 1995; Mynatt, Doherty, and Tweney, 1977); and (5) a computer microworld designed to capture the essential features of an historical discovery, such as a microworld in which participants, in effect, reenacted Jacob and Monod's discovery of the mechanism of genetic inhibition (Dunbar, 1993; Okada and Simon, 1997; Schunn and Dunbar, 1996).

5. Perhaps the most valuable characteristic of laboratory studies is that they enable us to look at failures as well as successes. The

historical record of scientific discovery focuses more on the latter than on the former. Although it has produced a literature that attempts explain why, in situations where a "race" for some discovery occurred, one lab succeeded while others failed (Crick, 1988; Judson, 1979), the myriad failures of scientific discovery remain underreported and underexamined. Laboratory studies can be of special value in this connection, for they allow investigators to control precisely the variables that are hypothesized to affect success and failure (e.g., Dunbar, 1993; Gorman, 1992; Penner and Klahr, 1996), or to examine some of the detailed differences in processes used by successful and unsuccessful participants.

Some observers have expressed doubt about the ecological validity of laboratory studies (Giere, 1993). They claim that the things being discovered in the laboratory are poor imitations of authentic scientific discoveries and are unlikely to invoke the same psychological processes that real scientists use as they go about their everyday work. But even the simplest of such studies taps the same everyday mental processes that are fundamental to scientific thinking. As I argued earlier in citing Francis Crick's account of the discovery of DNA, major scientific discoveries are not so labeled because they derive from any unusual thought processes, but rather because the knowledge that they produce is important.

One of the first psychologists to make the case for the "nothing special" view of scientific thinking was Simon (1966), who pointed out that information-processing theories of human problem solving could account for many of the "unique" characteristics of scientific discovery. This view has been elaborated more recently—particularly with respect to the issue of creativity—by several others, including Margaret Boden (1990, 1994), David Perkins (1981), Herbert Simon, Pat Langley, and Gary Bradshaw (1981), and Robert Weisberg (1993). The success of Simon's computational models—based as they are on a small set of relatively straightforward heuristics for finding regularity in existing data sets—provides further support for this position.

Note that I am not suggesting that the average person could walk into a scientist's lab and proceed to make discoveries. It is clear that practitioners of a scientific discipline must acquire an extensive portfolio of relatively particular methods and techniques during their long professional training. Furthermore, these techniques are applied in the context of an immense, cumulative, shared, and public knowledge base. This base includes facts about the discipline—its procedures, instrumentation, experimental paradigms, and data-analytic methods, not to mention its history, funding procedures, political implications, institutional structure, and even its publication practices (see Bazerman, 1988). But these all comprise what are called in the psychological literature "strong" or "domain-specific" methods. The mental processes we are focusing on are the "weak methods": domain-general, universal, problem-solving processes. Clearly, the strong methods used in scientific problem solving distinguish it from everyday thought. However, my claim is that the weak methods invoked by scientists as they ply their trade are the same ones that underlie all human cognition.

Thus, the challenge in creating discovery contexts with which to study the psychology of scientific discovery is to find a way to evoke these weak methods in contexts that mimic some of the richness and interconnectedness of the domain-specific knowledge and processes inherent in scientific discovery, while at the same time maintaining the experimental rigor that supports sound inferences about human cognition. This is not an easy task, and there have been several different approaches to understanding the cognitive psychology of scientific thinking. In the next section I review and categorize these different types of investigations.

A Taxonomy of Laboratory Investigations of the Cognitive Psychology of Science

Laboratory investigations of scientific reasoning can be classified along two dimensions: one representing the degree of domain-specificity or domain-generality, and the other representing the type of processes involved. Table 1.1 depicts this characterization of the field. The two rows correspond to the difference between domain-general knowledge and domain-specific knowledge, and the three columns correspond to the major components of the overall discovery process: generating hypotheses, designing experiments, and evaluating evidence.

Distinctions between Domain-General and Domain-Specific Knowledge
Both domain-specific and domain-general knowledge influence the scientific reasoning process. On the one hand, acquisition of domain-specific knowledge not only changes the substantive structural

Table 1.1
Types of foci in psychological studies of scientific reasoning processes.

	Hypothesis Generation	Experiment Design	Evidence Evaluation
Domain-specific knowledge	A	B	C
Domain-general knowledge	D	E	F

knowledge in the domain (by definition) but also influences the processes used to generate and evaluate new hypotheses in that domain (Carey, 1985; Keil, 1981; Wiser, 1989). Thus, it is not surprising that, after years of study in a specific domain, scientists exhibit reasoning processes that are purported to be characteristic of the field (e.g., "she thinks like a physicist") and very different from those used by experts in other fields, or by novices or children. On the other hand, in simple contexts that are nearly devoid of domain-specific knowledge, professional scientists are not distinguishable from lay persons (Mahoney and DeMonbreun, 1978), and even first graders can reason correctly about hypotheses and select appropriate experiments to evaluate them (Sodian, Zaitchik, and Carey, 1991).

Psychologists' attempts to disentangle the relative influence of general versus specific knowledge have produced two distinct literatures: one on domain-specific knowledge and the other on domain-general reasoning processes. This distinction, corresponding to the two rows in table 1.1, will be illustrated later, once I have described the other dimension in the table.

Processes in Scientific Reasoning
The three columns in table 1.1 reflect a view of scientific discovery as a problem-solving process involving search in a problem space (Newell and Simon, 1972). In the case of scientific discovery, there are two primary spaces to be searched: a space of hypotheses and a space of experiments (Klahr and Dunbar, 1988). In chapter 2 I will provide a detailed account of problem space search and these two spaces in particular. At this point I provide only a brief sketch. These spaces are sufficiently different that they require different representations, different operators for moving about in the space, and different criteria for what constitutes progress in the space. The distinction between searching the hypothesis space and searching the experiment space is sufficiently important that in the natural sciences people are often trained to be experts in one, but not the other, aspect of their discipline: for example, as theorists or as experimentalists. It is clear that the problems to be solved in each space are different, even though they have obvious and necessary mutual influences.

Search in the two spaces requires three major interdependent processes: hypothesis space search, experiment space search, and evidence evaluation. In searching the hypothesis space, the initial state consists of some knowledge about a domain, and the goal state is a hypothesis that can account for some or all of that knowledge. When one or more hypotheses are under consideration, it is not immediately obvious what constitutes a "good" experiment. In constructing experiments, scientists are faced with a problem-solving task paralleling their search for hypotheses. That is, they must search in the experiment space for an informative experiment. The third process—evidence evaluation—involves a comparison of the predictions derived from the current hypothesis with the results obtained from experimentation. The columns in table 1.1 correspond to these three processes.

Each of these processes will be further elaborated in chapter 2, but for now it suffices to think of them in terms of the conventional view of science as involving the generation of hypotheses, the formulation and execution of experiments, and the revision of hypotheses on the basis of empirical evidence. During the course of normal scientific discovery, the various cells in table 1.1 are traversed repeatedly. However, it is very difficult to study thinking processes that involve all of them simultaneously. Consequently, the early research in the field started out with investigations designed to constrain the topic of interest to just one or two cells. As the field has matured, more complex contexts involving multiple cells have been used. In the following brief review, I describe a few investigations that exemplify various cells and cell combinations from table 1.1.

Cell A: Domain-Specific Hypothesis Space Search   In a series of pioneering studies, Mike McCloskey (1983) investigated people's naive theories of motion. His basic paradigm was to present participants with depictions of simple physical situations (such as an object being dropped from an airplane, or a ball exiting a curved tube) and ask them to predict the subsequent motion of the object. McCloskey found that many college students held naive impetus theories (such as the belief that the curved tube imparted a curvilinear impetus to the ball, which dissipated slowly, and made the ball continue in a curved trajectory that eventually straightened out). Note that in this kind of study, participants are asked about their knowledge about a specific domain. They are not allowed to run experiments, and they are not presented with any evidence to evaluate. Nor is there an attempt to assess any domain-general skills, such as designing unconfounded experiments, making valid inferences, and so on. Thus McCloskey's work—as well as similar studies on children's understanding of the distinction between heat and temperature (Carey, 1985)—are classified as examples of research in cell A of table 1.1.

Cell B: Domain-Specific Experiment Space Search   In some investigations, participants are asked to decide which of a set of prespecified experiments will provide the most informative test of a prespecified hypothesis. There is no search of the hypothesis space and the experiment space search is limited to choosing from among the given experiments, rather than generating them. The goal of such investigations is to find out how participants map the features of the given hypothesis onto the features of the given set of experimental alternatives.

Judith Tschirgi (1980) investigated the ability of children and adults to make valid inferences in familiar, knowledge-rich contexts. Participants were presented with an everyday scenario—for example, a description of a successful (or unsuccessful) cake-baking situation in which some novel ingredients were used—and then provided with a hypothesis about a specific factor (e.g., honey rather than sugar made a great cake). Next, they were asked to decide which one of three possible variant recipes would best determine whether or not the hypothesized factor (honey) was the important one for a great cake. Tschirgi found that, at all ages, the extent to which people chose an unconfounded experiment depended on whether the outcome of the initial experiment was good or bad. That is, if the initial outcome was bad, the participants tended to vary the hypothesized culprit factor, while holding all other factors constant. (Tschirgi called this VOTAT: vary one thing at a time.) In contrast, if the initial outcome was good, then participants tended to keep the hypothesized single cause of the good outcome and vary many other things simultaneously (HOTAT: hold one thing at a time). Note that this study did not include any hypothesis space search (the sole hypothesis to be evaluated was provided by the investigator). Nor did it involve the actual evaluation of evidence, because participants did not get to see the outcome of the experiment that they chose.

VOTAT is a domain-general strategy for producing unconfounded experimental contrasts. Thus, Tschirgi's study could be placed in cell E of table 1.1. However, because its main purpose was to demonstrate the influence of domain knowledge on people's ability to design an experiment from which they could make a valid inference, it exemplifies the type of studies in cell B.

Cell E: Domain-General Experiment Space Search   Studies of people's ability to design factorial experiments (e.g., Case, 1974; Siegler and Liebert, 1975) focus almost entirely on effective search of the experiment space. The use of domain-specific knowledge is minimized as is search in the hypothesis space and the evidence evaluation process. For example, Deanna Kuhn and John Angelev (1976) explored children's ability to design unconfounded experiments to determine which combination of chemicals would produce a liquid of a specific color. Children had no particular reason to favor one chemical over another, nor were they supposed to propose any causal mechanisms for the color change. The goal of the study was focused on the development of children's domain-general skill at experimental design.

Cells C and F: Domain-Specific and Domain-General Evidence Evaluation
Studies in this category focus on people's ability to decide which of several hypotheses is supported by evidence. Typically, such studies present tables of covariation data, and ask participants to decide which of several hypotheses is supported or refuted by the data in the tables. In some cases, the factors are abstract and arbitrary (e.g., Shaklee and Paszek, 1985)—in which case we classify the studies in Cell F—and in others they refer to real world factors (such as studies that present data on plant growth in the context of different amounts of sunlight and water) (Amsel and Brock, 1996; Bullock, Ziegler, and Martin, 1992). In such cases participants have to coordinate their prior domain knowledge with the covariation data in the tables (e.g., Ruffman et al., 1993). These studies involve both cells C and F.

Cells A and C: Domain-specific Hypothesis Space search and Evidence Evaluation   In investigations that combine cells A and C, children are asked to integrate a variety of forms of existing evidence in order to produce a theory that is consistent with that evidence. They do not have the opportunity to generate new evidence via experimentation, and the context of their search in the hypothesis space is highly domain-specific. This type of investigation is exemplified by Stella Vosniadou and William Brewer's (1992) analysis of elementary schoolchildren's mental models of the earth. The challenge faced by children is how to reconcile adults' claims that the earth is round, with their firsthand sensory experience that it is flat, which, in turn, is contradicted by their secondhand sensory experience of photographs of the round earth. Based on an analysis of children's responses to an extensive clinical interview about features and aspects of the earth's shape, Vosniadou and Brewer were able to describe a progression of increasingly mature mental models of the earth, including a rectangular earth, a disc earth, a dual earth, a hollow sphere, a flattened sphere, and finally, a sphere.

  The work of Barbara Koslowski and her colleagues (Koslowski, 1996; Koslowski and Okagaki, 1986; Koslowski et al., 1989) also combines cells A and C as well as F. In these studies, participants are presented with a complex mixture of covariation data, possible causal mechanisms, analogous effects, sampling procedures, and alternative hypotheses from which they are asked to make a decision about a potentially causal factor. The results of these studies demonstrate that abstract consideration of the strength of covariation data is far from the only process that determines people's judgments about causality, as they draw on many other aspects of both their specific knowledge about the domain as well as domain-general features, such as sample size, in making their decisions.

Cells D, E, and F: Domain-General Hypothesis Space Search, Experiment Space Search, and Evidence Evaluation   Jerome Bruner, Jacqueline Goodnow, and George Austin (1956) created their classic concept-learning task in order to better understand people's appreciation of the logic of experimentation and their strategies for discovering regularities. Their participants' task was to discover an arbitrary rule (such as "large and red") that was being used to classify a set of predefined instances consisting of all possible combinations of shape, color, number, and so on. They ran several different procedures that collectively span the bottom row of table 1.1: participants had to generate hypotheses, choose among "experiments" (that is, select different cards that displayed specific combinations of attributes) and evaluate the evidence provided by the yes/no feedback that they received. Because the task is abstract and arbitrary, none of the domain-specific cells are involved in Bruner, Goodnow, and Austin's studies. We classify this type of study as mainly involving cells D and F. Cell E is implicated only marginally, because participants did not have to generate instances, only select them.

Another venerable task that spans cells D, E, and F is Wason's (1960) 2-4-6 task. In this task, participants are asked to discover a rule (predetermined by the investigator) that could classify sets of numerical triads. They are told that "2-4-6" is an example of a triad that conforms to the rule, and they are instructed to generate their own triads—which the investigator then classifies as an instance or noninstance of the rule. (See Klayman and Ha, 1987, for a review and theoretical integration of the extensive literature on this task.) This task *does* involve cell E (as well as D and F) because participants have to generate their own "experiments" (test triads) in their attempt to discover the classification rule. Like the Bruner, Goodnow, and Austin paradigm, the 2-4-6 task was designed to study people's reasoning in a context that "simulates a miniature scientific problem" (Wason, 1960, p. 139). Although one could argue that domain knowledge plays a role here (because knowledge of arithmetic is necessary for participants to propose hypotheses such as "even numbers," "increasing numbers," and so on), such knowledge has only a minor influence because the participants' task is not to discover anything about the domain.

A good example of the a study that spans cells D, E, and F is the pioneering investigation by Mynatt, Doherty, and Tweney (1977, 1978) in which people were asked to determine the laws governing the motion of "particles" in an arbitrary (and non-Newtonian) universe consisting of objects displayed on a computer screen. The participants' task was to infer the laws of motion by running experiments in which they fired particles at objects. This kind of task is a clear precursor of the kinds of microworld tasks we describe later, although—because participants knew that the "universe" was contrived by the experimenters—their domain-specific knowledge did not play a major role in their problem-solving activities.

Integrative Investigations of Scientific Reasoning
Research focusing on either domain-specific or domain-general knowledge has yielded much useful information about scientific discovery. However, such efforts are, perforce, unable to assess an important aspect of this kind of problem solving: the interaction between the two types of knowledge. Similarly, the isolation of hypothesis search, experimentation strategies, and evidence evaluation begs a fundamental question: how are the three main processes integrated and how do they mutually influence one another? The goal of the work described in this book is to integrate the six aspects of the scientific discovery process represented in table 1.1 while still being cast at a sufficiently fine grain so as not to lose relevant detail about the discovery process.

Several of our studies use tasks in which domain-general problem-solving heuristics play a central role in constraining search while, at the same time, participants' domain-specific knowledge biases them to view some hypotheses as more plausible than others. Furthermore, in these tasks, both domain-specific knowledge and domain-general heuristics guide participants in designing experiments and evaluating their outcomes. With respect to the integration of the three processes, such tasks require coordinated search in *both* the experiment space and the hypothesis space, as well as the evaluation of evidence produced by participant-generated experiments.

Conclusion

Science is a fundamental feature of human activity, and many of its aspects make it enormously appealing as an object of study. To some, science exemplifies the impenetrable mystery of creativity, whereas for others it epitomizes the best that systematic thought can produce. It has been an object of study by just about every one of the humanistic and social science disciplines, from anthropology to economics, from history to sociology, from education to philosophy.

Each of the four approaches that are employed in research on scientific discovery has its particular strengths and weaknesses (see Klahr and Simon, 1999, for an extended discussion of the contrasts and complementarities of these approaches). In this book, the focus will be on the psychology of science, with an emphasis on developmental aspects. Even within the area of psychology, there has been a wide diversity in the approaches that different researchers have taken. I have proposed a two-dimensional taxonomy of this work that crosses two types of domain knowledge with three main phases of the scientific discovery process and have provided illustrative examples of the resulting categories.

Although the earliest studies in this area tended to focus on highly selected aspects of the discovery process, it is now possible to do empirical studies of people performing tasks that capture—in abstracted and idealized form—all of the essential components of the discovery process. This book describes a series of such studies that my colleagues and I have conducted in the past decade. Some of the studies have been reported elsewhere (Dunbar, 1993; Klahr and Dunbar, 1988; Klahr, Fay, and Dunbar, 1993; Schunn and Klahr, 1992, 1995) and some are reported here for the first time. Our studies are not the only ones designed to traverse most of the cells in table 1.1. Other investigators have also been motivated—to varying degrees—by the same rationale that guides our work (e.g., Koslowski, 1996; Kuhn, 1989; Kuhn et al., 1995; Mynatt, Doherty, and Tweney, 1978; Krems and Johnson, 1995; Schauble, 1990, 1996; Schauble et al., 1991), and we will indicate the relationship between these studies and our own when appropriate.

Notes

1. For an analysis that compares the kinds of thinking processes underlying the great scientific discoveries, the basic mechanisms used in computational models of scientific discovery, and the problem solving of ordinary people faced with complex laboratory puzzles, see Klahr and Simon (1999). The focus of this book is almost entirely on the last of these three approaches to understanding scientific discovery.

2. However, those interested in sociological factors sometimes prefer instead to be ignorant of the substantive knowledge and scientific conventions of the laboratory under investigation. "Latour's knowledge of science was non-existent; his mastery of English was very poor; and he was completely unaware of the existence of the social studies of science. Apart from (or perhaps even because of) this last feature, he was thus in a classic position of the ethnographer sent to a completely foreign environment" (Latour and Woolgar, 1986, p. 273).

Chapter 2
Scientific Discovery as Problem Solving

It is understandable, if ironic, that "normal" science fits pretty well the description of expert problem solving, while "revolutionary" science fits the description of problem solving by novices. It is understandable because scientific activity, particularly at the revolutionary end of the continuum, is concerned with the discovery of new truths, not with the application of truths that are already well known. While it may incorporate some expert techniques in the manipulation of instruments and laboratory procedures, it is basically a journey into unmapped terrain. Consequently, it is mainly characterized, as is novice problem solving, by trial-and-error search. The search may be highly selective—the selectivity depending on how much is already known about the domain—but it reaches its goal only after many halts, turnings, and backtrackings.
(Simon, Langley, and Bradshaw, 1981, p. 5)

What does it mean to claim, as do Simon, Langley, and Bradshaw, that scientific discovery is a type of problem solving? The claim is neither controversial nor informative unless we go beyond a generic interpretation of "problem solving" as a synonym for "thinking," for it is unquestionable that scientific discovery involves some sort of thinking. Therefore, this chapter begins with a brief overview of some widely accepted (by cognitive psychologists) definitions and terminology associated with problem solving. This is followed by a description of the theoretical unification of the areas of problem solving and rule induction that was first suggested by Simon and Glen Lea (1974). Finally, I describe an extension of the Simon and Lea theory to the domain of scientific reasoning in which scientific discovery is characterized as a problem-solving process that involves search in two spaces: a space of hypotheses and a space of experiments.

Problem Solving, Search, and Weak Methods

Newell and Simon (1972) define a problem as consisting of an initial state, a goal state, and a set of permissible transformations from one state to another (called "operators") that, when executed in a correct sequence, result in a solution path from the initial state to the goal state, via a series of intermediate states and subgoals. Operators have constraints that must be satisfied before they can be applied. The set of states, operators, goals, and constraints is called a "problem space," and the problem-solving process can be conceptualized as a search for a path that links the initial state to the goal state.

This formal characterization can be applied to an extremely broad range of situations from laboratory puzzles to everyday situations and contexts. We begin with an example of the former type of problem, and then later in this section we provide an example of a naturally occurring problem-solving situation. Consider the well-known Tower of Hanoi puzzle. It consists of a stack of n disks of different size and three pegs (A, B, and C) on which they can be stacked. In the initial state, all the disks are stacked—in order of decreasing size—on peg A. That is, the largest disk is on the bottom of the stack, followed by the second largest, and so on. The goal state is to get them all stacked—in the same size order— on peg C. The only legal move (that is, the "move operator") is to take the top-most disk from the peg it is on and to place it on one of the other two pegs. The constraints on the move operator are (1) that a disk can only be moved if there is nothing on top of it and (2) that a larger disk can never be placed above a smaller disk. Although simply stated, this puzzle can be quite difficult for novices: the length of the most efficient solution is $2^n - 1$ moves. Thus, a three-disk problem can be solved in no fewer than seven moves, and a four-disk problem in no fewer than fifteen. (See Simon, 1975, for an elegant analysis of different strategies for solving this puzzle; see also Klahr and Robinson, 1981.)

Each of the basic components in a problem—initial state, goal state, operators, and constraints—can vary along a continuum from well- to ill-defined. For example, one could have a well-defined initial state and an ill-defined goal state and set of operators (e.g., make something with these materials), or one could have an ill-defined initial state and a well-defined final state (e.g., prove a particular mathematical conjecture). Scientific problems are obviously much less well defined than the Tower of Hanoi. Nevertheless, they can be characterized in the terms used here. Interestingly, the degree of well-definedness depends on the knowledge that is available to the problem-solver. For that reason, much of the training of scientists is aimed at increasing the degree of well-definedness of problems with respect to the scientists working on them.

In all but the most trivial problems, the problem solver is faced with a large set of alternative states and operators, so the search process can be quite demanding. For example, if we represent the problem space as a branching tree of m moves with b branches at each move, then there are b^m

moves to consider in the full problem space. As soon as m and b get beyond small values, exhaustive search for alternative states and operators is beyond human capacity.[1] Thus, effective problem solving depends in large part on processes that judiciously constrain search to the exploration of a few branches. These search constraint processes can be placed into two broad categories: *weak methods* and *strong methods*. Weak methods are

> so called because they require relatively little knowledge of the problem structure for their application, but are correspondingly unselective in the way in which they search through the problem space. One mark of expertise is the possession of strong methods specifically adapted to the problem domain, which may allow solutions to be found with little or no search. For example, if someone who knows the calculus is asked to find the maximum of a function, he or she applies a known algorithm (taking the derivative and setting it equal to zero), and finds the answer without search. (Simon, 1986, p. 162)

Scientific practice involves a plethora of strong methods, such as statistical tools, standard experimental paradigms, routine instrumentation processes, and even highly constrained publication formats. In this book we do not address those aspects of scientific discovery other than to acknowledge that they can be viewed, as in the maximization example earlier, as the direct application of a method with little or no search. Of more interest to us are the ways in which weak methods are used in scientific discovery. They are of interest because they are, by definition, heuristic: they may work, or they may not, but they are applicable in a wide variety of contexts. Unlike the strong methods, which are only acquired after extensive formal training, the weak methods are easily acquired (indeed, some may be innate), and they are domain-general. We will describe five major methods: generate and test, hill climbing, means-ends-analysis, planning, and analogy.

Generate and Test
This method is commonly called "trial and error." It consists of simply applying some operator to the current state and then testing to determine if the goal state has been reached. If it has been, the problem is solved. If it has not been, then some other operator is applied. In the most primitive types of generate-and-test methods, the evaluation function is binary: either the goal has been reached or it has not, and the next "move" does not depend on any properties of the discrepancy between the current state and the goal state, or the operator that was just unsuccessfully applied. An example of a "dumb" generating process would be one in which you are searching in a box of keys for a key to fit a lock, and

you sample with replacement: tossing failed keys back into the box without noting anything about the degree of fit, the type of key that seems to fit partially, and so on. A slightly "smarter" generator would, at the least, sample from the key box without replacement.

Hill Climbing

This method gets its name from the analogy to someone attempting to reach the top of a hill whose peak cannot be directly perceived (imagine a foggy day with severely limited visibility). One makes a tentative step in each of several directions, and then heads off in the direction that has the steepest gradient. More generally, the method computes an evaluation function whose maximum value corresponds to the goal state. Potential moves are generated and the evaluation function is applied to each potential state. The state that maximizes the increment to the evaluation function is chosen, that move is made, and then the process iterates from the new state. Hill climbing utilizes more information than generate-and-test about the discrepancy between the current state and the goal state. Instead of a simple all-or-none evaluation, it computes a measure of goodness of fit between the two, and uses that information to constrain search in the problem space. For the Tower of Hanoi, the hill-climbing evaluation function might be a simple count of the number of disks currently on the goal peg. The problem with this method is that it would be reluctant to remove any disks from the goal peg, even though that is a necessary part of the solution, as disks are temporarily placed there so that others can be moved.

Means-Ends Analysis

Of all the weak methods, perhaps the best known is means-ends analysis (Dunker, 1945; Newell and Simon, 1972). Means-ends analysis compares the current state and the goal state, and it produces a description of what differences exist. Then it searches for an operator that can reduce those differences. This search is effective only to the extent that the system already has indexed operators in terms of the types of differences they can reduce. It selects an operator that is designed to reduce the most important differences, and it attempts to apply that operator to the current state. However, it may be the case that the operator cannot be immediately applied, because the conditions for its applicability are not met. Means-ends analysis then formulates a subproblem in which the goal is to reduce the difference between the current state and a state in which the desired operator can be applied. Then it recursively attempts to solve the subproblem.

For the Tower of Hanoi, this method might define the most important difference between the initial state and the goal state as getting the largest disk (at the bottom of the initial stack of n disks) to the goal peg. But this move cannot be made unless the largest disk has nothing above it, and the goal peg is empty. The only state that fits this situation is one in which a stack of $n-1$ disks is on the "other" peg, and the biggest disk is on the start peg. Thus, means-ends analysis would establish this configuration as a subgoal and then attempt to achieve that subgoal.

Means-ends analysis is often used in everyday situations. Consider the problem faced recently by an unnamed psychologist in getting from an office at Carnegie Mellon University to a conference room at a Colorado resort in order to present a talk about scientific reasoning. The "difference" was one of distance, and among the set of distance-reduction operators were flying, walking, biking, and so forth. Flying was the operator that would most rapidly reduce distance, but it could not be applied to the initial condition: that is, one could not fly directly from the office to the conference site. This presented the subproblem of creating conditions for flying (i.e., getting to an airport). Getting to the airport could best be done via taxi, but there was no taxi at Carnegie Mellon. The sub-subproblem involved making a phone call to the cab company. But all the university phones were out of order for the day during a transition to a new system: only the pay phones worked. An even deeper subproblem: make a call on a pay phone. But a lack of coins made it impossible to apply that operator (no pun intended). However, a Coke machine was handy, and it accepted dollar bills and gave change. So the problem solver bought and discarded a Coke in order to get on the solution path to transport himself to Colorado.

The hierarchy of goals and subgoals generated by this method is called the "goal tree." At any point in the goal tree, if you asked *how* a goal was going to be achieved, the answer could be found in the subgoals (or, if possible, the immediately applied operators). If you asked *why* a goal was being attempted, the answer would lie in the parent goal for that subgoal. Thus: "Why do I need change?" "To make a phone call." (Or, more obscurely, because it skips a few levels in the goal tree: "To get to the airport.") "How will I get change?" "By using a vending machine."

One would not usually think of a vending machine as an means for distance reduction. However, as illustrated by this example, means-ends analysis can, in the process of proliferating subgoals, take the problem solver along unexpected paths into situations that might, at first blush, seem unlikely to bear any relevance to the initial goal. The nature of these paths can change so much that, in some cases they are more appropriately characterized as distinct problem spaces. Indeed, the determination of the number of distinct problem spaces involved in solving complex problems remains an unresolved issue, to which we will return at the end of this book. Later in this chapter we will characterize scientific discovery in terms of just two spaces, but that will be expanded later.

Planning

Newell and Simon (1972) define planning[2] as another problem-solving method consisting of (1) forming an abstract version of the problem space by omitting certain details of the original set of states and operators, (2) forming the corresponding problem in the abstract problem space, (3) solving the abstracted problem by applying any of the methods listed here (including planning), (4) using the solution of the abstract problem to provide a plan for solving the original problem, (5) translating the plan back into the original problem space and executing it.

For example, if we apply the planning method to the Tower of Hanoi puzzle we might get the following three-step plan: (1) Move the smallest disk to the intervening peg, (2) move a stack of $n-1$ disks to the goal peg, (3) move the smallest disk to the goal peg. Or for the Colorado problem, we might get (1) taxi to airport; (2) fly to Denver; (3) drive to Breckenridge. Because planning suppresses some of the detail in the original problem space, it is not always possible to implement the plan, for some of the simplifications result in planned solution paths that cannot be effected. For example, moving a stack of $n-1$ disks is not a legal move, so more problem solving is required to execute that part of the plan. Or, for the Colorado plan, there might be no rental cars at the Denver airport.

Analogy

Analogy involves a mapping between a new target domain (i.e., the current problem) and a previously encountered base domain (i.e., some similar, previously solved, problem). The mappings may vary in their complexity from surface mappings—involving only the simple recognition that the current problem can be solved by a known procedure—to relational mappings, to complex structural mappings (Forbus and Gentner, 1991; Gentner and Jeziorski, 1989; Halford, 1992). Although the potential power of solving a novel problem via analogy to a previously solved problem is obvious, the mapping process itself may fail. Thus, like the other weak methods, analogy is not guaranteed to produce a solution.

Although analogy is not included in Newell and Simon's list of problem-solving methods,[3] in the past twenty-five years, analogy has assumed a central role in theories of problem solving and scientific discovery and its underlying mechanisms have been studied in great detail. Keith Holyoak and Paul Thagard (1995) provide several examples of analogical problem solving in major scientific discoveries, ranging from a first-century analogy between sound and water waves to Turing's mind/computer analogy. Holyoak and Thagard also emphasize the role of analogical thinking in cognitive development. (See Goswami, 1996, for an extensive review.) Analogical reasoning also plays a central role in recent analysis of the thinking processes of contemporary scientists working in their labs (Dunbar, 1997; Thagard, 1997; Ueda, 1997), and, as we will argue in later chapters, it is often the method of choice for formulating initial hypotheses and experiments in a variety of discovery contexts.

Analogical mappings thus provide the principal bridge between weak and strong methods when the source of the analogy is a well-defined procedure. Used in conjunction with domain-specific knowledge, analogy may enable the search process to be greatly abridged when patterns are noticed in the current problem state. Prestored knowledge can be evoked and used to plan the next steps toward solution of the problem, provide macros to replace whole segments of step-by-step search, or even suggest an immediate problem solution. The recognition mechanism (with its associated store of knowledge) is a key weapon in the arsenal of experts and a principal factor in distinguishing their performance in the domain of expertise from that of novices.

Scientific Reasoning: Problem Solving or Concept Formation?

The problem-solving view of scientific discovery has its roots in the Gestalt tradition. For example, Wertheimer (1945) implicates search processes in his historical anecdotes about Einstein and Gauss, and Bartlett (1958) is quite explicit in structuring his discussion of the "thinking of the experimental scientist" in terms of search through a set of knowledge states.[4] Simon (1977) elaborates this position in characterizing scientific reasoning as a search process, similar in structure to any problem-solving task, albeit within a complex search space. Simon's contribution to the discovery-as-problem-solving view is to demonstrate how one could go beyond the search metaphor by explaining the discovery process in terms of an explicit theory of human problem solving (Newell, Shaw, and Simon, 1958). This basic idea has since been extended substantially by Simon and his colleagues in the computational models described in chapter 1.

There is another characterization of the process of scientific reasoning that was considered in the initial period when cognitive psychologists first began to study the topic. This view, exemplified by the Bruner and Wason tasks described in chapter 1, we call the *concept-formation view*. The argument here is that much of scientific reasoning consists of forming new concepts—via induction—on the basis of experimental evidence. This view tended to dominate the early laboratory investigations of the scientific discovery process.

Although the concept-formation and problem-solving views appear to be radically different characterizations of the scientific reasoning process, both traditions can be organized into a coherent theory of scientific reasoning. The key to this integration comes from Simon and Lea's (1974) insight that both concept learning and problem solving are information-gathering tasks and that both employ guided search processes. Simon and Lea have shown how a single information-processing system—called the Generalized Rule Inducer—can account for performance in problem-solving tasks and a range of rule-induction tasks, including concept attainment, sequence extrapolation, and grammar induction. The Generalized Rule Inducer uses the same general methods for both problem-solving tasks and rule-induction tasks. The main difference between problem solving and rule induction lies in the problem spaces that are used in the two tasks.

Consider a rule induction task such as the 2-4-6 task (Wason, 1960). In this task, the experimenter tells subjects that their goal is to figure out what rule the experimenter has in mind, and he tells them that 2-4-6 is an instance of that rule.[5] Subjects then propose a series of triads—such as 8-10-12 or 3-4-5—one at a time and, for each triad, the experimenter says whether or not it is an instance of the to-be-discovered rule. Whenever subjects are ready, they also can state what they think the rule is. (In the original form of this experiment, the rule was simply "increasing numbers," so that both of the triads proposed above would be positive instances of the rule.) Subjects typically start out with much more limited hypotheses about the rule, such as "increasing evens" or "the third is the sum of the first two."

This kind of task requires search in two problem spaces: a space of rules and a space of instances. That is, subjects have to search for hypotheses about what the rule underlying all the triples is, and they also have to search for a good instance—a particular triple—to test their hypotheses. Problem-solving search, however, takes place in a single space: a space of rules.

Thus, the distinctive feature of rule-induction tasks is that proposed rules (hypotheses) are never tested directly, but only by applying them to instances and then testing whether the application gives the correct result. In rule-induction tasks the participant selects (or is shown) an instance and checks to see whether the instance confirms or disconfirms the rule. Instance selection requires search of the instance space, and changing from one rule to another requires search of the rule space. Because rule induction requires two spaces, the tests operate in a different space from the hypothesis (rule) generator. Simon and Lea's analysis illustrates how information from each space may guide search in the other space. For example, information about previously generated rules may influence the generation of instances, and information about the classification of instances may determine the modification of rules.

The Generalized Rule Inducer view makes it possible to characterize some further differences between the previous research on concept formation and problem solving. Because the concept-learning research is concerned with rules derived from well-defined instances, the rule space is usually very simple: it consists of all possible combinations of the values and attributes in the instance space. Even when participants have some control over instance selection, as in the Bruner, Goodnow, and Austin (1956) work, the full set of permissible instances is predetermined. In problem-solving experiments, the structure of the problem space is usually much more complicated. Rather than being merely the concatenation of a new set of given features, it consists of a series of knowledge states that the participant can generate by following a wide variety of strategies.

The Goal Structure of the Scientific Discovery Process

The Generalized Rule Inducer was designed to account for the results of traditional laboratory studies of problem solving and rule induction. Recall that, in the Wason 2-4-6 task, participants have to search both a space of instances and a space of rules that might account for how the experimenter is classifying number triples. Analogously, in scientific discovery, one has to search both a space of observations or experiments, and a space of hypotheses that can account for them—"Nature's rules," in effect. In considering the complexity of the mental processes that support this kind of thinking, we applied one of the standard tools of cognitive psychology—task analysis—to the domain of scientific discovery. We formulated a framework that expands the top-level discovery goal into a hierarchically organized goal structure that elucidates the nature of this dual search and shows the relations among the components and subcomponents. In this chapter, we introduce that goal structure and in subsequent chapters we use it to account for people's behavior in a variety of scientific discovery tasks.

We start by summarizing the key features of our model of scientific discovery as dual search (SDDS). There are two parts to the presentation. First, we give a very broad overview of the model's main phases and then we give an elaborated description of its goal structure.

Dual Search

Searching the Hypothesis Space   The process of generating new hypotheses is a type of problem solving in which the initial state consists of some knowledge about a domain, and the goal state is a hypothesis that can account for some or all of that knowledge in a more concise or universal form. Once generated, hypotheses are evaluated for their initial plausibility. Expertise plays a role here, as participants' familiarity with a domain tends to give them strong biases about what is plausible in the domain. Plausibility, in turn, affects the order in which hypotheses are evaluated: highly likely hypotheses tend to be tested before unlikely hypotheses (Klayman and Ha, 1987; Wason, 1968). Furthermore, participants may adopt different experimental strategies for evaluating plausible and implausible hypotheses.

Searching the Experiment Space   One of the most important constraints on this search is the need to produce experiments that will yield interpretable outcomes. This requires *domain-general* knowledge about one's own information-processing limitations, as well as *domain-specific* knowledge about the pragmatic constraints of the particular discovery context. As we will see, there are important developmental differences in people's ability to constrain search in the experiment space.

Evaluating Evidence   Search in the two spaces is mediated by the evidence evaluation process. This process both assesses the fit between theory and evidence and guides further search in both the hypothesis space and the experiment space. In contrast to the binary feedback provided to participants in the typical psychology experiment, real-world evidence evaluation is not very straightforward. Relevant features must first be extracted, potential noise must be suppressed or corrected (Gorman, 1992; Penner and Klahr, 1996), and the resulting internal representation must be compared with earlier predictions. When people are reasoning about real world contexts, their prior knowledge imposes strong theoretical biases (Brewer and Chin, 1994). These biases influence not only the initial strength with which hypotheses are held—and hence the amount of disconfirming evidence necessary to refute them—but also the features in the evidence that will be attended to and encoded.

The Goal Structure of SDDS

This model is intended to depict the goal structure that is generated in a broad range of scientific reasoning contexts. The fundamental assumption is that scientific discovery involves search in problem spaces. In the case of scientific discovery, there are *two* primary spaces to be searched: a space of hypotheses and a space of experiments. Search in the hypothesis space is guided both by prior knowledge and by experimental results. Search in the experiment space may be guided by the current hypothesis, and it may be used to generate information to formulate hypotheses.

Before presenting the model, we need to briefly describe the format we use to depict the mental representation of hypotheses. We use Marvin Minsky's "frame" notation: data structures that have a set of elements with slots whose values can vary according to context, and whose set of elements bear fixed relations to one another. Initial hypotheses are constructed by a series of operations that result in the instantiation of a frame with default values. Subsequent hypotheses within that frame are generated by changes in values of particular slots and new frames are generated either by a search of memory or by generalizing from experimental outcomes.

SDDS consists of a set of basic *components* that guide search within and between these two problem spaces. In the following description of SDDS we sometimes refer to the components as goals and subgoals, and at other times as processes and subprocesses, depending on the context. Because we are proposing SDDS as a general framework within which to interpret human behavior in any scientific reasoning task, we introduce it at a very general level without reference to any particular discovery domain.

The full model is complex, so perhaps an advance organizer will help. The target we are aiming for in the next several pages is the fully-elaborated structure depicted in figure 2.9 (see page 37). Our approach is to describe various subcomponents of the full model in a piecemeal fashion—from left to right, and from top to bottom. Then, at the end of the chapter, we put it all together. So let us begin.

Three main components control the entire process from the initial formulation of hypotheses, through their experimental evaluation, to the decision that there is sufficient evidence to accept an hypothesis. The three components, shown in figure 2.1, are *Search Hypothesis Space, Test Hypothesis*, and *Evaluate Evidence*. The output from *Search Hypothesis Space* is a fully specified hypothesis, which provides the input to *Test Hypothesis*. The output of *Test Hypothesis* is a description of evidence for or against the current hypothesis, based on the match between the prediction derived from the current hypothesis and the actual experimental

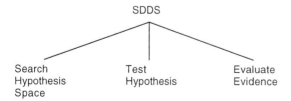

Figure 2.1
The three top-level components of SDDS.

result. Next, *Evaluate Evidence* decides whether the cumulative evidence—as well as other considerations—warrants acceptance, rejection, or continued consideration of the current hypothesis. Each of these three top-level components will be described more fully in the following paragraphs.

Search Hypothesis Space

This process, depicted in figure 2.2, has two components. One component generates the broad scope of a new hypothesis, and the second component refines it and further specifies it. Because we represent hypotheses as frames, we show this as first *Generate Frame* and then *Assign Slot Values*. Where do these initial frames and their associated slot values come from? We propose two different types of sources for new hypotheses. One source comes from prior knowledge stored in memory, and the other source comes from experimental (or observational) data. The two different sources are evoked in both *Generate Frame* and in *Assign Slot Values*.

Generate Frame   Depicted in figure 2.3, *Generate Frame* has two components corresponding to the two ways that a frame may be generated. The

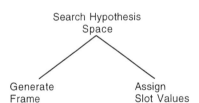

Figure 2.2
Top-level structure of Search Hypothesis Space.

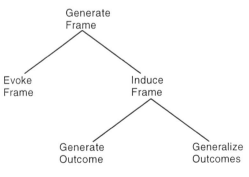

Figure 2.3
The structure of Generate Frame.

first component to be activated, *Evoke Frame,* is a search of memory for information that could be used to construct a frame. Prior knowledge plays an important role here. In cognitive psychology, several mechanisms have been proposed to account for the way in which initial hypotheses are generated, including analogical mapping (Gentner, 1983; Gick and Holyoak, 1983), heuristic search (Kaplan and Simon, 1990; Klahr and Dunbar, 1988), priming (Dunbar and Schunn, 1990; Schunn and Dunbar, 1996), remindings (Ross, 1984), and conceptual combination (Shrager, 1985, 1987). Each of these mechanisms emphasizes a different aspect of the way in which search in the hypothesis space is initiated.

But it is not always possible to evoke a new hypothesis from memory. In such cases, it is necessary to induce a frame from data. Thus, the second component of *Generate Frame* is *Induce Frame.* It generates a new frame by induction from a series of outcomes. The first subprocess in *Induce Frame* generates an outcome, and the second subprocess generalizes over the results of that (and other) outcomes to produce a frame. *Generate Outcome* will be described later.

The result from *Generate Outcome* is a data pattern that is input to *Generalize Outcomes,* which then attempts to generalize over the outcomes in order to produce a frame. The difference between *Evoke Frame* and *Induce Frame* is important. It corresponds to the difference between situations in which participants are able to recall similar situations and use them as the basis for constructing initial frames, and situations in which participants must observe some results before they can venture even an initial hypothesis.

Assign Slot Values   The second major component of *Search Hypothesis Space* is shown in figure 2.4. Its purpose is to take a partially instantiated

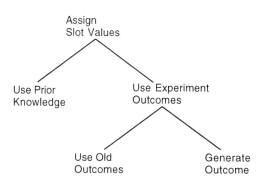

Figure 2.4
The structure of Assign Slot Values.

frame and assign specific values to the slots so that a fully specified hypothesis can be generated. Like *Generate Frame*, it also has two subcomponents corresponding to memory search or induction over data. Slot values may be assigned by using prior knowledge (*Use Prior Knowledge*) or by using specific experimental outcomes (*Use Experimental Outcomes*). As noted, the distinction here is parallel to the earlier distinction between evoking and inducing a frame, but now it is with respect to filling in slot values in an existing frame rather than generating a new frame. If there are already some experimental outcomes, then they can be examined to determine specific slot values (*Use Old Outcomes*). Alternatively, the system can use *Generate Outcome* to produce some empirical results solely for the purpose of determining slot values, that is, for refining a partially specified hypothesis.

In the early phases of the discovery process, *Use Prior Knowledge* plays the major role in assigning values, whereas later in the course of experimentation, *Use Experimental Outcomes* is more likely to generate specific slot values. If the system is unable to assign slot values to the current frame (because they have all been tried and rejected), then the frame is abandoned and the system returns to *Generate Frame* (see figure 2.3).

In figure 2.5, we have assembled all of these components of *Search Hypothesis Space* to show its full structure. The end result of *Search Hypothesis Space* is a fully specified hypothesis which is then input to *Test Hypothesis* (to be described in the next few paragraphs). Note that *Generate Outcome* occurs in two different subcontexts in the service of *Search Hypothesis Space*. This requires the running of "experiments" even though neither of these contexts involve the evaluation of an hypothesis, for it is still being formed. We will return to this point.

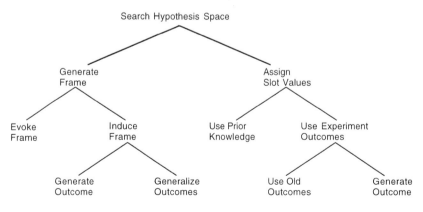

Figure 2.5
The full structure of *Search Hypothesis Space*.

Test Hypothesis
Now we describe the second of the three main components shown in figure 2.1: *Test Hypothesis* (figure 2.6). It generates an experiment (*Search E-Space*) appropriate to the current hypothesis, makes a prediction, runs the experiment, and matches the outcome to the prediction. *Test Hypothesis* uses three subcomponents. The first, *Search E-Space,* produces an experiment. It will be described later, as it is used in several places in the model. The second, *Make Prediction,* takes the current hypothesis and the current experiment and predicts specific results, centered on the current focal values. The third component, *Run,* executes the experiment, and then *Match* produces a description of a discrepancy between the prediction and the actual outcome. As depicted here, the expected outcome is generated prior to the running of the experiment (during *Predict*). However, SDDS allows the computation of what "should have happened" to occur *following* the running of the experiment, during the *Match* process. *Match* requires descriptions of both the expectation and the observation as input. When completed, *Test Hypothesis* outputs a representation of evidence for or against the current hypothesis; this representation is then used as input by *Evaluate Evidence.*

Evaluate Evidence
Evaluate Evidence (figure 2.7) determines whether or not the cumulative evidence about the experiments run under the current hypothesis is

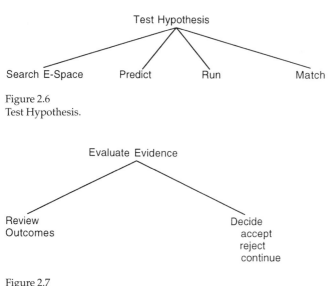

Figure 2.6
Test Hypothesis.

Figure 2.7
Evaluate Evidence.

sufficient to reject or accept it. It is possible that the evidence is inconclusive and neither situation obtains, in which case *Evaluate Evidence*
loops back to *Test Hypothesis*. Note that the input to the review process
consists of an accumulation of output from earlier *Test Hypothesis* cycles.
The scope of this accumulation could range from the most recent result,
to the most salient ones, to a full record of all the results thus far. The
content of this record could be one of either consistency or inconsistency.
Additional factors may play a role in *Evaluate Evidence*, for example,
plausibility, functionality, or parsimony. Although these factors appear
to influence evidence evaluation, we do not yet have a general understanding of how they work, and we will return to them in subsequent
chapters describing the results of specific studies.

Generate Outcome
This process, depicted in figure 2.8, starts with a *Search E-Space*, which
produces an experiment. Once produced, the experiment is *Run* and the
result is *Observed. Generate Outcome* occurs twice in the subgoal hierarchy
of *Search Hypothesis Space*: (1) when outcomes are being generated in order to induce frames and (2) when they are being run to refine hypotheses by assigning slot values (see figure 2.5). As noted, each time that
Generate Outcome is invoked, so is *Search E-Space*, which we describe next.

Search E-Space   Experiments are designed by *Search E-Space*. The most
important step is to *Focus* on some aspect of the current situation that the
experiment is intended to illuminate. "Current situation" is not just a
circumlocution for "current hypothesis," because there may be situations in which there is no current hypothesis, but in which *Search E-Space*
must function nevertheless. (This is an important feature of the model,
and it will be elaborated in the next section.) If there is an hypothesis,
then *Focus* determines that some aspect of it is the primary reason for the
experiment. If there is a frame with open slot values, then *Focus* will se-

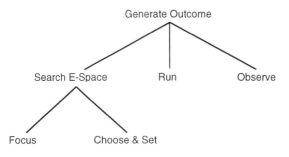

Figure 2.8
Generate Outcome.

lect any one of those slots as the most important thing to be resolved. If there is neither a frame nor an hypothesis—that is, if *Search E-Space* is being called by *Induce Frame,* then *Focus* makes an arbitrary decision about what aspect of the current situation to focus on. Once a focal aspect has been determined, *Choose* sets a value in the experiment space that will provide information relevant to it, and *Set* determines the values of the remaining, but less important, experimental features necessary to produce a complete experiment.

The Multiple Roles of Experimentation in SDDS
Examination of the relationship among all these processes and subprocesses, depicted in figure 2.9, reveals both the conventional and unconventional characteristics of the model. At the top level, the discovery process is characterized as a simple repeating cycle of generating hypotheses, testing hypotheses, and evaluating the accumulated evidence. Below that level, however, we can begin to see the complex interaction among the subprocesses. Of particular importance is the way in which *Search E-Space* occurs in three places in the hierarchy: (1) as a subprocess deep within *Generate Frame,* where the goal is to generate a data pattern over which a frame can be induced, (2) as a subprocess of *Assign Slot Values* where the purpose of the "experiment" is simply to resolve the unassigned slots in the current frame, and (3) as a component of *Test Hypothesis,* where the experiment is designed to play its conventional role of generating an instance (usually positive) of the current

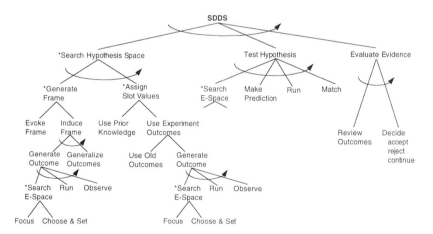

Figure 2.9
Complete SDDS Goal Structure. Components connected by an arrow are usually executed in the order shown. Component names preceded by an asterisk include conditional tests that subcomponents execute.

hypothesis. Note that the implication of the first two uses of *Search E-Space* is that, in the absence of hypotheses, experiments are generated atheoretically, by moving around the experiment space.

SDDS also elaborates the details of what can happen during the *Evaluate Evidence* process. Recall that three general outcomes are possible: The current hypothesis can be accepted, it can be rejected, or it can be considered further. In the first case, the discovery process simply stops, and asserts that the current hypothesis is the true state of nature. In the second case—rejection—the system returns to *Search Hypothesis Space*, where two things can happen. If the entire *frame* has been rejected by *Evaluate Evidence*, then the model must attempt to generate a new frame. If *Evoke Frame* is unable to generate an alternative frame, then the system will wind up in *Induce Frame* and will ultimately start to run experiments (in *Generate Outcome*) in order to find some empirical elements over which to do the induction. Having induced a new frame, or having returned from *Evaluate Evidence* with a frame needing new slot values (i.e., a rejection of the hypothesis but not the frame), SDDS executes *Assign Slot Values*. Here, too, if prior knowledge is inadequate to make slot assignments, the system may wind up making moves in the experiment space in order to make the assignments (i.e., *Generate Outcome* under *Use Experimental Outcomes*). In both these cases, the behavior we would observe would be the running of "experiments" without fully specified hypotheses. This is precisely what we see in several of the studies to be described later in this book. It is particularly common in children's experimentation. In the third case, SDDS returns to *Test Hypothesis* in order to further consider the current hypothesis. The experiments run in this context correspond to the conventional view of the role of experimentation. During *Move In E-Space, Focus* selects particular aspects of the current hypothesis and designs an experiment to generate information about them.

Conclusion

In this chapter we have elucidated our general claim that scientific discovery is a type of problem solving involving search in problem spaces. We then summarized the important weak methods used to control that search. Next, we argued that scientific discovery requires search in (at least) two problem spaces: a space of hypotheses and a space of experiments. Finally, we described a detailed goal structure consisting of three main components that coordinate the search in two spaces.

Each of these three components is a potential source of developmental change and, as indicated by the taxonomy presented in table 1.1, most psychologists have studied them in isolation. But such decomposition begs the very question of interest: the coordination of search in two spaces. We wanted to try a different approach in which we could study discovery behavior in situations that required coordinated search in *both* the experiment space and the hypothesis space. In order to do this, we set up laboratory situations that were designed to place participants in various parts of this framework and then look at how they managed the dual search process. In the next chapter, we describe our basic paradigm for such investigations.

Notes

1. For example, Newell and Simon (1972) note that in chess "there are something like 10^{120} continuations to be explored, with much less than 10^{20} nanoseconds available in a century to explore them" (p. 669).

2. Planning has had a very wide variety of definitions, ranging from "little computer programs that program the mind to perform certain cognitive tasks, such as long division, brushing your teeth, or generating a sentence" (Wickelgren, 1974, p. 357) to "any hierarchical process in the organism that can control the order in which a sequence of operations is to be performed" (Miller, Galanter, and Pribram, 1960, p. 16) to "the predetermination of a course of action aimed at achieving a goal" (Hayes-Roth and Hayes-Roth, 1979, p. 275). An elaboration and discussion of the many definitions can be found in Scholnick and Friedman (1987). We use the Newell and Simon definition here because (1) it is much better defined than the others, and (2) it fits nicely in the set of weak methods.

3. Instead, it is characterized by them as one of several sources of information that could be used to create a representation for the problem space. "If the given task bears a similarity to another task with which the problem solver is already familiar, then he may attempt to use the problem space and programs from the familiar one. To do so requires that the knowledge and structures be adapted to the new task. The result will be useful only if the initial recognition of similarity reflects fundamental isomorphisms between the structures of the tasks and if the adaption is successful. (Newell and Simon, 1972, p. 851)

4. In a remarkably prescient inquiry in 1932, Erika Fromm, then a young graduate student of Max Wertheimer, asked a sample of famous scientists and philosophers to reflect on their own "productive thinking processes" and to "write a few lines about the beginning and the course of a cognitive process from your concrete scientific research" (Fromm, 1998, p. 1194). Among the replies she received was one from Albert Einstein, who, in reflecting on the thinking that led to his special theory of relativity, said, "The psychological situation is comparable with the attitude of somebody who wants to solve a puzzle or a chess problem, who is convinced that the solution exists, because the creator of the problem possess the solution" (Einstein, 1932, quoted in Fromm, 1998, p. 1198).

5. There is an extensive literature on this task. See Klayman and Ha (1987) for an excellent review and theoretical reformulation.

Chapter 3

A Paradigm for Investigating Scientific Discovery in the Psychology Lab

with Kevin Dunbar

The scientist . . . is faced with the task of assimilating information, conserving cognitive strain, and regulating the risk of failure and folly. We have idealized the experimental situations employed in our investigations beyond what is normal in daily life, but that is the price one pays for experimenting at all. It is our hope that by reaching a fuller understanding of these more idealized forms of thinking in vitro, *the complexities of thinking as we observe it around us will be more readily understood.*
(Bruner, Goodnow, and Austin, 1956, p. 247)

In this chapter we describe our paradigm for studying the cognitive psychology of scientific discovery *in vitro* and we link it to the theoretical framework presented in chapter 2. We describe our basic procedure, a particular context for studying discovery processes in the psychology lab, the structure and content of the hypothesis space and the experiment space for that context, and the mapping between them. Because many of the discovery situations used in later chapters are direct isomorphs of the one introduced here, we present the context and its psychological representation in detail at this point.

Our procedure is to present people with situations in which they have to discover a rule that governs the behavior of a relatively complex system. In order to make the discovery, participants have to configure the system in various ways and observe its behavior. The thing to be discovered carries with it sufficient meaning that people are inclined to view some hypotheses as highly plausible, and others as implausible.

Because participants' verbalizations provide the basic information source for our analyses of their cognitive processes, the discovery task is preceded by a brief training in how to give concurrent verbal protocols. Next, participants are given basic instruction about the system so that they learn about its basic properties and characteristics. Finally, they are given a challenge to discover something new about the system. They are told that their task is to formulate hypotheses and to design, run, and interpret experiments that bear on their hypotheses. Participants can terminate the process whenever they believe that they have discovered the new rule or principle. We record all participant verbalizations and behaviors, as well as the behavior of the system being investigated. This enables us to track participants' goals, hypotheses, experiments, and evaluations. Our tasks typically take between thirty and ninety minutes, depending on the participants and on the particular context being investigated.

This paradigm has several features that make it a useful way to investigate scientific thinking in the psychology laboratory. Each of the following features captures an important aspect of real science:

> 1. The discovery contexts are sufficiently complex to ensure that hypotheses and experiments cannot be characterized in the same underlying representation. That is, the elements and relations that comprise the hypothesis space are not the same as those comprising the experiment space. Consequently, the heuristics used to search the two spaces are not identical. Moreover, the mapping between experiments and hypotheses is nontrivial. In contrast, in a classical concept learning experiment, instances (e.g., large-red-triangle) and hypotheses (e.g., red things) are represented in exactly the same form, and search proceeds in a single space.

> 2. Prior knowledge can influence the form, content, structure, and strength of belief of hypotheses. As a result, different standards of proof and refutation may be applied to different hypotheses.

> 3. Participants design their own experiments. They are not simply presented with predetermined patterns of covariation or a set of fixed alternatives. Instead, they have to decide on the size and complexity of their experiments.

> 4. Participants decide when they have discovered "truth." They must base their conclusions upon a combination of their prior biases and the evidence that they have generated, because they are never told whether they are right or wrong.

In addition to these similarities to real science, our materials are designed to be interesting and challenging for a wide range of ages, from elementary schoolchildren through college adults, because we are interested in the developmental course of scientific reasoning skills.

The Basic Paradigm

In our earliest studies, we used a robotic toy called BigTrak (Dunbar and Klahr, 1989; Klahr and Dunbar, 1988). It was a self-contained, self-propelled, "laser tank"—depicted in figure 3.1a—that could be programmed to move around the floor of the laboratory through a simple

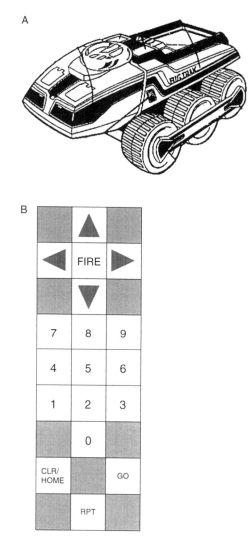

Figure 3.1
(a) The BigTrak device. (b) Simplified BigTrak keypad.

programming language. The user could press a series of buttons on the BigTrak's keypad that would control sequences of forward and backward movements, turns, and "firings" of its "cannon."[1]

Participants were taught how to program BigTrak's basic commands (move forward, move backward, turn left, turn right, fire cannon), and how to get it to make specific maneuvers. Once they were familiar with the device's programming conventions and its behavior, participants were asked to figure out how a new function operated. In the standard configuration, the new function was labeled RPT, and it worked by repeating the last n steps in the program one time.[2] The participant's task was to discover and report how the RPT key functioned. Participants did this by writing a series of programs and observing the device's behavior. Because participants usually generated a variety of hypotheses about how RPT works (e.g., repeat the whole program n times, repeat the last n steps, repeat the nth step once, repeat the next n steps n times, etc.) the task challenged their ability to generate informative experiments and to relate the outcomes of those experiments to their hypotheses.

As participants attempted to discover how RPT works, they formulated hypotheses and generated experiments (by writing and executing programs) to evaluate those hypotheses. In this chapter we will describe how the hypothesis space can be represented as a set of frames consisting of slots and values. We will also describe the experiment space for BigTrak in terms of the essential features of experiments, and we will summarize the relation between search in the two spaces.

A simplified version of the BigTrak keypad is depicted in figure 3.1b. The basic execution cycle involves first clearing the memory by pressing the CLR key and then entering a series of up to sixteen instructions (or steps), each consisting of a function key (the command) and a one- or two-digit number (the argument). The five command keys are: ↑ move forward, ↓ move backward, ← rotate left, → rotate right, and FIRE. When the GO key is pressed BigTrak executes the program.[3]

For example, suppose you pressed the following series of keys: CLR ↑5 ←7 ↑3 →15 FIRE 2 ↓8 GO. When the GO key was pressed, BigTrak would move forward five feet, rotate to the left seven "minutes" (counterclockwise 42 degrees), move forward 3 feet, rotate to the right fifteen minutes (clockwise 90 degrees), fire twice, and back up eight feet.

Our procedure had three phases. In the first, participants were instructed in how to generate verbal protocols and then were introduced to BigTrak. In the second, they were instructed on the use of each basic command. During this phase, the RPT key was not visible. Participants were trained to criterion on how to write a series of commands to accomplish a specified maneuver. The end of this phase corresponded to a scientist having a basic amount of knowledge about a domain.

In the third phase, participants were shown the RPT key. They were told that it required a numeric parameter (n), and that there could be only one RPT n in a program. They were told that their task was to find out how RPT worked by writing programs and observing the results. This corresponded to a new problem in the domain—an unresolved question in an otherwise familiar context. Then participants began to formulate hypotheses about RPT and run experiments to test those hypotheses. This required a coordinated search of the Hypothesis Space and the Experiment Space. Participants were never told whether or not they had discovered how RPT worked. They had to decide that for themselves.

The Influence of Prior Knowledge

One purpose of the instruction phase was to familiarize participants with the device and the experimental context so that they could function comfortably in the discovery phase. A more important goal of the instruction phase was to establish a realistic but tractable analog to a real scientific problem. Scientific work goes on in the context of previously developed theories that provide a background both for the generation of hypotheses and the design of experiments. Analogously, by the time our participants encounter the RPT key, they have various mental models of BigTrak's functioning as well as general knowledge about what "repeat" means. In the BigTrak context, three categories of prior knowledge may influence participants' hypotheses about how RPT works.

1. Linguistic Knowledge about the Meaning of "Repeat"   Participants know that repeating something means doing it again and that various linguistic devices are needed to determine both *what* is to be repeated and *how many times* the repetition is to occur. There is some ambiguity about whether the number of repeats includes or excludes the initial execution or occurrence (i.e., does "he repeated it twice" mean two or three utterances of the same sentence?).

2. Programming Knowledge about Iteration   BigTrak is a computer-controlled device, and participants with some programming experience may draw on knowledge about different kinds of iteration constructs from familiar programming languages. Typically, n plays the role of determining the number of repetitions, while the scope is determined by syntactic devices.

3. Specific Knowledge about BigTrak   Based on what they learn during the training phase, participants know that there are two types of keys: regular *command* keys that correspond to specific observable actions and take numerical arguments ($\uparrow$, $\rightarrow$, etc.), and *special* keys that take no argument (CLR, GO, etc.). For all command keys, the numerical argument corresponds to the number of repetitions of a unit event (moving a foot, turning a six-degree unit, firing the cannon once, etc.). Although all command keys have an eventual observable consequence, they do not have an immediate action. The GO key does have immediate observable consequences: It executes the entire program that has been entered.

These different knowledge sources suggest misleading and conflicting analogies. In most programming conventions, the element(s) to be repeated follow the repeat indicator, the scope is determined by syntax, and the number of repetitions is controlled by a variable. On the other hand, a common linguistic form for "repeat" implicitly sets the number of repetitions to a single one and the scope to an immediately preceding entity (e.g., "could you repeat that?"). Even the specific experience with other BigTrak commands provides contradictory clues to RPT's precise function. One potential conflict concerns the cues for classification of the type of command. RPT is "regular" in that it takes a parameter and does not cause any immediate action, and yet unlike any other regular key, it corresponds to no particular behavior. Another potential conflict concerns the meaning of the parameter. The participant has to determine whether n corresponds to what is to be repeated or to how many times it is to be repeated. Finally, prior knowledge about special keys may leave participants uncertain about which parts of the program might be affected by the RPT key. For example, the domain of CLR and GO is the entire program, but the domain of RPT remains to be discovered.

All of these factors conspire to produce a discovery context in which prior knowledge is likely to influence the initial plausibility of certain classes of hypotheses. We believe that this increases the external validity of BigTrak as a productive context in which to investigate discovery processes.

Hypothetical Behavior
Before describing the behavior of a real participant, we present a simple idealized example of how you might attempt to figure out how RPT works. In table 3.1 we have listed a hypothetical sequence of hypotheses, predictions, and experiments and their outcomes. In this example we will assume that, unlike most of our participants, you follow the canons of good science: you formulate two contrasting hypotheses and set out to test them. Hypothesis A says that when you put in a RPT and a number, the whole program repeats that many times. Many participants start out with this hypothesis, or something very similar to it. Hypothesis B is a little odd: it says that RPT n takes the nth step in the program and repeats it one more time. Very few participants start out with this hypothesis. Nevertheless, let us assume that these are the two that you want to test.

What about experiments? What kind of program should you write in order to test your hypotheses? Suppose you decide that one good strategy for searching the space of experiments (in this case, programs that use the RPT function) is to start simple, with a minimally complex pro-

Table 3.1
Hypothetical sequence of hypotheses, experiments, and outcomes.

	Experiment 1	Experiment 2
	↑ 1 RPT 1	↑ 1 FIRE 2 ↓ 1 RPT 2
Hypotheses about RPT n		*Predictions*
H_A: repeats the entire program *n* times.	↑ 2	↑ 1 FIRE 2 ↓ 1 ↑ 1 FIRE 2 ↓ 1
H_B: repeats the *n*th step once.	↑ 2	↑ 1 FIRE 2 ↓ 1 FIRE 2
		BigTrak Behavior
	↑ 2	↑ 1 FIRE 2 ↓ 1 FIRE 2 ↓ 1

gram. Thus, you write the program shown at the top of the experiment 1 column in table 3.1: (↑ 1 RPT 1). Although this is indeed a simple to construct and easy to observe experiment, it is not very informative, because the prediction from both hypotheses (shown in the center of the experiment 1 column) is that BigTrak will go forward two times, which is precisely what it does (as shown at the bottom of the column). This is clearly a poor experiment because it fails to discriminate between predictions of the two hypotheses. The experiment might not be a total loss if BigTrak did something inconsistent with both hypotheses, but it doesn't.

For your second experiment, you try something more complex: ↑ 1 FIRE 2 ↓ 1 RPT 2. Now the two hypotheses do make distinctive predictions: H_A predicts ↑ 1 FIRE 2 ↓ 1 ↑ 1 FIRE 2 ↓ 1 and H_B predicts ↑ 1 FIRE 2 ↓ 1 FIRE 2. Experiment 2 has some additional desirable properties; it is pretty short, so you can keep track of what is going on, and it has easily distinguishable components, so each piece of behavior is highly informative.

However, when the second experiment is run, BigTrak goes like this: ↑ 1 FIRE 2 ↓ 1 FIRE 2 ↓ 1. This behavior is inconsistent with both theories. Thus, from experiment 1, you could conclude that both theories were still viable, but from experiment 2, you have evidence that neither is correct. But you can go beyond this kind of binary evaluation of truth or falsity by examining some of the features of BigTrak's behavior. For example, you might notice that BigTrak repeated the last two steps of the program. You might also notice that you used 2 as the value of *n*. From this critical observation that RPT 2 caused BigTrak to repeat the last 2 steps in a program, you might generalize to the hypothesis that RPT *n* repeats the last *n* instructions. And that *is* the way the original BigTrak really worked.

Typical Participant Protocol

Now let us look in detail at some real performance on this task. This example also illustrates how we extract and encode information from the video tape record and how we go about our protocol analysis. The example used here, although typical in many respects, is shorter than most, because it was generated by a participant who very rapidly discovered how RPT works. The entire protocol is listed in table 3.2.

Table 3.2
Example of a complete protocol from a successful adult.

		So how do you think it might work?
		Uh . . . it would repeat all of the steps before it, however many times I told it to repeat it.
		Well . . . so start working on it now then.
		OK.
		And tell me everything that's going on in your mind.
		OK.
		Now press CLEAR.
Exp. 1		
↑ 2 RPT 2	0:30	OK, um . . . I'm gonna make it go forward two, and then I'm gonna make it repeat that twice.
→		
↑ 4		
		Maybe not, uh . . .
Exp. 2		
	2:00	. . . repeat once
↑ 1 ← 15 ↑ 1 HOLD 2 RPT 1		Hmm . . . guess that was it.
→		*So what are you thinking?*
↑ 1 ← 15 ↑ 1 HOLD 4		Um . . . actually I have no idea now. I'm trying to figure out what it is.
		Um . . . maybe it repeats the last step.
Exp. 3		
		OK, I'm gonna try that. . . . repeat once
↑ 2 ← 30 RPT 1	3:30	
→		All right, that backs up my theory.
↑ 2 ← 60		
Exp. 4		
	4:00	Let me see if I can somehow make sure that that's what it does . . .
↑ 2 ← 30 RPT 4		it repeats the last step however many times that I tell it to,
→		so I'm gonna . . . repeat it four times . . .
↑ 2 ← 30 ↑ 2 ← 30		That was strange, hmm . . .

Table 3.2 (continued)

Exp. 5		um . . . let me see that again
	4:30	
↑ 2 ← 30 RPT 4		
→		OK, maybe it means repeat the last number . . .
↑ 2 ← 30 ↑ 2 ← 30		however many steps before it that I put in, that'll be the number after the repeat. For instance, if I put repeat two, it'll repeat the last two steps. If I put repeat five, it'll repeat the last five steps, and if there's too many . . . if the five is more than the number of steps in the program, it'll just end it at whatever number of steps in the program,
Exp. 6		
	6:00	so . . . repeat one, no, repeat two.
↑ 2 ← 15 ↑ 2 FIRE 3 RPT 2		All right, I think I might have gotten it.
→		
↑ 2 ← 15 ↑ 2 FIRE 3 ↑ 2 FIRE 3		
Exp. 7		
	6:30	
↑ 2 ← 15 ↑ 2 FIRE 3 RPT 3		OK, I think I've gotten it.
→		
↑ 2 ← 15 ↑ 2 FIRE 3 ← 15 ↑ 2 FIRE 3		
Exp. 8	7:30	I'm gonna make it repeat four times . . . wanna repeat four . . .
↑ 2 ← 15 ↑ 2 FIRE 3 RPT 4		
→		
↑ 2 ← 15 ↑ 2 FIRE 3 ↑ 2 ← 15 ↑ 2 FIRE 3		
		OK, now I'm trying to figure out which order the repeat step goes.
Exp. 9		If it does the first part of the program or if it does . . . if it starts
↑ 2 ← 15 ↑ 2 FIRE 3 RPT 1	9:00	from the last part of the program, where repeat . . . if I say repeat one, does it repeat the
→		first step in the program,
↑ 2 ← 15 ↑ 2 FIRE 6		or does it repeat the last step I pressed in? Um . . . repeat that step It goes from the last step, and I don't understand why it doesn't go backwards.
		Maybe it counts back two steps.
		If I put repeat two, it would count back two steps, starting from there and go until the
Exp. 10		last step. All right,
	10:00	. . . um . . . the last two steps were forward
↑ 2 ← 15 ↑ 2 FIRE 3 RPT 2		two and fire three,
→		so let me try and repeat that again.
↑ 2 ← 15 ↑ 2 FIRE 3 ↑ 2 FIRE 3		

Table 3.2 (continued)

Exp. 11		
	11:00	All right, now if I . . . repeat five . . .
↑ 2 ← 15 ↑ 2 FIRE 3 RPT 4		so if I put repeat four, it should do the whole
➔		program over again.
↑ 2 ← 15 ↑ 2 FIRE 3 ↑ 2		
← 15 ↑ 2 FIRE 3		
		Well, I think I figured out what it does.
		So how does it work?
		OK, when you press the repeat key and then the number,
		it comes back that many steps and then starts from there
		and goes up to, uh . . . it proceeds up to the end of the program
		and then it hits the repeat function again.
		It can't go through it twice.
		Great!

Note: CLR and GO commands have been deleted. The left-hand column shows the program, followed by (➔) BigTrak's behavior. The right-hand column shows the participant's comments (with experimenter's comments italicized).

Before his first experiment, the participant (ML) forms the hypothesis that RPT n will repeat the entire program n times. The prediction associated with the first experiment is that BigTrak will go forward six units. The prediction is consistent with the current hypothesis, but BigTrak does not behave as expected: it goes forward only four units, and the participant comments on the possibility of a failed prediction just before experiment 2. This leads him to revise his hypothesis after experiment 2: RPT n repeats only the last step. At this point, it is not clear whether ML thinks there will be one or n repetitions of the last step, and experiment 3 does not discriminate between the two possibilities. (We call this kind of hypothesis "partially specified," because of the ambiguity. In contrast, the initial hypothesis stated earlier is "fully specified.") However, his comments following experiment 3 clarify the issue. Experiment 3 produces results consistent with the hypothesis that there will be n repetitions (BigTrak goes forward two units and turns left sixty units), and ML explicitly notes the confirming behavior. But experiment 4 disconfirms the hypothesis. Although he makes no explicit prediction, we infer from statements made before experiment 4 that ML expected BigTrak to go forward two and turn left 120. Instead, it executes the entire ↑ 2 ← 30 sequence twice. ML finds this "strange," and he repeats the experiment.

Following his fifth experiment, ML begins to formulate and verbalize the correct hypothesis—that RPT n causes BigTrak to execute one repe-

Table 3.3
Common hypotheses for the effect of RPT *n*.

		Role of *n*
C1:	*n* repeats of entire program	Counter
C2:	*n* repeats of the last step	Counter
C3:	*n* repeats of subsequent steps[1]	Counter
S1:	One repeat of last *n* steps	Selector
S2:	One repeat of first *n* steps	Selector
S3:	One repeat of the *n*th step	Selector
U1:	One repeat of entire program	Unspecified
U2:	One repeat of the last step	Unspecified

1. BigTrak allowed RPT to occur at any position in a program, and some subjects conjectured that RPT had its effect on instructions *following* rather than *preceding* its location. Although we include this type of hypothesis here and in figure 3.2, most subjects did not propose such a rule, and we disallowed it in our subsequent microworld designs.

tition of the *n* instructions preceding the RPT, and he even correctly articulates the special case where *n* exceeds the program length, in which case the entire program is repeated once. ML then does a series of experiments where he only varies *n* in order to be sure he is correct (experiments 6, 7, and 8), and then he explores the issue of the order of execution in the repeated segment.

Dual Search in Discovering How RPT Works

Having described both hypothetical and real behavior on the BigTrak discovery task, we now turn to a theoretical analysis of how dual search is executed in this context. We present, first, a description of space of hypotheses associated with this task, then a description of the experiment space, and finally, a summary of how the search in the two spaces is coordinated. Only the formal structure of these spaces is presented in this chapter. In subsequent chapters we go on to quantify various aspects of the spaces and their search, based on a series of empirical investigations.

The BigTrak Hypothesis Space

Except for its brevity, ML's performance is typical of the participants to be described later in most respects, and his proposed hypotheses are among the more common hypotheses that participants proposed (see table 3.3). On the right side of the table, hypotheses are classified according to the *role* that they assign to the parameter (*n*) that goes with the RPT command. In hypotheses C1 to C3, *n* *counts* the number of times that something (i.e., program, last step, first step, etc.) gets repeated. We call these "counter" hypotheses. In hypotheses S1 to S3, *n* determines

which segment of the program will be *selected* to be repeated again. We
call these "selector" hypotheses. (Recall that the correct rule is S1 in
table 3.3: Repeat the last *n* steps once.) The distinction between counters
and selectors turns out to be very useful in our subsequent analyses. Finally, there are some hypotheses that don't assign any role at all to *n* (e.g.,
U1 and U2).

These eight hypotheses about RPT *n* (as well as many others) can be
represented in a space of "frames" (Minsky, 1975). A frame is simply an
organized data structure with a set of attributes—or "slots"—that can
take on values according to what the frame is representing. The basic
frame for discovering how RPT works is depicted at the top of figure 3.2.
It consists of four slots, corresponding to four key attributes. The most
important slot is the role of *n* (*n*-ROLE). Is it a counter or is it a selector?
The second slot defines the number of repetitions: 1, *n*, some other function of *n*, or none. The third slot defines the *unit* of repetition: is it a step
(as in C2 and S3), the entire program (as in U1 and C1), or a group of
steps (as in S1)? The final slot determines the boundaries of the repeated
segment: for example, beginning of program, end of program, *n*th step
from beginning or end, and so on.

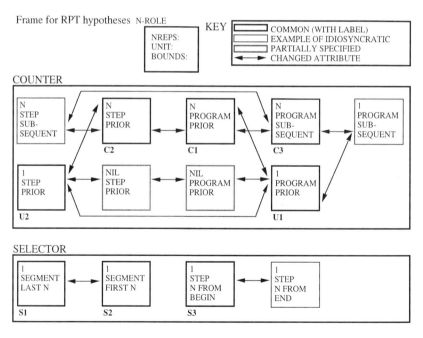

Figure 3.2
Hypothesis space for BigTrak. Labels on some hypotheses (e.g., C1, S3, etc.) correspond to
the hypothesis descriptions in table 3.3.

A fully instantiated frame corresponds to a fully specified hypothesis, several of which are shown in figure 3.2. The hypotheses are clustered according to role they assign to n: counter or selector. Within each of these frames, an arrow connects those hypotheses differing along only a single attribute. All other pairs of hypotheses in figure 3.2 differ by more than one attribute. Of particular importance is the fact that no arrows appear between the counter hypotheses at the top and the selector hypotheses at the bottom. This is because the values of some attributes are linked to the values of others and a change in n-role requires a simultaneous change in more than a single attribute. For example, if n-role is *counter*, the number of repetitions is n, whereas, if n-role is *selector*, then number of repetitions is 1.

This frame representation is a convenient way to capture a number of aspects of the scientific reasoning process. First, it characterizes the relative importance that participants give to different aspects of an hypothesis. This is consistent with Klayman and Ha's (1987) suggestion that "some features of a rule are naturally more 'salient,' that is, more prone to occur to a hypothesis-tester as something to be considered" (p. 11). In our context, a frame is constructed according to those features of prior knowledge that are most strongly activated, such as knowledge about the device or linguistic knowledge about "repeat." When a frame is constructed, slot values are set to their default values. For example, having selected the n-role: counter frame, values for number of repetitions, units and boundary might be chosen so as to produce C1 (see figure 3.2).

Second, the frame representation suggests a way in which experimentation can be focused on the production of specific information. Once a particular frame is constructed, the task becomes one of filling in or verifying slots in that frame. The current frame will determine the relevant attributes. That is, the choice of a particular role for n (e.g., *counter*), also determines what slots remain to be filled (e.g., number of repetitions: n), and it constrains the focus of experimentation.

Third, the structure of these frames captures an important aspect of most theories of conceptual change and scientific discovery: the distinction between local theoretical changes and radical hypothesis revision. The frame representation used here makes it clear that some hypotheses are very closely related whereas others require a major restructuring. More specifically, several changes within the set of counter hypotheses, shown in the middle panel in figure 3.2, or the set of selector hypotheses, shown at the bottom of figure 3.2, require only a change in a single slot value. In contrast, a change between any counter and any selector requires simultaneous change in the value of more than one slot. Thus, search in the BigTrak hypothesis space can involve local search among counters or among selectors, or it can involve more far-ranging search between counter frames and selector frames.

The BigTrak Experiment Space

Participants can test hypotheses by conducting experiments, that is, by writing programs that include RPT and observing BigTrak's behavior. In order to decide which programs to write, they must search in a space of experiments. The BigTrak experiment space can be characterized in many ways: the total number of commands in a program, the location of RPT in a program, value of n, the specific commands in a program, the numerical arguments of specific commands, and so on. For example, counting only commands, but not their numerical arguments, as distinct, there are over 30 billion (5^{15}) distinct programs that participants could choose from for each experiment. Even if we consider programs with no more than four steps, there are nearly eight hundred different experiments to choose from ($5^4 + 5^3 + 5^2 + 5$). It is clear that, even for this little domain, there is a vast search space, and participants must bring to bear effective heuristics for constraining that search.

But this space can be reduced still further, and our participants appear to quickly realize that there are just two key dimensions to the experiment space for this task. The first is λ—the length of the program preceding RPT. The second is the value of n—the argument that RPT takes. Because both parameters must have values no greater than fifteen, there are 225 "cells" in the λ–n space. Within that space, we identify three distinct regions. Region 1 includes all programs in which $n = 1$. Region 2 includes all programs in which $1 < n < \lambda$. Region 3 includes all programs in which $n \geq \lambda$. Of the 225 cells in the 15×15 experiment space, 15 (7%) are from region 1, 91 (40%) are in region 2, and 119 (53%) are in region 3. The regions are depicted in figure 3.3, together with illustrative programs.

Interaction between the Two Spaces

Programs from different regions of the experiment space vary widely in how effective they are in providing useful evidence with which to evaluate hypotheses. Table 3.4 indicates how hypotheses and experiments interact. The entries in each column under the four hypotheses show what these hypotheses would predict for the program (i.e., the experiment) listed at the left of a row. Programs are depicted by generic commands (e.g., X, Y, Z). To illustrate, the second example shows a program with $\lambda = 2$ and $n = 1$. This is a region 1 experiment. Under hypothesis C1, the two-step program would be executed once and then repeated one more time. Under hypothesis C2, only the last step (Y) would be repeated one additional time. Under hypothesis S1, the last n steps (in this

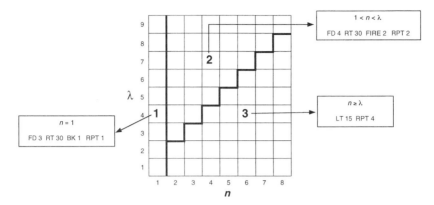

Figure 3.3
Structure of the BigTrak experiment space, showing the three regions. λ = number of commands preceding RPT. n = argument for RPT. (Only a segment of the space is shown here: the full space is 15×15.)

Table 3.4
Predicted behavior of BigTrak under four hypotheses and programs from each of the experiment space regions.

					Hypotheses			
					Counters		Selectors	
					C1: Program n times	C2: Last step n times	S1: Last n steps once	S2: nth step once
No.	Region	λ	n	Program				
1	1	1	1	X **R1**	**XX**	**XX**	**XX**	**XX**
2	1	2	1	X Y **R1**	**XYXY**	XY**Y**	XY**Y**	XY**X**
3	1	3	1	X Y Z **R1**	**XYZXYZ**	XYZ**Z**	XYZ**Z**	XYZ**X**
4	2	3	2	X Y Z **R2**	**XYZXYZXYZ**	XYZ**ZZ**	XYZ**ZYZ**	XYZ**ZY**
5	3	3	3	X Y Z **R3**	**XYZXYZXYZ**<u>XYZ</u>	XYZ**ZZZ**<u>Z</u>	XYZ**XYZXYZ**	XYZ**ZZZ**
6	3	2	3	X Y **R3**	**XYXYXYXY**<u>XY</u>	XY**YYY**<u>Y</u>	XY**XY***	XY**Y***
7	3	1	3	X **R3**	**XXXX**<u>X</u>	X**XX**<u>X</u>	X**X***	X**X***
8	3	3	4	X Y Z **R4**	**XYZXYZXYZXYZ**<u>XYZ</u>	XYZ**ZZZZ**<u>Z</u>	XYZ**XYZ***	XYZ**Z***

Note: Each row shows a generic program and how BigTrak would behave under each of the four rules shown at the head of the column. For each entry, executions under control of RPT are shown in boldface, executions under the $n + 1$ interpretation of "repeat n times" are underlined, and the effects of not allowing n to be greater than λ in selector hypotheses are indicated by an asterisk.

case, the last step, because $n = 1$) would be repeated once and under hypothesis S2, the first step would be repeated once. This program cannot discriminate between hypotheses C2 and S1. More specifically, suppose that, in the second program in table 3.4 (X Y R1), X is ↑2 and Y is →15. The program would be ↑2 →15 RPT 1 and the four different hypotheses would generate the following predictions for that program: C1 (repeat the program once) would predict ↑2 →15 ↑2 →15; both C2 (repeat the last step once) and S1 (repeat the last step once) would predict ↑2 →30; and S2 (repeat the first step once) would predict ↑2 →15 ↑2.

Each of the generic examples in table 3.4 can represent a continuum of discriminating power. The most highly differentiated programs are obtained if we substitute distinct commands for X, Y, and Z (for example, X = ↑ 2, Y = FIRE 1). The least informative programs are those in which both the command and the parameter are the same (e.g., X = Y = Z = → 15). Intermediate between these two extremes are programs in which the commands are the same but the parameters are different, such as FIRE 1 FIRE 2 FIRE 3. For many such programs the different hypotheses do, in fact, make distinct predictions, but it is extremely difficult to keep track of BigTrak's behavior.

Two important and subtle features of the hypotheses are included in the notation in table 3.4. The first potentially confusing feature has to do with the ambiguity inherent in the phrase "repeat it n times" when $n > 1$. Does it mean n or $n + 1$ total executions of the repeated entity? That is, if a program is supposed to repeat something twice, a participant might expect to observe either two or three occurrences of that item or segment. The underlined segments in Table 3.3 show the behavior generated by the $n + 1$ interpretation (which is the one we use in our simulations). If participants use the n interpretation, then they would not expect to see these extra segments. The second feature involves hypotheses S1 and S2 when $n > \lambda$. For these programs (indicated by an asterisk), BigTrak behaves as if n equals λ.

Experiments in the three regions interact with hypotheses as follows: (1) Programs in region 1 have poor discriminating power. We have already described example 2, and example 3 similarly fails to discriminate C2 from S1. Example 1—a minimalist program with $\lambda = n = 1$—has no discriminating power whatsoever. (2) Region 2 provides maximal information about each of the most common hypotheses because it can distinguish between counters and selectors, and it can distinguish *which* selector or counter is operative. It produces different behavior under all four hypotheses for any program in the region, and varying n in a series of experiments in this region always produces different outcomes. (3) Under hypotheses S1 and S2, results of experiments in region 3 may be confusing because they are executed under the subtle additional rule that values of n greater than λ are truncated to $n = \lambda$. Therefore, varying

n in this region will give the impression that n has no effect on the behavior of the device (compare examples 1 and 7 or 5 and 8). Although some of the programs in this region are discriminating (such as example 5 with $\lambda = n = 3$), others either do not discriminate at all (S1 versus S2 in example 7) or depend on the truncation assumption to be fully understood (such as examples 6 to 8).

SDDS in the BigTrak Context
Dual search in the BigTrak context is illustrated in figure 3.4. The hypothesis space and experiment space are represented on the left as two interrelated planes, and the activated components of the SDDS subgoal structure are shown in ovals. The figure depicts the processes surrounding ML's first three experiments. (Thus, the following description requires the coordination of table 3.2 and figure 3.4.) As described earlier, ML starts with the very common initial hypothesis that RPT n repeats the entire program n times. Having selected this hypothesis (shown in the upper plane of figure 3.4a), ML selects his first experiment (in the $\lambda = 1, n = 2$ cell of the experiment space shown in the lower plane of figure 3.4a). Then follows the predict, run, match, and evaluate cycle, leading to a second search of the hypothesis space. The first subgoal in this search is to assign a new value to the "repeated segment" slot of the counter frame, and the next subgoal is to generate an outcome via E-Space search. ML's second experiment, shown in figure 3.4b, is a four-step program with $n = 1$. Its outcome leads ML to the hypothesis that RPT n instructs BigTrak to repeat only the last step of the program. This hypothesis, and the experiment ML used to test it, are shown in figure 3.4c.

As the depiction in figure 3.4 indicates, the searches in the two spaces provide mutual constraint: experiments are designed to evaluate the current hypothesis, and hypotheses are constrained by current (and prior) experimental results. But this characterization is only at a global level, and many questions remain about how the dual search is conducted. What determines participants' initial starting points in these spaces? What determines how they move from one part of the space to another? How does the location in one space determine the constraints on the next move in the other space? Finally, but importantly, how do these processes change with development? These questions motivate the series of empirical studies to be described in the next several chapters.

Reiteration: The Two Aspects of Scientific Discovery

The successful scientist, like the successful explorer, must master two related skills: knowing where to look and understanding what is seen. The

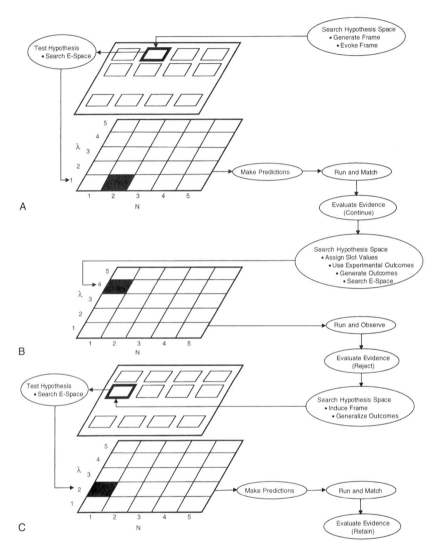

Figure 3.4
Dual search by a participant exploring the BigTrak spaces.

first skill—*experimental design*—involves the design of experimental and observational procedures; the second—*hypothesis formation*—involves the formation and evaluation of theory. Historical analyses of scientific discoveries suggest that the interaction between experimental design and hypothesis formation is crucial to the success of the real scientific endeavor and that both activities are influenced by the semantics of the discovery context. However, this interaction can be quite complex; consequently, the implicit research strategy in most psychological studies of scientific reasoning has been to investigate each skill in isolation and in semantically lean contexts. This strategy has yielded many important findings about distinct stages of the scientific reasoning process, but much remains to be learned about how the stages interact and about how the interaction is influenced by prior knowledge.

The work described in this book extends the earlier laboratory studies by investigating scientific reasoning in contexts that require a rich interaction among the many processes that support the formation of hypotheses and the design of experiments. Our goal is to create such contexts while maintaining the positive advantages of laboratory studies of psychological processes. In the remaining chapters, we provide detailed examples of such investigations.

Notes

1. Note that the BigTrak language is very similar to the widely used LOGO programming language (Klahr and Carver, 1988; Papert, 1980).
2. In the computer-based microworlds to be described later, the function can be set—under experimenter control—to operate in several different ways (e. g., to repeat the entire program n times).
3. In addition to the keys depicted in Figure 3.1*b*, BigTrak has three special function keys not shown here: (1) CLS clears the last step that was entered. (2) HOLD n makes Big-Trak pause for n tenths of a second. (Most subjects did not use HOLD, although ML, the subject described later in the chapter, did use it once.) (3) CK checks the most recently entered step by executing it in isolation. These special keys played no important role in this or subsequent studies, and, with one exception, they will not be mentioned again.

Chapter 4

Coordinating Dual Search: The Role of Evidence

with Kevin Dunbar

It is a capital mistake to theorize before one has data.
(Arthur Conan Doyle, *The Adventures of Sherlock Holmes*, 1891)

Working with theories is not like skeet shooting, where theories are lofted up and bang, *they are shot down with a falsification bullet, and that's the end of that theory. Theories are more like graduate students—once admitted you try hard to avoid flunking them out, it being much better for them and for the world if they can become long-term contributors to society.*
(Newell, 1990, p. 14)

Arthur Conan Doyle's warning gives primacy to the role of evidence by reminding us that theories should be constructed only after collecting data, whereas Allen Newell's remark suggests that no single piece of evidence should be considered so important as to constitute the fatal "falsification bullet." What, then, is the proper balance between theory and evidence in the scientific discovery process? Is there some "best way" to make a discovery? We think not, because, as we indicated in chapter 2, the subgoal hierarchy for scientific discovery is surprisingly complex, and it can be traversed in many ways that depend on strategic preferences, domain knowledge, and a host of other factors. Nevertheless, we believe that different discovery strategies can be identified and that they will have distinctive consequences. These strategies differ with respect to how they traverse the three main components in the SDDS framework; that is, in the way in which hypotheses are generated, experiments are designed, and evidence is brought to bear on hypotheses.

In the previous chapter we introduced our paradigm for investigating discovery strategies in the psychology lab, and we described the behavior of a single adult participant who was attempting to discover the function of BigTrak's RPT key. The purpose of that description was to indicate the richness and complexity of the cognitive processes that are involved in making discoveries in our task domain. Now we begin a more detailed and systematic analysis of how people approach this task. In this chapter, we look at the performance of Carnegie Mellon undergraduates. In chapter 5, we expand the participant population to include middle-school children and non-technical college adults, and we also extend our paradigm to a computer-based microworld. In chapter 6 we report on several variations in both the "cover story" for the discovery task and the type of participant populations being studied. The final empirical chapter (chapter 7) describes a new microworld, one that is sufficiently complex that it requires participants to search not only in the hypothesis and experiment spaces, but also in some additional spaces and to apply some discovery strategies that we had not previously identified.

In this chapter we describe two studies[1] in which adult participants attempted to discover how BigTrak's RPT key operated, using the paradigm described in chapter 3. These studies serve two functions. At the methodological level they provide empirical support for our claims about the merits of using microworlds to better understand discovery processes. At the substantive level they reveal two distinct strategies for traversing the SDDS goal hierarchy. More specifically, we will contrast a strategy that utilizes an empirical orientation and focuses on search in the experiment space with a theory-oriented strategy that emphasizes search in the hypothesis space. The results reported in this chapter will indicate the differences between these two types of search and the consequences they have for the discovery process. Of particular interest is the extent to which participants' behavior during the Evaluate Evidence phases departs from the "win-stay lose-shift" strategy that dominates normative views of the scientific method.

Study 1: Theorists and Experimenters

Participants and Procedure
The participants in this first study were twenty Carnegie Mellon undergraduates who were representative of the cross-section of students taking introductory psychology courses. The only additional selection factor was that participants had to have had prior experience in at least one programming language. We added that requirement so as to minimize the time required in phase I, when participants were learning how to do the basic BigTrak programming. (Subsequent analysis did not reveal any reliable differences between participants who had one or many programming courses, or between participants from the engineering, science, humanities, or fine arts colleges at Carnegie Mellon. Later studies provide a more systematic exploration of possible population differences.)

Study 1 followed the three-phase procedure described in chapter 3. First, participants were given instruction and practice in how to generate a good verbal protocol. These instructions were derived from the standard procedures suggested by Ericsson and Simon (1993). Next, the participants learned how to use BigTrak. The experimenter explained each of the basic commands. Then participants were asked to write programs to accomplish specific tasks (e.g., move to the corner of the room, turn around and come back) that would demonstrate their mastery of the basic commands. These two phases were completed within about twenty minutes.

The third—and focal—phase began when the experimenter asked the participant to find out how the RPT key works. Participants were asked to say what they were thinking and what keys they were pressing. All participant behavior during this phase, including all keystrokes, was videotaped. At the outset of this phase, participants had to state their first hypothesis about how RPT worked before using it in any programs. When participants claimed that they were absolutely certain how the repeat key worked, or when forty-five minutes had elapsed, the phase was terminated.

The experimenter interacted with the participant under the following conditions: If the participant was pressing buttons without talking, the experimenter would ask what the participant was thinking. If the participant forgot to bring BigTrak back to the starting position, the experimenter would ask the participant to do so. Finally, if the participant tested the same incorrect hypothesis with the same type of program more than three consecutive times, the experimenter would suggest writing "a different kind of" program.

Aggregate Results
Protocols were transcribed in the format illustrated in appendix 5.1. We coded each experiment in terms of the hypothesis held by the participant at the time of the experiment. Hypotheses could be partially specified or fully specified, depending on how explicitly the various slot values were mentioned. For experiments with active hypotheses, we derived the predicted behavior of BigTrak, and coded whether or not the outcome matched the prediction.

In this section, we first present a coarse-grained aggregate analysis of the data including descriptive statistics about how participants behaved with respect to the major categories of the SDDS model: generating hypotheses, formulating experiments, and evaluating evidence. Then we focus on how participants searched the hypothesis space, and we identify two distinct approaches to discovery. In subsequent sections we look carefully at the evidence evaluation process and show that, although our participants are generally successful at this task, their behavior diverges widely from most normative models of scientific reasoning. Then we turn to the specific content of hypotheses and experiments that were generated during the discovery process. We conclude the analysis of study 1 by shifting our focus from how participants generated and revised hypotheses to how they designed experiments.

Overall Performance
Nineteen of the twenty participants discovered how the RPT key works within the allotted forty-five minutes. The mean time to solution (i.e., when the correct rule was finally stated) was about twenty minutes. In the process of discovering how RPT worked, participants proposed, on average, between four and five hypotheses and conducted, on average, about fifteen experiments.

The twenty participants wrote a total of 364 programs. Fifty-one of these did not include a RPT, but they were immediately followed by an identical program with a RPT. For purposes of analysis, we collapsed these paired contrasts into a single "experiment." Another seven programs were calibration trials in which participants attempted to determine (or remember) what physical unit is associated with n for a specific command (e.g., how far does BigTrak move for ↑ 1?). Two programs that did not contain a RPT were unclassifiable. This left us with 304 experiments on which the following analyses are based.

On their paths to discovering the correct hypothesis, participants entertained a variety of hypotheses. These hypotheses, and their "popularity" are listed in table 4.1. We defined a "common hypothesis" as a fully-specified hypothesis that was proposed by at least two different participants. Across all participants, there were eight distinct common hypotheses. These hypotheses, previously described in chapter 3 (table 3.3), are listed in the first column of table 4.1. The second column in table 4.1 shows the proportion of all study 1 experiments that were run while a particular hypothesis was held. (The final two columns in table 4.1 will be explained later.)

Participants proposed, on average, between four and five hypotheses (including the correct one). Fifty-five percent of the experiments were conducted under one of the eight common hypotheses. Partially specified hypotheses, which account for 3 percent of the experiments, are defined as those in which only some of the attributes of the common hypotheses were stated by the participant (e.g., "It will repeat it n times"). An idiosyncratic hypothesis is defined as one that was generated by only one participant (e.g., "The number calls a little prestored program and runs it off"). Such hypotheses are not listed separately in table 4.1. For 28 percent of the experiments there were no stated hypotheses. For some experiments classified in the "no hypothesis" category, participants may have actually had a hypothesis, but failed to state

Table 4.1
Experiments conducted under different types of hypotheses in study 1 and study 2.

Hypothesis	Study 1	Study 2	
	Percentage of experiments under each hypothesis	Percentage of experiments under each hypothesis	Number of participants mentioning hypothesis in search phase
Counter n-role			
C1: *n* repeats of entire program	14	13	5
C2: *n* repeats of the last step	20	26	9
C3: *n* repeats of subsequent steps	2	0	3
Selector n-role			
S1: One repeat of last *n* steps	2	0	5
S2: One repeat of first *n* steps	4	0	1
S3: One repeat of the *n* th step	3	5	5
Unspecified n-role			
U1: One repeat of entire program	6	11	1
U2: One repeat of the last step	4	9	2
Other types of hypotheses			
Partially specified	3	0	1
Idiosyncratic	14	5	10
No hypothesis	28	26	

it; however, for reasons to be discussed later, we believe that for most of these cases, participants did, in fact, conduct experiments without any hypothesis in mind.

Hypothesis Space Search

Recall that participants were asked to state their hypothesis about RPT before actually using it in an experiment. This enabled us to determine the influence of prior knowledge on the evocation of initial hypotheses. In chapter 3, we discussed the possibility that linguistic knowledge of "repeat," programming knowledge about iteration, and specific knowledge about BigTrak might conspire to produce inappropriate analogies to RPT. This was indeed the case; no participant started out with the correct rule. Seventeen of the twenty participants started with a counter hypothesis. That is, participants initially assumed that the role of *n* is to specify the number of repetitions, and their initial hypotheses differed only in whether the repeated unit was the entire program or the single instruction preceding RPT (C1 and C2). This suggests that participants drew their initial hypotheses by analogy from the regular command keys, all of which determine the number of repetitions of a unit.

Having proposed their initial hypotheses, participants then began to revise them on the basis of experimental evidence. Subsequent hypotheses were systematically related to initial hypotheses. By representing knowledge in terms of frames, we can specify the relation among subsequent hypotheses. Of the 55 percent of all experiments that were conducted with a fully specified hypothesis, nearly two-thirds were conducted in the n-role: counter frame. As shown in table 4.1, these experiments dealt with C1, C2, and C3, which assign n the role of counter; another 10 percent dealt with U1 and U2, which assign it no role at all. When participants were exploring a particular frame, changes in hypotheses usually differed only in the value of a single attribute. (This transition is indicated by connecting arrows in figure 3.2.) For example, if participants were using the n-role: counter frame, changing the unit of repetition from program to step would correspond to a change from C1 to C2, or changing the bounds from prior to subsequent would correspond to a C1 to C3 transition.

In our earlier description of the frame representation for elements of the hypothesis space, we noted that any change from a counter frame to a selector frame is accompanied by changes not only in the values of the n-role slot, but also in the unit-of-repetition slot, the number-of-repetitions slot, and the bounds slot (see figure 3.2). Thus, whenever there is a shift from one frame to the other, at least three slots must change value simultaneously. Fifteen of the participants made only one frame change, and four of the remaining five made three or more frame changes. This suggests that participants were following very different strategies for searching the hypothesis space. We will return to this issue later in this chapter.

Strategic Variation in Scientific Discovery: Theorists and Experimenters
There is abundant evidence demonstrating strategic variation in problem solving—ranging from Bruner, Goodnow, and Austin's (1956) discovery of different strategies for concept-learning, to more recent work on strategic differences in chess, puzzles, physics problems, and scientific reasoning tasks (Chase and Simon, 1973; Klahr and Robinson, 1981; Klayman and Ha, 1989; Kuhn et al., 1995; Larkin et al., 1980; Lovett and Anderson, 1995, 1996; Simon, 1975), and even to such apparently straightforward domains as elementary arithmetic (Siegler, 1987; Siegler and Jenkins, 1989). Thus, we were particularly interested in whether a clear strategic difference would emerge in our discovery task. It did: our participants' protocols yielded two distinct discovery strategies.

As noted earlier, all participants started with the wrong general frame. Consequently, their early efforts were devoted to attempting to refine the details of this incorrect frame. The most significant representational change occurred when n-role was switched from counter to selector and a new frame was constructed. For most participants, once this frame change occurred, the discovery of how RPT worked followed soon after.

How did participants do this? We classified participants into two groups according to the strategy suggested by their activities preceding the switch from the counter frame to the selector frame. We called the first group "experimenters." These thirteen participants induced the correct frame only after observing the result of an experiment in region 2 of the experiment space. We call the participants in the second group "theorists." Theorists did not have to conduct an experiment in region 2 of the experiment space in order to propose the correct frame. These seven participants discovered the correct frame not by searching the experiment space, but instead by searching the hypothesis space. To summarize: the operational distinction between experimenters and theorists was whether or not they conducted an experiment in region 2 immediately prior to proposing a selector hypothesis.

Performance Differences between Experimenters and Theorists
Having categorized participants this way, we then compared them on several other performance measures, listed in table 4.2. There were several notable differences. First, theorists took, on average, less than half as much time as experimenters to discover how RPT worked. They worked at about the same rate as experimenters, so this meant that theorists also produced about half as many experiments as did the experimenters. However, when these experiments are categorized according to whether or not they were conducted under an explicitly stated hy-

Table 4.2
Performance summary of experimenters and theorists in study 1.

	Experimenters	Theorists	Combined
n	13	7	20
Time (minutes)	24.5	11.4	19.4
Experiments	18.4	9.3	15.2
Experiments with hypotheses	12.3	8.6	11.0
Experiments without hypotheses	6.1	0.8	4.2
Different hypotheses	4.9	3.9	4.6
Hypothesis switches	4.8	3.0	4.2
Experiment-space verbalizations	5.9	0.9	4.1
n-λ combinations used	9.9	5.7	8.5

pothesis, another important difference appears: Experimenters conducted significantly more experiments without hypotheses than did Theorists.[2] They also made more explicit comments about the experiment space. There were no differences between the two groups in the number of different hypotheses stated or in the number of hypothesis switches.

Strategic Differences

Experimenters: General Strategy   Participants classified as experimenters went through two major phases. During the first phase they explicitly stated the hypothesis under consideration and conducted experiments to evaluate it. In contrast, during the second phase they conducted many experiments without any explicit hypotheses. Experimenters used a variety of approaches during the first phase. Some proposed new hypotheses by abstracting from the result of a prior experiment, and they proposed many hypotheses. These were the participants, described above, who made more than a single frame change; four of them made three or more such changes. Others stuck doggedly to the same hypothesis, abandoning it only after much experimentation.

The second phase was an exploration of the experiment space. We infer this from the number of experiments conducted without explicit statement of a hypothesis: prior to the discovery of how the RPT key works, experimenters conducted, on average, six experiments without stating any hypothesis. Furthermore, these experiments were usually accompanied by statements about the potential utility of varying n or λ. By pursuing this approach, the experimenters eventually conducted an experiment in region 2 of the experiment space. As described earlier, the results of experiments in this region rule out all the common hypotheses and are consistent only with S1. When participants conducted an experiment in this region, they noticed that the last n steps were repeated and proposed S1—the correct rule.

Theorists: General Strategy   Theorists also started out by proposing hypotheses within the counter frame. Then they conducted experiments that tested the slot values of the frame. When they had gathered enough evidence to reject a hypothesis, Theorists switched to a new value of a slot in the frame. For example, a participant might switch from saying that the prior step is repeated n times to saying that the prior program is repeated n times. When a new hypothesis was proposed, it was always in the same frame, and it usually involved a change in only one attribute.

However, for theorists construction of a new frame was not preceded by an experiment in region 2, nor was it preceded by a series of experiments where no hypothesis had been stated. Theorists switched frames by searching memory for information that enabled them to construct a new frame, rather than by further experimentation. Knowing that sometimes the previous step and sometimes the previous program was repeated, the theorists could infer that the unit of repetition was variable and that this ruled out all hypotheses in the counter frame—these hypotheses all require a fixed unit of repetition. This enabled theorists to constrain their search for a role for n that permits a variable unit of repetition. The memory search produced the selector frame and allowed theorists to propose one of the hypotheses within it. They usually selected the correct one, but if they did not, they soon discovered it by changing one attribute of the frame when their initial selector hypothesis was disconfirmed.

Strategy Differences: Summary   Although both groups started by using hypotheses to guide search in the experiment space, they diverged in the way they searched for new hypotheses once the initial hypotheses—almost always counters—were abandoned: Theorists searched the hypothesis space for a new hypothesis, but experimenters explored the experiment space without an active hypothesis, that is, while traversing the lower left branches of the SDDS goal structure depicted in figure 2.9, to see if they could induce some regularities from experimental outcomes.

Evidence Evaluation
Thus far, our analysis has focused on two of the three main processes in SDDS: on searching the hypothesis space and on searching the experiment space. Now we turn to the third of these processes: evidence evaluation. The crucial decision made by this process is how to interpret the evidence in terms of the current hypothesis. According to the classical norms of the scientific method one should reject disconfirmed hypotheses and retain confirmed ones (cf. Bower and Trabasso, 1964; Popper, 1959). However, our participants' behavior showed substantial departures from this norm.

For the 219 (out of 304) cases where it was clear what participants' current hypotheses were, we classified their responses to confirming and disconfirming evidence. As shown in table 4.3, in nearly one quarter of

Table 4.3
Proportion of rejections and retentions of current hypotheses, given confirming or disconfirming evidence in study 1.

| | Disposition of current hypothesis | | |
	Retain	Reject	n
Experimental outcome			
Confirms current hypothesis	.75	.25	84
Disconfirms current hypothesis	.56	.44	136

the instances where the experimental outcome confirmed the current hypothesis, participants changed that hypothesis, and in over half of the disconfirming instances, they retained the disconfirmed hypothesis. This is not to say that participants were entirely insensitive to confirmation/disconfirmation information, for their responses were in the direction of the normative model, especially in the tendency to retain confirmed hypotheses. Nevertheless, both theorists and experimenters showed severe departures from the canons of "good science."

Experiment Space Search
The strategies that the two groups use to search the experiment space also can be compared. In moving from one program to the next, participants could vary either n alone, λ alone, both n and λ, or neither n nor λ. Here, the normative model would favor a conservative strategy of not varying both λ and n on successive experiments. Both experimenters and theorists avoided such nonconservative changes on all but 20 percent of their E-space moves (see table 4.4). Overall, there were no significant differences in how the two groups searched the experiment space. Thus, although the two groups differed in *when* they decided to search the experiment space, they did not differ in *how* they searched it, at least at this aggregate level of analysis.

However, a finer-grain analysis does reveal an interesting difference between experimenters and theorists. The number of different n–λ combinations that are used is a measure of the extent to which the experiment space is explored by participants. There are 225 different n–λ combinations that could be explored, but only a small fraction of this experiment space is actually used. Recall that the experimenters conducted twice as many experiments as the theorists. If they were using those extra experiments to explore the experiment space more widely than the theorists, rather than to revisit E-space cells, then they should have explored more n–λ combinations. This was indeed the case; overall, the theorists explored nineteen distinct n–λ combinations, whereas the experimenters explored fifty.

Table 4.4
Proportion of cases in which n, λ, neither, or both changed from one experiment to the next by experimenters and theorists, study 1.

	Changed only n	Changed only λ	Changed neither	Changed both	Total number of experimental changes
Experimenters	.40	.18	.20	.22	226
Theorists	.36	.31	.14	.19	58

In summary, the main difference in how theorists and experimenters search the experiment space is that the latter group conduct more experiments than the theorists and that this extra experimentation is often conducted without explicitly stated hypotheses. Moreover, this extra experimentation is used to search the experiment space more extensively. We have argued that instead of conducting a search of the experiment space, the theorists search the hypothesis space for an appropriate role for n. This is an important claim for which there was no direct evidence in the protocols. Therefore, we conducted a second study to test our hypothesis that it is possible to think of a selector hypothesis without exploration of the experiment space.

Study 2: Forced Search in the Hypothesis Space

Our interpretation of participants' behavior in study l generated two related hypotheses: (1) it is possible to think of the correct rule via pure hypothesis-space search, without using any experimental results; and (2) when hypothesis-space search fails, participants switch to experiment-space search. In study 2, we tested each of these hypotheses.

We tested the first hypothesis—that participants could generate the correct rule without any experimentation—by introducing a hypothesis-search phase into our procedure. During this phase we asked participants to state not just one, but several, different ways that RPT might work before doing any experiments. We reasoned that if participants were able to think of the correct rule without any experimentation, then this would support the view that the theorists in study 1 did indeed construct the appropriate frame without using experimental input. The hypothesis-search phase was followed by the experimental phase, in which participants were allowed to conduct experiments as in study 1. We expected that participants who mentioned the correct rule during the hypothesis-space search phase would discover that it was indeed correct with relatively little experimentation.

Our second hypothesis asserts that if hypothesis-space search is unsuccessful, then participants switch to a search of the experiment space. We argued that this was the strategy used by the experimenters in study 1. This hypothesis predicts that participants who fail to discover the correct rule during the first phase of study 2 should not be able to discover the correct rule by hypothesis-space search during the second, experimental, phase of the task. Thus, we predicted that participants who are unable to generate the correct rule in the hypothesis-space search phase will behave like the experimenters of study 1, that is, they will search the experiment space without a hypothesis and will discover the correct rule only after conducting a region 2 experiment.

A further goal of study 2 was to discover whether generation of several hypotheses prior to experimentation would change the way participants searched the experiment space and evaluated evidence. In study 1 participants always tested hypotheses one at a time; they never stated they were conducting experiments to distinguish between hypotheses. Study 2 was designed to determine whether, after having considered a number of different hypotheses before entering the experimental phase, participants would then test multiple hypotheses in a single experiment. Generating hypotheses before the experimental phase may also influence the process of evidence evaluation by making participants more willing to abandon their preferred hypotheses in the face of disconfirming evidence. If so, then even those participants who do not generate the correct hypothesis during the hypothesis-space search phase should conduct fewer experiments than the participants in study 1 and should show less perseveration with disconfirmed hypotheses.

Participants and Procedure
Ten Carnegie Mellon undergraduates participated in study 2. Five of them had taken at least one programming course, and the other five had no programming experience. We used the same familiarization procedure as in Study 1, in which participants learned how to use all the keys except the RPT key. Familiarization was followed by two phases: hypothesis-space search and experimentation. The hypothesis-space search phase began when the participants were asked to think of various ways that the RPT key might work. In an attempt to get a wide range of possible hypotheses from the participants, we used three probes in the same fixed order: (1) "How do you think the RPT key might work?" (2) "We've done this experiment with many people, and they've proposed a wide variety of hypotheses for how it might work. What do you think they may have proposed?" (3) "When BigTrak was being designed, the designers thought of many different ways it could be made to work. What ways do you think they may have considered?" After each question, participants responded with as many hypotheses as they could generate. Then the next probe was used. After the participants had generated all the hypotheses that they could think of, the experimental phase began: Participants conducted experiments while attempting to discover how the RPT key works. This phase was nearly identical to the discovery phase of study 1.[3]

Results
During the hypothesis-space search phase, participants proposed, on average, 4.2 hypotheses. All but two participants began with the counter frame, and seven of the ten participants switched to the selector frame

during phase 1. The correct rule (S1) was proposed by five of the ten participants.

The last column in table 4.1 shows the number of participants who proposed each hypothesis at least once. These numbers are only roughly comparable to the other entries in the table because the first two columns indicate the proportion of experiments run under each hypothesis for study 1 and study 2, while the final column is simply frequency of mention during the hypothesis-space search phase. Nevertheless, some similar patterns emerge. First, all but one of the common hypotheses was mentioned by at least two of the participants. Furthermore, as in study 1, hypotheses C1 and C2 were among the most frequently mentioned hypotheses (indeed, all but one participant proposed C2). However, in study 2 half of the participants proposed selector hypotheses, whereas in study 1 fewer than 10 percent of the experiments dealt with selector hypotheses.

During the experimentation phase, all participants discovered how the RPT key works. They were again classified as experimenters or theorists according to whether or not they discovered the correct rule after conducting an experiment in region 2 of the experiment space. This time, there were six experimenters and four theorists. Interestingly, all of the theorists stated the correct rule during the hypothesis-search phase, and all had prior programming experience. In contrast, the only experimenter who stated the correct rule during the hypothesis-space search phase was the one who had prior programming experience. The performance of the two groups on a number of measures is shown in table 4.5. Mean time to solution was 6.2 minutes, and participants generated, on average, 5.7 experiments and proposed 2.4 hypotheses during phase 2. Although the differences between the means of the two groups on all the measures mirror

Table 4.5
Performance summary of experimenters and theorists in phase 2 of study 2.

	Experimenters	Theorists	Combined
n	6	4	10
Prior programming experience	1	4	5
Stated S1 in phase 1	1	4	5
Time (minutes)	8.2	3.3	6.2
Experiments	7.5	3.0	5.7
Experiments with hypotheses	5.7	2.0	4.2
Experiments without hypotheses	1.8	1.0	1.5
Hypothesis switches	3.0	1.5	2.4
Experiment-space verbalizations	2.2	1.0	1.7
n-λ combinations used	5.7	2.5	4.4

Table 4.6
Proportion of rejections and retentions of stated hypotheses, given confirming or disconfirming evidence, by experimenters and theorists, study 2.

Experimental Outcome	Experimenters			Theorists		
	Retain	Reject	n	Retain	Reject	n
Confirm current hypothesis	.58	.42	12	1.00	0.0	1
Disconfirm current hypothesis	.41	.59	17	.14	.86	7

the earlier pattern from study 1, none of them are significant, due to the small sample size and large within-group variances.

The experiment-space search patterns in this study are radically different from those in study 1. Both experimenters and theorists made their discoveries much faster in study 2 than did their counterparts in study 1. For experimenters, there were 7.5 experiments in 8.2 minutes in study 2 versus 12.3 experiments in 18.4 minutes in Study 1. For theorists, there were 3 experiments in 3.3 minutes in study 2 versus 9.3 experiments in 11.4 minutes in study 1.

In addition to these experiment-space search differences, there were differences in the way that evidence evaluation took place. Study 2 participants switched hypotheses more readily than did study 1 participants. In study 1 both experimenters and theorists changed their hypothesis after disconfirmation only 44 percent of the time (see table 4.3). In contrast, in study 2 (see table 4.6), the theorists changed hypotheses after disconfirmation 86 percent of the time and the experimenters changed after disconfirmation 59 percent of the time. Furthermore, the participants in study 2 moved to region 2 earlier than the participants in study 1, and thus generated a much higher proportion of region 2 experiments than did participants in study 1.

Discussion
The results of the hypothesis-space search phase of study 2 show that participants are able to generate the correct hypothesis (among others) without conducting any experiments. This result is consistent with the view that the theorists in study 1 thought of the correct rule by searching the hypothesis space. The results of the experimental phase of study 2 further support our interpretation of study 1. All participants who failed to generate the correct rule in the hypothesis-space search phase behaved like experimenters in the experimental phase: They discovered the correct rule only after exploring region 2 of the experiment space. This is consistent with the view that when hypothesis-space search fails, participants turn to a search of the experiment space.

The contrast between the results of study 1 and study 2 is striking. The main difference is that participants conducted far fewer experiments in study 2. A prior search of the hypothesis space allowed the participants to generate selector hypotheses much more readily than in study 1. This was true even for participants who could not think of the correct rule in the hypothesis-space search phase. Furthermore, participants in this study, unlike those in study 1, did attempt to conduct experiments that would allow them to distinguish between two hypotheses. This approach tended to guide E-space search into region 2. For example, consider a participant who was trying to distinguish between two counter hypotheses: "repeats the previous step n times" and "repeats the previous program n times." If he wrote a series of programs in which the value of n varied, he would quickly wander into region 2 of the experiment space, and discover how the RPT key works. Participants in study 1 rarely designed hypothesis-discriminating experiments, for they usually were dealing with only a single hypothesis at a time. Thus it took them longer to abandon hypotheses, and they conducted fewer experiments in region 2.

The influence of prior knowledge is suggested by the finding that all of the theorists, but only one of the experimenters, had prior programming experience. Knowing something about programming may have helped theorists to construct the correct frame before performing any experiments, although it is not clear precisely what aspect of programming knowledge was crucial. We find it interesting that the effect of differential prior knowledge propagates through the initial hypothesis-formulation stage to influence differences in experimental strategies.

In sum, prior exploration of the hypothesis space had two main effects on the experimental phase. First, it allowed participants to generate an initial set of hypotheses that included some from the n-role: selector frame. As a result, participants quickly switched to the n-role: selector frame in the experimental phase. Second, because participants were aware that a number of hypotheses could account for their results, they conducted experiments designed to discriminate among them. Often the best way to do this is to conduct an experiment in region 2. Once participants conducted such an experiment, they quickly discovered the correct rule.

Summary of Studies 1 and 2

In chapter 2 we argued that scientific discovery requires search in two problem spaces and in chapter 3 we described a general paradigm for studying dual search in the laboratory. In this chapter we reported the results of two studies using that paradigm with BigTrak. There were three important findings. First, participants' verbalizations and experimental designs provided clear evidence that when people attempt to discover something in a moderately complex environment, they do indeed search in two problem spaces: one of these spaces—the hypothesis space—contains hypotheses about the aspect of the environment under investigation, and the other space—the experiment space—contains possible configurations of the environment that might produce informative evidence related to those hypotheses. Second, people can use (at least) two different strategies for searching these spaces that can be distinguished by which of the two spaces are searched preferentially. Third, during the phase of evidence evaluation, when active hypotheses are being reconciled with the empirical results, people often violate the normative canons of "rational" scientific reasoning. We briefly discuss these last two findings here, and we will return to them—and others— in the final chapter of this book.

Strategic Differences in Dual Search
Our theorist and experimenter strategies are similar to strategic differences first reported in Bruner, Goodnow, and Austin's (1956) classic work on concept formation. Those investigations revealed two basic strategies used by participants. In one strategy, called *focusing,* participants focus on a positive instance and change the values of instances one attribute at a time until they discover the concept's defining values. In our terms, Bruner, Goodnow, and Austin's "Focusers," by systematically attending to the relevance of individual attributes, were cautiously searching the experiment space. Our experimenters pursued a strategy similar to focusing. They searched the experiment space, not with a hypothesis in mind, but only with an encoding of the last few instances of BigTrak's behavior. Their goal was to discover the attributes common to all the instances that they generated.

The second strategy that Bruner, Goodnow, and Austin discovered was *successive scanning* in which participants test a single hypothesis at a time. Both our experimenters and our theorists used this strategy, though the difference between our two groups was that the experimenters switched from testing hypotheses to collecting information that would allow them to generate a new hypothesis. Bruner, Goodnow, and Austin argued that participants adopt one strategy rather than another because some strategies impose more of a cognitive strain, or short-term memory load, than others. However, in our task the source of difference between experimenters and theorists is in long-term memory: Participants who managed to construct the correct frame from information in long-term memory were classified as theorists. Those who were unable to construct the correct frame from information in long-term memory, and therefore had to search the experiment space were classified as experimenters.

Our experimenter/theorist distinction is roughly analogous to one that has developed in the area of computational models of discovery (mentioned briefly in chapter 1). In these models the distinction is between data-driven versus model-driven approaches to inductive inference. The former correspond roughly to our experimenters and the latter to our theorists. However, for most machine learning models, both the amount and the accuracy of information required far exceeds the capacity of our participants. This fallibility may account for the kind of strategy differences—similar to ours—that have been observed in other discovery tasks. For example, Jens Rasmussen (1981) found two different types of strategies used by operators trying to find faults in a complex system (such as a power plant). Some operators search the experiment space trying to find the faulty component. Other operators search a hypothesis space in order to think of a set of symptoms that are similar to the observed symptoms. Rasmussen also found that use of these strategies varies with the amount of domain knowledge that the operators have: experts tend to search the hypothesis space, and novices tend to search the experiment space. It is likely that in Rasmussen's case, as in ours, the different strategies result from differences in prior knowledge rather than from a stable individual difference.

Generating, Using, and Ignoring Evidence

Much of the research on scientific reasoning has been concerned with the extent to which people behave "logically" when presented with formal reasoning tasks. In particular, researchers have devoted an enormous amount of effort to understanding two aspects of disconfirmation. The first aspect is usually studied in terms of so-called confirmation bias. The question here is why people tend to avoid the Popperian edict of falsification and fail to test potentially disconfirming instances when evaluating hypotheses. The second question is why people fail to change their hypotheses when disconfirming evidence does appear. A third question is raised by our results: Why do participants change hypotheses that have just been confirmed? In this section, we will suggest how these questions can be answered in terms of the SDDS model.

Failure to Seek Disconfirmation   One of the most venerable claims in the scientific reasoning literature is that participants exhibit a pervasive confirmation bias. That is, they prefer to select experiments that are expected to confirm rather than disconfirm their hypothesis. The general issue of confirmation bias has been substantially advanced by Klayman and Ha's (1987) elegant analysis and review of three decades of work on

Wason's famous "2-4-6" rule induction task (Wason, 1960). To review the Wason task briefly: the participant is trying to guess a "rule" that classifies number triples into exemplars and non-exemplars of that rule. The experimenter provides an initial instance that conforms to the rule, and then participants propose their own instances and the experimenter says "yes" or "no." When participants think that they know the classification rule, they announce their hypothesis and the experimenter tells them whether or not their hypothesis is correct. In its original form, the starting example was 2-4-6 and the experimenter's rule was simply "increasing numbers." The (intentionally misleading) initial instance influences participants to spend a lot of time with rules such as "evens," "a + b = c," "increasing evens," and so on. Dozens of empirical studies show that participants typically generate instances of the rule that they expect to be classified as "yes." This tendency has been called "confirmation bias."

As Klayman and Ha point out, it is important to disentangle the type of instance (experiment, in our terms) used by a participant from whether it is, or is not, an instance of the correct rule (i.e., the correct hypothesis). Thus, people can choose what they believe to be either a positive or a negative instance of a rule, and it can turn out to be, indeed, a positive or negative instance. For example, if your hypothesized rule is "even numbers," then for a positive instance, you might propose 4-10-12, or for a negative instance you might propose 5-9-7. In both cases, your expectation would be supported: your positive instance would receive a "yes" and your negative instance would receive a "no." You would be tempted to conclude that your hypothesis had been "proven." However, this feedback only provides what Klayman and Ha call "ambiguous verification" because many other rules might also be consistent with your proposed positive instance or inconsistent with your proposed negative instance. Indeed, we know that the correct rule ("increasing numbers") is *not* the one that led you to generate each of the instances ("even numbers").

However, if you choose an instance that is a positive example of your hypothesized rule and the feedback is that it is *not* an example of the correct rule, then the experiment has produced, in Klayman and Ha's terms, "conclusive falsification." For example, if, while holding your "even numbers" hypothesis, you propose 10-4-2, you would expect a "yes," but you would get a "no." One can also get conclusive falsification by proposing an instance that is a negative instance of one's current hypothesis and receiving—unexpectedly—positive feedback. For example, you would expect 5-7-9 to get a "no," but it would get a "yes." The fundamentally important point here is that *falsificationist goals and outcomes are orthogonal to whether one uses positive or negative instances of one's hypothesized rule.*

Klayman and Ha argued that most people follow a heuristic they call a "positive test strategy"—"a tendency to examine cases hypothesized to be targets." Moreover, Klayman and Ha showed that, when the probability of a hypothesis being confirmed is small, this strategy can provide useful information. Furthermore, a positive test strategy provides at least a sufficiency test of one's current hypothesis. However, if, as in Wason's "2-4-6" task, the probability of confirming one's hypothesis is high, then positive tests will not provide any useful information. Klayman and Ha's analysis suggests that the appropriateness of the strategy depends on the distribution of positive and negative instances, although such information is not available to the participant at the outset.

In our task, participants almost invariably followed the positive test strategy: They reasoned that "my theory is that RPT does X. If I am right, and I write program Y, then BigTrak will do Z." According to Klayman and Ha's argument, our participants' strategy was appropriate, because for about 60 percent of the experiments in study 1 and study 2 participants received disconfirming evidence (see tables 4.3 and 4.6). That is, BigTrak did *not* do Z. Thus, even though participants were looking for confirming evidence their hypotheses were frequently falsified.

SDDS provides an interesting extension of this view of confirmation bias. As Klayman and Ha note, participants' strategies should depend on what they think the nature of the instances they encounter will be; if there are many positive instances, a negative test strategy will be more useful than a positive test strategy. Following a positive test strategy and producing a predominance of disconfirming evidence forces participants to either search memory in order to construct a new frame or search the experiment space for a data pattern that can suggest a new hypothesis. When experimenters discovered that regions 1 and 3 of the experiment space disconfirmed their initial hypotheses, they switched to region 2. A positive test strategy enabled them to avoid further search of uninformative regions of the experiment space.

Tolerating Disconfirming Evidence   Recall that our participants maintained their current hypotheses in the face of negative information. In study 1, fewer than half of the disconfirming outcomes led to immediate hypothesis changes. SDDS suggests some possible explanations for this behavior. One contributing factor is the probabilistic nature of the basic processes in *Evaluate Evidence*. An unanticipated consequence of the complexity of our procedure was that—due to the fallibility of memory and of the *Run & Observe* processes—the feedback participants received had some probability of error. That is, from the participants' perspective, there might be error in either the device behavior, their encoding of that behavior, or their recall of the current program and associated prediction. Thus, some cases of perseveration may result from participants simply not believing the outcome and attributing the apparent disconfirmation to one of several fallible processes (see Gorman, 1989; Penner and Klahr, 1996b). Examples consistent with this explanation are those cases in which the participant not only retains a disconfirmed hypothesis, but also repeats exactly the same experiment (see experiments 4 and 5 in table 3.2). Another error-related cause of perseveration may be even simpler: Participants erroneously encode the disconfirming behavior as confirming behavior.

The nondeterministic nature of experimental evidence can also have an effect on the decision mechanism in *Evaluate Evidence*. This process is based not only on whether the result of the prior experiment rules out the hypothesis, but also on whether enough evidence has accumulated to accept or reject the hypothesis. The amount of evidence in favor of a hypothesis and the strength of the hypothesis both determine when participants will continue to hold or will switch a hypothesis. Only when the cumulative disconfirming evidence exceeds a criterion will a hypothesis be changed. In the present study, participants had general sources of prior knowledge that predisposed them to the counter frame. We infer that these hypotheses had a high *a priori* strength because they were the most popular and they needed much disconfirming evidence to be rejected. However, once the initial hypotheses were rejected, participants conducted few experiments on subsequent hypotheses. Because these subsequent hypotheses had lower strength, any evidence that appeared to contradict them quickly led to their rejection.

Other authors have made similar observations. O'Brien, Costa, and Overton (1986) for example, note that "participants are less likely to take evidence as conclusive when their presuppositions about the content domain discourage them from doing so" (p. 509). Chinn and Brewer (1998) provide a detailed taxonomy of different types of responses to anomalous data—that is, experimental results that should, in the narrow sense, provide "conclusive falsification" of a hypothesis. These responses range from outright rejection of the data without justification to various levels of partial acceptance without substantial theory revision to, finally, acceptance of the anomalous data and its "inevitable" consequence: theory revision.

An alternative explanation that has been offered for the finding that participants tend to stick to disconfirmed hypotheses is that they cannot think of alternative hypotheses. Einhorn and Hogarth (1986), suggest that

> because the goal of causal inference is to find some explanation for
> the observed effects, the discounting of an explanation by specific

alternatives still leaves one with the question, "If X did not cause Y, what did?" . . . In fact, the distinction between testing hypotheses and searching for better ones can be likened to the difference between a "disconfirmation" versus "replacement" mode of inference. The replacement view is consistent with the Kuhnian notion that theories in science are not discarded, despite evidence to the contrary, if they are not replaced by better alternatives (Kuhn, 1962). Indeed, the replacement view is equally strong in everyday inference. (pp. 14–15)

The results from our studies provide a basis for elaborating this view. We know that when participants do have alternatives readily available—as in study 2—they are more likely to drop disconfirmed hypotheses than when they do not—as in study 1 (cf. tables 4.3 and 4.6). On the other hand, when participants could no longer think of any new hypotheses, they could decide to search the experiment space and not hold any hypotheses at all. Thus, participants did not have to stick with their hypotheses once they had accumulated enough evidence to reject them, because it was permissible in our study to replace something with nothing.

Abandoning Verified Hypotheses   The other side of perseveration in the face of disconfirmation is changing hypotheses in the face of confirmation. Recall that, on average, participants in study 1 changed their current hypothesis in about 25 percent of the cases where the most recent experimental outcome confirmed it. Strictly speaking, this is not a departure from logical norms, as we noted earlier, positive experimental results can provide only ambiguous verification, rather than "confirmation," as we have been calling it. Our interpretation of this behavior also invokes memory processes, but this time in a positive way. That is, participants do have memory for previous outcomes, and the current result may not only confirm the current hypothesis, but also, when added to the pool of previous results, may be consistent with some other hypothesis that appears more plausible or interesting. In order to account for this fully, we would have to elaborate the processes involved in *Evaluate Evidence* so that it could look for global, as well as local, consistency in deciding what to do with the current hypothesis.

Conclusion

In chapter 2 we proposed that scientific reasoning requires search in two problem spaces. In this chapter we reported participants' behavior in a complex discovery task and observed different patterns of search in these two problem spaces caused by two different strategies for scientific discovery. We used SDDS as a framework for interpreting these results. Clearly, there are many aspects of the scientific reasoning process that we need to investigate further, but we believe that SDDS offers a potentially fruitful framework for discovering more about discovery. Of particular interest to us is the extent to which there are developmental differences and other kinds of individual differences in the way this dual search is coordinated. In the next chapter, we report on two additional studies in which a wider range of participants, including middle-school students and nontechnically trained adults, attempted to make discoveries in the BigTrak domain.

Notes

1. Throughout the book, we use the term *study* rather than *experiment* in order to distinguish our studies from our participants' experiments. In addition to identifying these studies by number, we have given each study a distinctive label that captures its main focus.
2. Statistical detail is not provided in this book, although appropriate analyses were conducted and only those that reached conventional levels of significance are reported as such. (See original technical articles for detail.)
3. There were a few variations in how the data were collected. Instead of videotape recording, we used an audio tape for subjects' verbalizations. Key presses were also captured on the audio tape by having subjects tell the experimenter what keys to press. Otherwise, the procedure was the same as that used in study 1.

Chapter 5

Developmental Aspects of Scientific Reasoning

with Kevin Dunbar and Anne L. Fay

The large amount of variability in children's discovery processes may seem surprising. However, similar variability is evident in other accounts of discovery, notably in accounts of the discovery processes of great scientists. . . . Both noble scientific discoveries and mundane everyday discoveries seem to be based on opportunistic, catch-as-catch-can cognitive processes that take a variety of forms and occur in a variety of situations.
(Siegler and Jenkins, 1989, p. 107)

In this chapter and the next we report several studies in which we investigated the scientific reasoning skills of elementary, middle, and high school children and compared their performance to the performance of adults having different levels of scientific training. We used the same basic paradigm described in chapter 4. However, starting with Study 4 we introduced a computer-based version of the BigTrak device in order to support some variations on the to-be-discovered rule.

Child-as-Scientist Revisited

As we noted in Chapter 1, the developmental literature has tended toward a polarization of views about the ontogenesis of scientific thought—or, to put it more simply, about "the child as scientist" debate. One position—emphasizing domain-specific knowledge—is that improvements in scientific reasoning abilities are a consequence of a knowledge base that grows as the child develops (e.g., Carey, 1985; Keil, 1981). For example, Carey (1985) argues,

> The acquisition and reorganization of strictly domain-specific knowledge (e.g., of the physical, biological and social worlds) probably accounts for most of the cognitive differences between 3-year-olds and adults. I have argued that in many cases developmental changes that have been taken to support format-level changes, or changes due to the acquisition of some tool that

crosscuts domains, are in fact due to the acquisition of domain-specific knowledge. (p. 62)

Under this extreme view, the *processes* that children use only appear to be qualitatively different from those of adults because children do not have the necessary knowledge to perform at adult levels. In effect, children *do* think like scientists, albeit scientists who don't know much about their domain.

The other position, exemplified by the work of Piaget (1952), purports that although there are obviously changes in the knowledge base as children grow older, they are not the primary source of the radical differences in the behavior of children and adults. Rather, children have qualitatively different strategies for reasoning about the world (e.g., Inhelder and Piaget, 1958; Kuhn and Phelps, 1982). Flavell (1977) succinctly describes the difference between the reasoning strategies of adults and children:

> The formal-operational thinker inspects the problem data, *hypothesizes* that such and such a theory or explanation might be the correct one, *deduces* from it that so and so empirical phenomena ought logically to occur or not occur in reality, and then tests his theory by seeing if these predicted phenomena do in fact occur. . . . If you think you have just heard a description of textbook scientific reasoning, you are absolutely right. Because of its heavy trade in hypotheses and logical deduction from hypotheses, it is also called *hypothetico-deductive* reasoning, and it contrasts sharply with the much more nontheoretical and nonspeculative *empirico-inductive* reasoning of concrete-operational thinkers. (pp. 103–104, emphasis in original)

Research in this tradition has used tasks in which the role of knowledge has been minimized and the different developmental strategies are made transparent. In particular, strategies associated with experimental design and valid inference are viewed as domain-general developmental acquisitions. Under this view, children fail to think like scientists because they simply lack the domain-general cognitive capacity to do so.

The principal obstacle in determining which of these views (if either) is correct is that domain-specific knowledge interacts with domain-general processes when people attempt to make inferences from data. In an insightful summary of this interaction, Leona Schauble (1996) notes,

> At the heart of the debate between the experimentation strategies versus conceptual change approaches is a disagreement about normative models of reasoning. The experimentation strategies approach tends to emphasize concern for logical validity, for

example, whether the patterns of evidence that participants cite do, in fact, bear logically on the hypothesis being tested. When such criteria are applied, preadolescent children perform less well than adults, and adults themselves, even professional scientists, frequently make errors (Kuhn et al., 1988; Tweney, Doherty, and Mynatt, 1981). In contrast, the conceptual change approach tends to be more concerned with plausibility and explanatory coherence as tests for deciding whether new knowledge should be adopted (Thagard, 1989). When these criteria are applied, even young children's reasoning seems quite rational (Carey, 1985; Samarapungavan, 1992; Vosniadou and Brewer, 1994). Yet, validity and coherence play complementary roles in appropriate belief change. An individual who focuses exclusively on finding logical relations between patterns of evidence and outcomes may over interpret observed variance, because variance in outcomes is sometimes due to measurement or other kinds of error, instrumentation problems, spurious correlations, or other confounding variables in the system. Logic alone cannot prescribe whether variance in outcomes is due to a change in an underlying causal variable or to some other irrelevant fluctuation; these decisions must be guided by prior belief and theory. In contrast, if plausibility and coherence are the sole criteria applied, belief change could hardly occur. A refusal to entertain beliefs that seem implausible with respect to the current knowledge system might result in a person dismissing relevant evidence and clinging rigidly to current beliefs even when they are incorrect. (p. 102)

Indeed, this is precisely the kind of behavior we observed in the two studies described in the previous chapter. Both perseveration in the face of disconfirming evidence and abandonment of verified hypotheses can be seen as instances of Schauble's general point about coherence and belief change. In this chapter, we explore this issue further in the context of age-related differences in the components of SDDS.

When we started our investigations (Klahr and Dunbar, 1988) there were few studies that allowed children to cycle repeatedly through the phases of hypothesis formation, experiment generation, and evidence evaluation as they endeavored to converge on an empirically supported explanation of some phenomenon. Moreover, because the definition of "scientific" thinking remained quite imprecise and global, it was difficult to provide a satisfactory account of the developmental course of such thinking. Indeed, Gopnik (1997) makes the intriguing proposal that the child-as-scientist issue should be stood on its head: "[it] is not that children are little scientists but that scientists are big children." Even after nearly a decade of attention these issues remain unresolved, in no small part because of this lack of definition.

Our approach to this problem has been to provide a detailed characterization of the components of both the domain knowledge base and the general discovery processes. Only after these have been specified is it possible to ask about their development. Thus, in this chapter, our focus is on developmental differences in the specific components of the SDDS framework introduced earlier.

Study 3: Dual Search by Children

The results of studies 1 and 2 with adults enables us to pose the developmental questions in a more specific form than has traditionally been possible. One set of questions deals with searching the hypothesis space. First, given the same training experience as adults, will children think of the same initial hypotheses as adults? If they do, then this would suggest that the processes used to construct an initial frame are similar in both adults and children. Second, when children's initial hypotheses are disconfirmed, will the children assign the same values to slots as the adults? That is, are the processes that are used to search the hypothesis space similar in both adults and children? Finally, will children be able to change frames or will they remain in the same frame? Given that some adults—theorists—were able to construct frames from a search of memory, will children be able to do so too? Failing that, will they be able to switch their strategy to a search of the experiment space, as did the experimenters, or will they stay within their initial frame?

Another set of questions concerns children's search of the experiment space. Children may search different areas of the experiment space than did the adults, or they may even construct a different type of experiment space. Such a finding would suggest that the strategies used to go from a hypothesis to a specific experiment are different in adults and children. Another possibility is that children may evaluate the results of experiments in a different way from adults. That is, the evidence evaluation process may use a different set of criteria for revising, rejecting, or retaining hypotheses.

Method

Twenty-two third to sixth graders from a private school participated in the study. All of the children had forty-five hours of LOGO instruction before participating in this study. We selected this group partly as a matter of convenience, because they were participating in another study on the acquisition and transfer of debugging skills (Klahr & Carver, 1988). More important, because we will be contrasting the children's performance with adult participants—all of whom had some programming experience—our participants' experience provided at least a rough control for prior exposure to programming instruction. In a pilot study we also discovered that children with no programming experience had great difficulty understanding what was expected of them on the task. Furthermore, the participants' age range (between 8 and 11 years old) spans the putative period of the emergence of formal operational reasoning skills, the hallmark of which is, as noted earlier, the ability to "reason scientifically."

Because some of our participants were as young as eight, we modified BigTrak slightly in order to make it more appealing and interesting to children. We created a "dragon costume" that fit over BigTrak while leaving it free to move as before, and leaving its keypad fully exposed (See figure 5.1). The only change in the instructions was that the "Fire" button now corresponded to the dragon's "breathing fire," instead of firing its "laser cannon."

As in studies 1 and 2, the participants were taught how to use BigTrak and were then asked to discover how the RPT key works. The session ended when the children stated either that they were satisfied that they had discovered how the RPT key works, or that they could not figure out how it worked. Two changes to our procedure made it more suitable for working with children. First, if the children did not spontaneously state what they were thinking about, then the experimenter asked them how they thought the RPT key worked. Second, if a child persisted with the same incorrect hypothesis and did exactly the same type of experiment (i.e., λ and n were not changed) four times in a row, the experimenter asked the child what the purpose of the number with the RPT key was.

Figure 5.1
BigTrak in dragon costume.

Results

In this section, we first present a protocol from an eleven-year-old. Then we present several aggregate performance measures, followed by a summary of types of hypotheses and experiments that the children proposed. We also point to some of the more important differences between the strategies used by the children and the adults.

Protocol of a Child Discovering how RPT Works on the BigTrak Dragon   The full protocol is presented in appendix 5.1 on page 121. The participant is an eleven-year-old girl (RJ) who is fairly representative of the other children in study 3 with respect to total time taken, number of experiments, and initial hypotheses. But RJ's protocol is not entirely typical for two reasons. First, the experimenter gave RJ a few important hints about how to constrain her search in both the experiment space and the hypothesis space.[1] Although the experimenter did not go so far as to suggest specific hypotheses, his hints did draw RJ's attention to particular slot values. The second reason that RJ is not typical is that these hints in turn enabled her to discover the correct rule, which, as we will see in the next section, was very unusual for third graders. However, RJ's protocol provides a clear example of the type of false starts that characterize the other children, as well as of the moment of discovery.

RJ starts off with a simple counter hypothesis that RPT n repeats the last step n times (0:30). This hypothesis would predict that, for RJ's first program, BigTrak will repeat the FIRE 6 command six times. Because $n > \lambda$ in this program, BigTrak simply repeats the entire program one time, yielding two executions of the $\uparrow 1$ FIRE 6 sequence. This leaves RJ somewhat confused (1:30) because she expected only a single step to be repeated. Although there is less repetition than she expected, she decides that this is a sensible response and changes to a "repeats program" hypothesis.

Experiment 2 is potentially very informative because it is in region 2 (i.e., $n < \lambda$). If RJ maintained her second hypothesis, then she would make the prediction shown in appendix 5.1, that is, she would expect the entire program to be repeated three times. Instead BigTrak only repeats the last three steps one time. This is a rather complex sequence that takes almost thirty seconds to be executed. RJ observes that the program got repeated but she doesn't seem very confident about this and decides to run a program with smaller parameters (2:00). This type of comment reflects an explicit awareness of the need to design experiments from which reliable observations can be made.

Experiment 3 is also a region 2 program and it is particularly well designed because it has distinctive components that will allow RJ to parse the behavior of the device. In this particular case, the use of the FIRE command makes for a very clear distinction between what would be predicted under the current—although weakening—hypothesis of repeating the entire program and the actual behavior because there is only one FIRE command in the sequence that is executed.

At this point (4:30), RJ is silent for a while and the experimenter probes with the standard non-directive question "what are you thinking?" For the next minute or so, RJ seems to be struggling with the way to articulate the apparent irrelevance of the value of n because she has noticed that whether she uses a large number such as six or a small number such as two she does not seem to be getting the expected n repetitions of the entire program. She even starts to speculate on what the function or the purpose of the RPT key might be. In this case, RJ's search in the hypothesis space is guided by consideration of what kind of efficiencies might be introduced by a RPT key. Right before 6:00 she formulates the idea of having the RPT key function over a segment of a program as a sort of subroutine executor when she postulates that RPT might be useful for allowing one to repeatedly execute $\leftarrow$, $\uparrow$, $\leftarrow$, $\uparrow$, and so on. In other words, she begins to consider a selector hypothesis even though she is unable to articulate its details. However, when pressed by the experimenter (6:00) she reverts back to a simple counter hypothesis, although without much confidence.

Experiment 4 has $\lambda = n$. Given the ambiguity of whether there should be two or three total repetitions of the entire program, RJ may have interpreted the outcome as a confirmation of her theory. However, she realizes that this program is also hard to track and makes another comment (7:00) about the experiment space in the context of understanding her own memory failures.

Consequently, experiment 5 is extremely simple. But here RJ runs into an observational, or encoding, difficulty resulting from the fact that Big-Trak does not pause after each of the executions of the $\uparrow$ 2, but rather runs them off continuously. Thus, although RJ's hypothesis predicts that BigTrak should move forward six units, it only moves forward four units. However, RJ has not calibrated precisely just how far a single forward command should take BigTrak. Here the experimenter intervenes and suggests that she try a command that is easier to quantify (8:30).

Experiment 6 is particularly interesting because it is an instance of the "reject-confirm" behavior described in chapter 4. That is, even though the current outcome is entirely consistent with RJ's hypothesis that RPT 2 should repeat the entire program two times, she proposes an alternative hypothesis that is also consistent with the behavior she just saw: perhaps RPT only repeats the first instruction.

Experiment 7 has $n = \lambda = 2$. The outcome is consistent with her current hypothesis, which she now reaffirms (9:00–9:30). Because RJ was one of the last children to participate in this study, we were fairly confident that, at this point, RJ was likely to terminate the experiment convinced that she had discovered how RPT worked. In order to see how RJ might respond to an informative experiment at this point, the experimenter intervened (10:00) and suggested an experiment that would soon destroy RJ's current theory.

Following experiment 8, RJ is clearly confused, and she repeats the exact same experiment at experiment 9. The discrepancy between the predicted and the actual behavior is so great that RJ now proposes that n has no effect at all and that RPT simply repeats the program regardless of the value of n. Notice that this is not an unreasonable conclusion given that she has run so many programs with $n > \lambda$. From her perspective, the truncation function on BigTrak has led to some inexplicable behavior. Once again, the experimenter intervenes (11:30) and suggests that RJ focus on the effect on the value of n.

We interpret RJ's "nothing happened" comment following E11 (12:30) to mean that there is no difference between the result of the experiment at E10 and E11 (because both of them are truncated). Note that this is consistent with RJ's current hypothesis—however tentative—that the value of n has no effect at all. She pursues this idea in Experiment 12 and again notices that RPT 4, RPT 3, and RPT 5 have all produced exactly the same type of behavior.

But now, at E13, RJ does a crucial experiment that gets her on the path to discovering how RPT works. She notices that the second command, but not the first, was repeated twice. However she does entertain the possibility that maybe she misobserved or misremembered this outcome so she repeats it essentially identically at E14. Now she is sure of the observation (15:00), but unsure of the interpretation. RJ knows that RPT is repeating only the second command and not the first one, but she doesn't know what to make of that. Again, focusing on the effect of n, she uses the same program as she did at E14 but she increases the value of n to 2. At this point we have indicated two possible predictions because it is not clear whether she has quite discovered the selector frame or whether she is still entertaining the counter frame.

Finally, between 15:30 and 16:30, RJ articulates the correct selector hypothesis. Notice that her account is essentially a redescription of the specific outcomes that she has seen. The experimenter then pushes her to come up with a generalization and just after 16:30 the "a-ha" experience sets in. Although it is not represented in the printed transcription, the emphasis on the audio tape indicates an unmistakable increase in confidence and excitement. Moreover, RJ's rate of speech during this next thirty seconds is more than double what it has been throughout the earlier part of the protocol. At E16 she runs a well-designed region 2 experiment and finds that the behavior is exactly as predicted. At E17 she runs another region 2 experiment and finds the behavior to be entirely consistent with the correct selector hypothesis. RJ concludes with great enthusiasm about her discovery.

Hypothesis Space Search   Having presented a detailed example of one child's performance, we now turn to an analysis of the aggregate results for the full set of children. We start with a discussion of search in the hypothesis space.

Only two of the twenty-two children correctly concluded that RPT n repeats the last n instructions once. Nevertheless, fourteen children (including the two who were correct) asserted that they were absolutely certain that they had discovered how RPT works. Four gave up in confusion, and four thought that it worked in a particular way some of the time. The children spent, on average, twenty minutes trying to determine how the RPT key works. They generated an average of thirteen programs. Of the 285 programs run by the participants, 240 were experiments. Of the rest, twenty-three were control experiments, one was a calibration, and twenty-one were unclassifiable. Children proposed 3.3 different hypotheses during the course of a session. Given that nearly all of these were incorrect, this is about the same number of incorrect hypotheses proposed by adults. (Mean number of hypotheses for adults in study 1 was 4.6—including the correct hypothesis, which most of them discovered.) However, as shown in table 5.1, there were substantial differences between children and adults in the proportion of experiments run under different types of hypotheses.

One difference was that although nearly 10 percent of the adults' experiments were run under a selector hypothesis, only 1 percent of the children's were. Another striking difference was that nearly 30 percent of the children's experiments were conducted under partial hypotheses, whereas adults proposed fully specified hypotheses for all but 3 percent of their experiments (see table 5.1). Of those experiments children conducted under partial hypotheses, 51 percent did not mention the unit of repetition (i.e., whether it was a step, a program, or a segment), and 49 percent did not mention the number of repetitions.

The relatively large proportion of partial hypotheses could be the result of differences in the children's ability to articulate fully specified hypotheses, or it could result from children's tendency to disregard the attributes of number of repetitions and the unit of repetition. With respect to the number of repetitions, the latter interpretation is supported by the finding that the children often failed to type in a number after pressing the RPT key, indicating that they did not see a number as being a necessary part of the RPT command. With respect to the unit of

Table 5.1
Proportion of experiments conducted by adults and children under each common hypothesis.

		Proportion of experiments under each hypothesis	
	Hypothesis	Adults* (Study 1)	Children (Study 3)
C1:	n repeats of entire program	.14	.21
C2:	n repeats of the last step	.20	.08
C3:	n repeats of subsequent steps	.02	0
C4:	$n-1$, $n/2$, or $+n$ repeats	0	.17
C5:	n repeats of last 2 steps	0	.07
S1:	One repeat of last n steps	.02	0
S2:	One repeat of first n steps	.04	0
S3:	One repeat of the n th step	.03	.01
U1:	One repeat of entire program	.06	.03
U2:	One repeat of the last step	.04	.05
	Partially specified	.03	.27
	Idiosyncratic	.14	.01
	No hypothesis	.28	.10

*This column is taken from column 1 of table 4.1

Note: Hypotheses are labeled according to the role of n: S-selector; C-counter; U-unspecified.

repetition, the issue is unclear. In any event, children's tendency to omit either the unit of repetition or the number of repetitions suggests some ambiguity in their understanding of the role of these two features.

All of the twenty children who failed to discover how RPT works proposed hypotheses that were solely in the n-role: counter frame. Even though the children observed many experimental outcomes that were consistent with the n-role: selector frame and not with their current frame, none of the children were able to induce the selector frame. This suggests two things: First, the children did not have sufficient knowledge available to generate the n-role: selector frame by searching the hypothesis space. Second, the children did not use the results from their experiment-space search to induce a new frame. Instead, they used it to induce new slot values for their current frame. As a result, the children generated a number of hypotheses within the n-role: counter frame that were not generated by the adults.

For example, many of the children who originally had an hypothesis with n-role: counter abandoned it in favor of an unspecified role for n or invented a new number of repetitions to account for the data. Seventeen percent of their experiments were conducted using one of these hypotheses (C4 in table 5.1). These hypotheses were generated when the children were trying to account for the finding that RPT 2 only repeats the prior program once, not twice. These children either said that n had no role, or tried to accommodate the slot for the number of repetitions to fit the data. The children stated that the program was repeated $n - 1$ times, $n/2$ times, or stated that the value of n replaced the value that was bound to the previous command (e.g., FIRE 3 RPT 8 will do a FIRE 3 FIRE 8). No adult generated such hypotheses.

Another type of hypothesis that appeared only in the children's data was that the last two steps of the program were repeated n times. Three of the twenty-two children proposed this type of hypothesis after conducting an experiment in region 2 with $n = 2$. Thus, the children proposed an hypothesis that was within the n-role: counter frame, yet was consistent with the observation that the last two steps of a program were repeated. Each of these hypotheses is a way of staying within the n-role: counter frame while accounting for the finding that there were not n repetitions of a command or a program. These hypotheses were generated even though there was a large amount of evidence available that could disconfirm both the individual hypotheses and the frame itself. However, the children were content with hypotheses that could account for the results of the most recent outcome. That is, local consistency was sufficient, and global inconsistency was ignored. It is not clear to what extent this myopia derives from faulty logic, strong biases, or limited memory capacity.

Experiment-Space Search   One question that we raised earlier was whether children's search in the experiment space would be different from that of the adults. The distribution of experiments over the experiment space is shown in table 5.2. Children were significantly more likely than adults to choose region 1 experiments, and significantly less likely to run them in region 3. As noted in chapter 3, programs in region 1 have poor discriminating power, whereas experiments in region 3 suggest

Table 5.2
Percentage of programs in each area of the experiment space for adults (study 1) and children (study 3)

	Region		
	1	2	3
Adults	40	17	43
Children	51	17	32

that n is irrelevant, because they repeat the entire program once, whatever the value of n.

Even though both adults and children conducted the same proportion of their programs in the (potentially) highly informative region 2 of the experiment space, adults were able to induce the correct rule from experiments in this region, whereas children were not. In the following paragraphs we will explore these interactions between search of the experiment and hypothesis spaces in more detail.

Differences in Search Strategies   Only two children generated the n-role: selector frame, so it is difficult to classify the other twenty children as either experimenters or theorists according to the same criteria used in study 1. The earlier classification was based on how participants switched from one frame to another, but when participants use only one frame it is impossible to make this categorization. However, even without this criterion we can see that all twenty of the children who failed to generate the correct hypothesis can be classified as a type of Experimenter. The children were within the n-role: counter frame and their search of the hypothesis space consisted of changing the values of the slots within the n-role: counter frame. This was achieved by searching the experiment space to determine a value for the number of repetitions slot within the frame.

Although children—like adults—searched the experiment space in order to induce new hypotheses, their search was different from that of the adults: The adults searched the experiment space once they had abandoned the n-role: counter frame, and the goal of their search was to induce a new frame. In contrast, the children used experiments to find new slot values within a frame that they were reluctant to abandon. Some experiments, because they were in uninformative regions of the experiment space, did confirm their incorrect hypotheses. Others did not, but children responded to disconfirmation either by misobservation or by ignoring the results and running yet another experiment that they were sure would confirm their prediction. This indicates that although the children were exploring both the hypothesis and the experiment space, their search of the hypothesis space was limited—it was constrained to staying within one frame, the n-role: counter frame.

Study 3 Discussion
This study revealed three main differences between adults and children. First, children proposed hypotheses that were different from those proposed by adults even though they had equal access to the most informative region of the experiment space. Second, the children did not abandon their current frame and search the hypothesis space for a new

frame, nor did they use the results of experiment-space search to induce a new frame. Third, the children did not attempt to check whether their hypotheses were consistent with prior data. Even when children knew that there was earlier evidence against their current hypothesis, they said that the device *usually* worked according to their theory.

Each of these results indicates that children had greater difficulty than adults at discovering a highly implausible rule for RPT. As noted at the outset of this chapter, however, domain knowledge deficits can influence our assessments of children's grasp of valid inference and good experimental design. Suppose that instead of being a highly implausible selector, RPT worked according to the one of the more commonly proposed counter rules. What kinds of differences and similarities would we find between children and adults in that case? This question motivated our fourth study, in which we varied the plausibility of the to-be-discovered rule.

Study 4: Designing Good Experiments to Test Bad Hypotheses: A Developmental Study

Results from the first three studies suggest that, over the range of ages and technical experience included thus far, all participants are likely to share domain-specific knowledge that biases them in the same direction with respect to the relative plausibility of different hypotheses. We decided to use this consistent preference for some hypotheses and aversion to others as a means of determining how search in the experiment space is influenced by hypothesis plausibility. More specifically, we wanted to see how age and scientific training influence differences in the domain-general heuristics used to constrain search in the experiment space. Such domain-general heuristics might include rules for effecting normative approaches to hypothesis testing as well as pragmatic rules for dealing with processing limitations in encoding, interpreting, and remembering experimental outcomes.

Method
Four participant groups participated in study 4: twelve university undergraduates, twenty community college students, seventeen "sixth" graders (a mixed class of fifth to seventh graders, mean age eleven years) and fifteen third graders (mean age nine years). The adult groups were selected to contrast participants with respect to technical and scientific training. Sixth graders were selected because they represent the age at which many of the components of "formal reasoning" are purported to be available, and the third graders were chosen because study 3 had indicated they were the youngest group who could perform

reliably in our task. In addition, the two younger groups match the ages of children studied in many other investigations of children's scientific reasoning skills (e.g., Kuhn, Amsel, and O'Loughlin, 1988; Kuhn et al., 1995).

The university students were mainly science or engineering majors who received partial course credit for participation. They reported having taken about two programming courses, and they rated themselves between average and above average on technical and scientific skills. All community college students were non-science majors (general studies, para-legal, communications, pre-nursing, and so on). They were recruited by posted advertisements and were paid for their participation. Community college students had little training in mathematics or physical sciences beyond high school, and less than half of them had taken a college course in biology or chemistry. Although 70 percent of them had used computer-based word processors and 45 percent had used spreadsheets, only three of the twenty had ever taken a programming course.

Children were volunteers from an urban private school and came primarily from academic and professional families. They were selected to be young "equivalents" of the university students with respect to both the likelihood of ultimately attending college and age-appropriate computer experience. All sixth graders had at least six months of LOGO experience, and most had more than a year of experience. All but one of the third graders had at least one month of LOGO, with the majority having six months to a year of experience. Note that community college students had less programming experience than the third graders.

The BT Microworld   In this study we shifted from using BigTrak to the first of its computer-based isomorphs (see appendix 5.3). We used a computer microworld—called BT^2—in which participants enter a sequence of commands to a "spaceship" which then responds by carrying out various maneuvers. The BT interface is shown in figure 5.2.

The spaceship moves around in the left-hand panel according to instructions that are entered in its memory when participants "press" (point and click) a sequence of keys on the keypad displayed on the right. The full execution cycle involves (1) clearing the memory and returning BT to "base" with the CLR/HOME key; (2) entering a series of up to sixteen instructions, each consisting of a function key (the command) and a one- or two-digit number (the argument); (3) pressing the "GO" key and observing BT's behavior as it executes the program. The commands all correspond to a similar function on the BigTrak keypad, with the one added constraint that when the BT reaches the edge of the panel, it does not go off the screen, or wrap the screen.

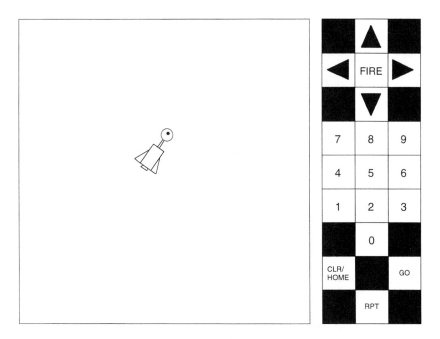

Figure 5.2
BT interface. Participants enter commands by pressing the keypad in the panel on the right, and the BT "spaceship" maneuvers in the panel on the left.

Design   Recall that our earlier studies revealed that there were two very popular counter hypotheses about the effect of RPT N in a program: Repeat the entire program, or the last step, n times. In contrast, there were two hypotheses—both selectors—that participants were unlikely to propose at the outset: Repeat the nth step, or the last n steps, once. This age-independent preference for counters over selectors was exploited in our design.

We provided each participant with an initial hypothesis about how RPT might work. The suggested hypothesis was always wrong. However, depending on the condition, participants regarded it as either plausible or implausible. In some conditions the suggested hypothesis was only "somewhat" wrong, in that it was from the same frame as the way that RPT actually worked. In others, it was "very" wrong, in that it came from a different frame than the actual rule.

The BT simulator was programmed so that each participant worked with a RPT command obeying one of the two "counter" rules or two "selector" rules described above. We used a 2 Given (Counter or Selector) × 2 Actual (Counter or Selector) × 4 Education level (third grade, sixth grade,

Table 5.3
Four types of Given-Actual conditions (study 4).

Frame Type			Specific Rule		
Given	→	Actual	Given	→	Actual
Counter	→	Counter	C2: Repeat last step n times	→	C1: Repeat entire program n times
Counter	→	Selector	C1: Repeat entire program n times	→	S1: Repeat the last n steps once
Selector	→	Counter	S1: Repeat the last n steps once	→	C1: Repeat entire program n times
Selector	→	Selector	S2: Repeat the nth step once	→	S1: Repeat the last n steps once

community college, and university) between-participants design. The given-actual conditions are listed in table 5.3. The given hypothesis is the one that was suggested by the experimenter, and the actual rule is the way that BT was programmed to work for a particular condition. The important feature of this design is that RPT *never worked in the way that was suggested by the given hypothesis*. In each given-actual condition, there were three university students,[3] five community college students, four sixth graders, and four third graders (except for the counter-counter condition, which had three third graders and five sixth graders).

Procedure   The study had three phases. In the first, participants were introduced to BT and instructed on the use of each basic command. During this phase, the display did not include the RPT key shown in figure 5.2. Participants were trained to criterion on how to write a series of commands to accomplish a specified maneuver.

In the second phase, participants were shown the RPT key. They were told that it required a numeric parameter (n) and that there could be only one RPT N in a program. They were told that their task was to find out how RPT worked by writing at least three programs and observing the results. At this point, the experimenter suggested a specific hypothesis about how RPT might work:

> One way that RPT might work is: (one of the four hypotheses described in the next section). Write down three good programs that will allow you to see if the repeat key really does work this way. Think carefully about your program and then write the program down on the sheet of paper. . . . Once you have written your program down, I will type it in for you and then I will run it. You can observe what happens, and then you can write down your next

program. So you write down a program then I will type it in, and then you will watch what the program does. I want you to write three programs in this way.

Next, the third—and focal—phase began. Participants wrote programs (experiments) to evaluate the given hypothesis. After each program had been written, but before it was run, participants were asked to predict the behavior of BT, indicating the extent of their understanding or acceptance of the given hypothesis. Participants had access to a record of the programs they had written (but not to a record of BT's behavior).

Participants were instructed to give verbal protocols. This gave us a record of (1) what they thought about the kinds of programs they were writing while testing their hypotheses, (2) what they observed and inferred from the device's behavior, and (3) what their hypotheses were about how RPT actually worked. When participants had written, run, and evaluated three experiments, they were given the option of either terminating or writing additional experiments if they were still uncertain about how RPT worked. The entire session lasted approximately forty-five minutes.

Results
As we have done earlier, we preface our quantitative analyses with an examination of the verbal protocol of a single participant in order to illustrate a variety of interesting qualitative aspects of participants' behavior. (The full protocol is listed in appendix 5.2 on page 127.) Our goal is to convey a general sense of participant's approach to the task. In subsequent sections, we provide a detailed analysis based on the full set of protocols.

DP was a male university student in the Counter → Selector condition, and he was given Rule C1: *Repeat entire program n times*. The actual rule was Rule S3: *Repeat nth step once*.[4] DP discovered the correct rule after five experiments. Two characteristics of DP's protocol make it interesting (but not atypical). First, even before the first experiment, DP proposed an alternative to the given hypothesis: "I want to test to see if repeat repeats the statements before it. . . . and I'll put a statement after the repeat to see if it has any effect on that." That is, he is testing, in addition to C1, another hypothesis: C3 – *n* repeats of subsequent step(s) (see table 3.3). Second, throughout the experimental phase, DP made many explicit comments about the attributes of the experiment space. He clearly attended to the properties of a "good" experiment.

DP's goal in his first experiment is unambiguous: to determine whether RPT acts on the instruction before or after the RPT command. (That is, C1 versus C3.) To resolve this question DP conducts an experiment with easily distinguished commands before and after the RPT key.

(This ability to write programs that contain useful "markers" is an important feature of participants' behavior, and we will return to it later.) This experiment allows DP to discriminate between two rival hypotheses and DP extracts from the first experiment the information he sought: "It appears that the repeat doesn't have any effect on any statements that come after it."

For the second experiment DP returns to the question of whether the given hypothesis (C1), or the Current hypothesis (C3) was correct, and he increases λ from 1 to 2. In designing experiment 2, he also includes one step following the RPT "just to check" that RPT had no effect on instructions that follow it. Thus, even though experiment 1 provided evidence inconsistent with C3, DP designs an experiment that could provide another disconfirmation of it. Once again he uses commands that could be easily discriminated and writes another program from region 3 of the experiment space ($λ = 2, n = 2$). When experiment 2 is run, DP observes that there were two executions of the ↑ 2 instruction, and he concludes (2:30–3:00) that "it only repeats the statement immediately in front of it." Although this conclusion is consistent with the data that DP had collected so far, it appears to leave him entertaining U2: One repeat of the last step, rather than the correct rule.

For the third experiment, DP continues to put commands after RPT just to be sure they are not affected. However, given that his current hypothesis (U2) had been confirmed in the previous experiment he next writes a program that further increases λ. This is his first experiment in region 2. The goal of this experiment is to "see what statements are repeated" (3:30). He realizes that, although the outcome of experiment 3 is inconsistent with U2, the outcome of the previous experiment is not: (5:30–6:00: "it seemed to act differently in number two and number three"). The unexpected result led DP to abandon hypothesis U2 and to continue beyond the mandatory three experiments.

For the fourth experiment DP uses a different value of n (6:00–6:30: "repeat three instead of a repeat two, and see if that has anything to do with it.") Here, too, DP demonstrates another important characteristic of many of our participants' approaches to experimentation. He uses a conservative incremental strategy in moving from one experiment to the next, similar to the VOTAT (vary one thing at a time) strategies described by Tschirgi (1980) and the conservative focusing strategy described by Bruner, Goodnow, and Austin (1956). This approach still leads him to put commands after the RPT, even though he was confident that RPT has no effect on them, and even though they placed greater demands on his observational and recall processes. (At the $λ$-n level, DP executed VOTAT consistently throughout his series of five experiments. That is, he never varied *both* λ and n on successive experiments. The λ-n pairs were: 1-2, 2-2, 3-2, 3-3, 3-1. For his last three experiments, even the specific commands and their parameters remained the same, and only n varied.) This moved him from region 2 into region 3, and while analyzing the results of this experiment (7:00–10:00) in conjunction with earlier results, DP changes from the counter frame to the selector frame. First he notices that "the number three" statement (i.e., the ↓ 1) was repeated twice in this case but that "the turning statement" was repeated (i.e., executed) only once (7:00–7:30). The implied comparison is with the previous experiment in which the turning statement (i.e., "the right 15 command" [5:30]) was the command that got repeated.

The next sentence is of particular interest: "because when I change the number not only did it change . . . it didn't change the uh . . . the number that it repeated but it changed the uh . . . the actual instruction" (9:00–9:30). A plausible paraphrase of this comment is as follows: "When I changed the value of n, it didn't change the *number* of repetitions, but it did change *which* commands got repeated." This is precisely the insight required to shift from the counter frame to the selector frame.

DP goes on to clearly state two instantiated versions of the correct rule by referring to previous results with $n = 2$ and $n = 3$, and he designed his fifth experiment to test his prediction with $n = 1$. The outcome of this final experiment, from region 1, in conjunction with earlier results was sufficient to convince him that he had discovered how RPT worked.

Aggregate Results   Having presented an illustrative example of the performance of one participant, we now turn to a detailed analysis of the full set of participants. Group differences are investigated with respect to four questions. First, how successful were participants in discovering how RPT actually worked in the different experimental conditions? Second, how did participants' interpretation of the task affect their goals and implicit constraints? Third, how did they search the experiment space? Fourth, how did their search of the experiment space affect the hypothesis that they finally stated?

In the following analyses, for those cases where the data from the two older groups were not significantly different and the data from the two younger groups were not significantly different, the data were collapsed into adult (university students and community college student) versus children (grades three and six). For other analyses, the data from the two adult groups and the sixth graders all revealed the same pattern, but the third graders showed an opposite pattern. In these situations, the groups were collapsed into Older (university students, community college students, and sixth graders) versus Youngest (third graders).

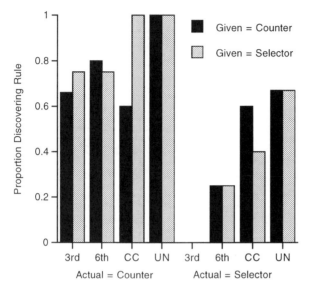

Figure 5.3
Proportion of participants in each group discovering the correct rule for each Given-Actual condition.

SUCCESS RATES   Domain-specific knowledge—as manifested in participants' expectations about what "repeat" might mean in this context—played an important role in participants' ability to discover the Actual rule (see figure 5.3). Regardless of what the given hypothesis was, participants found it easier to discover counters (81%) than selectors (35%). There was also a main effect for group: the correct rule was discovered by 83 percent of the university students, 65 percent of the community college students, 53 percent of the sixth graders, and 33 percent of the third graders. This group effect is attributable to the Actual = Selector conditions, in which 56 percent of the adults but only 13 percent of the children were successful. For Actual = Counter, adults and children were roughly equal in their success rates (88% versus 75%).[5]

The main effect for plausibility of the Actual rule can also be attributed primarily to the children's performance in the Actual = Selector condition. Whereas 75 percent of the children discovered the rule when it was a counter, only 25 percent of the sixth graders and none of the third graders discovered the rule when it was a selector. Adults were also better at discovering counters than selectors, although the effect was not as strong as for children due to the surprisingly poor performance by the community college participants in the counter-counter condition.

The main effect for grade resulted from three of the six possible pair-wise comparisons among the four participant groups: University students did better than sixth graders, they also did better than third graders, and the community college students did better than third graders, also. Thus, overall success rate was affected only when grade level differences were extreme (both adult groups versus third graders) or when they were combined with training differences (university students versus sixth graders).

HYPOTHESIS INTERPRETATION: INITIATING SEARCH IN THE HYPOTHESIS SPACE   Our purpose in presenting participants with a given hypothesis was to determine the extent to which search in the hypothesis space was influenced by the plausibility of the hypothesis being considered. This is one of the points at which domain-specific knowledge (which determines plausibility) might affect domain-general knowledge about experimental strategies, such as attempts to disconfirm, discriminating between rival hypotheses, and so on.

Before running the first experiment, participants were asked to predict what would happen. Their predictions indicated the extent to which they understood or accepted the given hypotheses. Each participant's response to the given hypothesis was assigned to one of three categories: I, accept the given hypothesis; II, accept the given, but also propose an alternative (see the protocol for participant DP, presented earlier); and III, reject the given, and propose an alternative. The proportion of participants responding in each category is shown as a function of grade level and type of given hypothesis in table 5.4.

Table 5.4
Proportion of participant responses in each category when given either counter or selector hypothesis.

			Group							
			UN		CC		Sixth		Third	
	Response category	Given	C	S	C	S	C	S	C	S
I	Accept Given		.50	.50	.90	.57	.56	.50	.86	.14
II	Accept Given and propose alternative		.50	.50	.10	.43	.11	.13	0	0
III	Reject Given and propose alternative		0	0	0	0	.33	.37	.14	.86

Note: UN—University students: CC—Community college students; C—Counter hypothesis; S—Selector hypothesis. One third grader and three community college students did not respond to the "what will it do?" question.

There was a main effect of given hypothesis (counter versus selector) on type of response. This effect was attributable entirely to the third graders, 86 percent of whom either accepted a given counter or rejected a given selector. There was also a main effect for group. This effect remained when analyzed separately for both Given = Counter and Given = Selector. In both conditions, the two adult groups always accepted the given hypothesis, either on its own (Category I) or in conjunction with a proposed alternative (Category II) (the difference between university students and community college students in their response patterns was not significant). In contrast, no third grader and only about 10 percent of the sixth graders ever proposed an alternative to compare to the given (Category II). Children were approximately evenly divided between accepting the given (Category I) or rejecting it (Category III). Sixth graders were about as likely to accept as reject the given hypothesis, regardless of whether it was a counter or a selector, but third graders almost always accepted counters and rejected selectors. Overall, adults were more likely to consider multiple alternatives (Category II) than children.

Of the twenty-five participants who proposed alternatives to the given hypothesis, three proposed alternatives that could not be coded as either counters or selectors. For the remaining twenty-two, there was a strong effect of the type of given hypothesis on the type of alternative proposed (see table 5.5). All of the eight Given = Counter participants who proposed alternatives proposed another counter, regardless of group. In contrast, across all four groups, only two of the twelve Given = Selector participants proposed alternatives from the selector frame.

Table 5.5
Number of participants in each group who generated alternatives from the same or different frame as given hypothesis.

Type of alternative	Given	Group									
		UN		CC		Sixth		Third		All Groups	
		C	S	C	S	C	S	C	S	C	S
Same frame as Given		3	1	1	0	3	1	1	0	8	2
Different frame from Given		0	2	0	3	0	3	0	4	0	12

Note: UN—University students; CC—Community college students; C—Counter hypothesis; S—Selector hypothesis. One sixth grader and two third graders generated alternatives that were unclassifiable.

In summary, when responding to the given hypothesis, adults were able to consider more than a single hypothesis, whereas children were not. When participants did propose alternatives, they tended to propose plausible rather than implausible alternatives (i.e., counters rather than selectors). As we shall see in the next section, this propensity to consider multiple versus single hypotheses can affect the type of experimental goals set by the participants, which in turn can be used to impose constraints on search in the experiment space.

SEARCH IN THE EXPERIMENT SPACE   How did participants solve the problem of designing a "good experiment" to discover how the RPT key worked? We address this question by analyzing the kinds of experiments that participants designed. We start with an analysis of how domain-general knowledge about their own cognitive limitations was used by participants to impose pragmatic constraints on the complexity of their experiments. Next, we do a static analysis of the distribution of experiments in the experiment space, and then we look at the *dynamics* of experiment space search by examining transitions from one experiment to the next. Finally, we examine the *interaction* between the experiment space and the hypothesis space by analyzing the ability of participants to extract useful information from the outcomes of experiments and to use that information to evaluate their hypotheses.

CONSTRAINTS DERIVED FROM DOMAIN-GENERAL KNOWLEDGE   Participants' use of domain-general knowledge to constrain search in the experiment space can be investigated by analyzing (1) what they say about experiments and (2) the features of the experiments that they actually write. Each of these knowledge sources, in turn, can be analyzed at the $\lambda - n$ level, or at a finer grain of analysis that looks at the details of program content. In this section, we first summarize the results from the verbal protocols, and then we look at the features of participants' programs.

Participants' comments include many statements indicating both explicit understanding of the experiment space dimensions and what might be called a general notion of "good instrumentation": designing interpretable programs that contain easily identifiable markers. Participants made explicit statements about both kinds of knowledge. The following statements by different adult participants are typical: (1) "I don't want to have two of the same move in there yet, *I might not be able to tell if it was repeating the first one or if it was doing the next part of my sequence*"; (2) "I'm just going to make up some random but different directions *so that I'll know which ones get executed*"; (3) "I'm going to use a series of commands that will . . . *that are easily distinguished from one another*, and won't run it off the screen"; (4) "so I'm going to pick two [commands] that are the direct opposite of each other, to see if they don't really have to be direct opposites but I'm just going to write a program that consists of two steps, *that I could see easily*" (emphasis added).

Sixth graders were somewhat less articulate, but still showed a concern for both experiment space dimensions and program interpretability. Typical comments were (1) "I should have done FIRE because that was something *more standing out*"; (2) "Can I write one that has less steps so I can see if I can figure it out that way easier?" (3) "This time I'm not going to make it so long so it'll be easier." (4) "Maybe I should not go all the way [to the screen boundary] so I can tell if it does it again." Third graders rarely made such metacognitive comments. We quantified participants' appreciation of the dimensions of the experiment space by tabulating the frequency with which they made comments about "using longer programs," "using a different value of n," and so on. Eighty-three percent of the university students made at least one such comment, compared to 60 percent of the community college students, 53 percent of the sixth graders, and 20 percent of the third graders.

In addition to these verbal statements, participants demonstrated the effects of constraint imposition in their limited exploration of the experiment space. Permissible values for both λ and n range from one to fifteen. However, all participants tended to constrain both the length of programs they ran and the value of n. Although the $\lambda \leq 4$ by $n \leq 3$ region of the experiment space represents only 5 percent of the full space, 50 percent of the university students' 44 experiments were within it, as were 63 percent of the community college students' 117 experiments, 31 percent of the sixth graders' 68 experiments, and 31 percent of the third graders' 55 experiments. That is, participants at all grade levels clustered their experiments in a small region of the experiment space, although adults did it more than children.

At a finer level of detail, good instrumentation was assessed by the extent to which participants observed three pragmatic constraints: (1) using small numeric arguments (values < 5) on move commands, so that the actions of BT are not distorted by having it hit the boundaries of the screen; (2) using standard units of rotation, such as fifteen or thirty "minutes" (90 and 180°), for turn commands; and (3) using distinct commands in a program where possible.[6] Programs constrained in these ways produce behavior that is easier to observe, encode, and remember.

Participants were scored as observing a constraint if they violated it on no more than one of their experiments. For both turns and moves, there was a main effect of group. On move commands, 92 percent of the university students, 85 percent of the community college students, 65 percent of the sixth graders, and 47 percent of the third graders used small numeric arguments. On turn commands, 92 percent of the university students, 95 percent of the community college students, 71 percent of the sixth graders, and 53 percent of the third graders used standard rotational units. In contrast, there was no significant difference in the proportion of participants in each group who observed the distinct command constraint, although for all groups the proportion was much lower than for the other two constraints: 42 percent of the university students, 45 percent of the community college students, 24 percent of the sixth graders, and 53 percent of the third graders observed this constraint. The main effect of grade level for the first three analyses is not simply a domain-specific training effect, because even when the university participants are eliminated, it remains and, as mentioned earlier, the children had more computer programming training than the community college students.

It is possible that group differences on explicit statements about the experiment space are a consequence of older participants' general superiority at verbalization. However, none of the other three measures depend on verbalization ability. Thus, both what participants said and what they did support the conclusion that older participants—even those with weak technical backgrounds—were better able than children to constrain their search in the experiment space and to design interpretable experiments.

CONSTRAINTS DERIVED FROM DOMAIN-SPECIFIC KNOWLEDGE   Participants may establish different goals in response to hypotheses that their domain-specific knowledge leads them to interpret as plausible or implausible. These different goals, in turn, should lead to different types of search constraints in the experiment space. More specifically, if the goal is to identify which of the program steps are repeated for selector hypotheses, or to discriminate between selectors and counters, then participants should write programs having more than n steps (i.e., programs with $\lambda > n$). In programs where λ is several steps greater than n, it is easy to distinguish among repeats of all steps, first step, last step, and n steps. On the other hand, if the goal is to demonstrate the effect of a Counter, then participants should use larger values of n and (for pragmatic reasons) relatively short programs (i.e., programs with $\lambda < n$). Both of these effects should be strongest for the first experiment, before participants have any direct evidence for the actual rule.

Both of the adult groups' responses and sixth graders' responses were consistent with the normative account given above: Combining the three groups, only ten of the twenty-five older participants given counters wrote $\lambda > n$ programs, whereas twenty of the twenty-four given selectors did so. Third graders showed the opposite pattern: Six of the seven given counters, but only two of the eight given selectors had first programs with $\lambda > n$. Figure 5.4 shows the proportion of participants in each age group and each given condition whose first programs had $\lambda > n$.

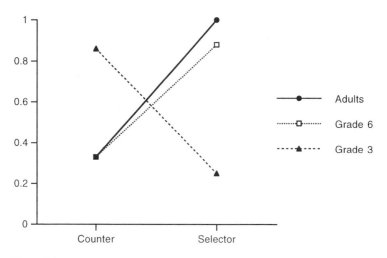

Figure 5.4
Proportion of participants in each age group given counters or given selectors whose first experiments had $l > n$.

These results show that whereas participants at all grade levels used both domain-general and domain-specific knowledge to constrain their search, the groups differed in how they used the two kinds of knowledge. Adults and sixth graders, when given a plausible counter, produced short programs with large values of n, suggesting a focus on the number of repetitions, rather than on what was to be repeated. On the other hand, when given an implausible selector, older participants were likely to start with longer programs with smaller n's (i.e., programs with $\lambda > n$), suggesting a focus on what was to be repeated rather than the number of repetitions, which would allow them to discriminate between counters and selectors.

We interpret the third graders' reversal of this pattern as evidence for their apparent inability to even consider a selector hypothesis. When given one, they wrote relatively short programs with relatively large values of n, a strategy that is consistent with a goal of trying to convincingly demonstrate a counter. When given a counter, third graders used less extreme values of n, perhaps because they had less motivation to "prove a point."

Different experimental strategies can also be inferred by classifying experiments in terms of experiment space regions (see figure 3.4). As noted in chapter 3, region 2 is the most informative region, and adults appear to have understood its potential informativeness better than the children. Ninety-two percent of university students, 75 percent of community college students, 59 percent of sixth graders, and 53 percent of third graders wrote at least one region 2 experiment. Another way to extract useful information from the experiment space is to write experiments from more than a single region. Adults were more likely to sample different regions than were children. Ninety-one percent of the adults (100% of university students and 85% of the community college students) wrote experiments from at least two different regions of the experiment space. In contrast, only 29 percent of the sixth graders and 60 percent of the third graders sampled from more than one region. Staying in one region of the experiment space is only detrimental if the region fails to discriminate between hypotheses—region 1 for hypotheses C2 (last step N times) versus S1 (last N steps once)—or if it fails to adequately demonstrate the correct hypothesis—region 3 for S1. All of the third graders in Actual = Selector conditions who stayed in one region were in either region 1 or 3. For the sixth graders in Actual = Selector conditions, 75 percent who stayed in one region were in region 3. Thus, for the children, the failure to run experiments from different regions of the experiment space severely limited their ability to extract useful information from the outcomes of their experiments.

The common pattern here is that there is little or no difference between the university and community college participants, who, when combined, tend to differ from the two children's groups. For some measures, the sixth graders cluster with the adult participants. Taken as a whole, this pattern suggests a developmental effect, rather than a training effect, for participants' sensitivity to the potential informativeness of different types of experiments as a function of the given hypothesis. Moreover, for some of our measures, this effect appears between third and sixth grades.

DYNAMICS OF SEARCH IN THE EXPERIMENT SPACE   The analysis of the experiment space in terms of λ-n combinations or experiment space regions gives a picture of the properties of experiments aggregated over the entire search process, but it does not describe the dynamics of search in the experiment space. In this section we look at the search dynamics at two levels: (1) changes in n and λ from one experiment to the next, independent of program-content change, and (2) program-content change across experiments, independent of changes in λ and n.

One type of domain-general knowledge that participants might bring to this task is the "vary one thing at a time" (VOTAT) strategy mentioned earlier. When applied to the λ and n dimensions of the experiment space, VOTAT produces conservative moves: changes from one experiment to the next that do not vary both λ and n at the same time (including moves that vary neither). Overall, participants were conservative on 56 percent of their moves, and this did not vary according to group or actual hypothesis.

If we look at a finer level of detail—at the specific program content—then we can define a conservative move as one that keeps program content constant (except for additions or deletions) so that the effects of changes in λ and n would be easy to detect. Under this definition, the university adults are more likely to make conservative moves than the community college adults and the children. The mean percentage of conservative moves at the program-content level was 48 percent for university students, but only 13 percent, 12 percent, and 9 percent for community college students, sixth graders, and third graders, respectively. University students were significantly different from all other groups, but the community college students, sixth, and third graders were not significantly different from each other.

ENCODING EXPERIMENTAL OUTCOMES   The biases induced by domain-specific knowledge create expectations about BT's behavior. These expectations might affect participants' ability to encode accurately outcomes inconsistent with those expectations. Participants' descriptions of experimental outcomes were scored as misencodings if they contained unambiguous errors in reporting BT's behavior during program execution (i.e., if they contained explicit descriptions of events that did not actually occur, or if they described a sequence of events, but omitted an important one).

There was a main effect of the actual condition on misencoding: 63 percent of the participants in the Actual = Selector but only 35 percent of the participants in the Actual = Counter conditions misencoded at least one experiment. Within-group analyses showed that third graders misencoded more programs when the actual rule was a selector than when it was a counter. The other three groups were as likely to misencode programs when the Actual rule was a selector as when it was a counter. Even though the third graders' misencodings were more prevalent when the rule was implausible, they were not systematically distorted in the direction of their current hypotheses. For all the groups, when misencodings did occur, distortions of the actual results were as likely to occur in the direction of confirming the current hypothesis as disconfirming it.

There was also a main effect of group on misencoding: Twenty-five percent of the university students, 40 percent of the community college students, 53 percent of the sixth graders, and 73 percent of the third graders misencoded at least one experimental outcome. To determine whether the tendency to misencode experimental outcomes differed between specific groups, we compared misencoding rates among all six

pairings of the four participant groups. The analysis yielded three significantly different pairs: university students versus sixth, university
students versus third, and community college students versus third.

These results are almost identical to the pattern of between-group differences in overall success rates reported earlier, and they suggest the
possibility that third-graders' inability to discover selectors is a consequence of their well-known encoding and mnemonic deficiencies. However, the interaction of BT rules and regions produced encoding and
mnemonic demands that were more difficult in counter conditions,
where the third-graders did very well, than in the selector conditions,
where they all failed to discover the correct rule. In general, participants
in Actual = Counter conditions, who are always working with C1 (Repeat entire program N times), tend to have much more complex behaviors to observe, encode, and remember than do participants in Actual =
Selector conditions. For example, consider the region 2 program shown
in figure 3.3: $\uparrow$ 4 $\rightarrow$ 30 FIRE 2 RPT 2. This program would execute nine
instructions under C1, but only five under Rule S1 (repeat the last n steps
once).[7]

Encoding demands for participants working under counter versus
selector rules were estimated by calculating the mean number of executed instructions for each participant's correctly and incorrectly encoded program outcomes.[8] A 2 (Actual Rule: Selector versus Counter)
× 2 (Encoding: Correct versus Incorrect) ANOVA revealed that, on average, participants in the counter condition had to observe and encode
significantly more instruction executions than participants in the selector condition (25 executions versus 6.5 executions) but there was no
difference in program length for correctly versus incorrectly encoded
programs, and no interaction effect. Furthermore, whereas children in
the Actual = Counter conditions could correctly encode programs with
a mean length of twenty-two executions, children in the Actual = Selector conditions misencoded programs that had only seven executed instructions.

Thus, children's failures in the selector condition cannot be attributed
to general encoding and observation deficits. A more plausible explanation is that their counter bias led them to focus on the verification that n
repetitions (of something) had occurred. This attention to *number* of repetitions rather than what was being repeated caused them to misencode
the outcome. However, it did not lead them to distort their encodings to
fit a counter rule. N was given a counter role in only four of the thirty-
two Actual = Selector programs where children stated their hypotheses
and in three of these cases the value of n was 1, and the encoding was
correct.

INDUCING HYPOTHESES FROM EXPERIMENTAL OUTCOMES   We began this analysis with a presentation of overall success rates, followed by a detailed analysis of the statics and dynamics of search in the experiment space. Throughout, we have pursued the theme that domain-specific knowledge about "repeat" determined the initial plausibility of hypotheses and that, in turn, hypothesis plausibility influenced the kind of domain-general knowledge that participants brought to bear in imposing constraints on their search of the experiment space. One remaining question is whether or not, when their experiment space search did lead them into region 2, participants were able to make use of its maximally informative results. In other words, how successful were participants at coordinating the searches in the hypothesis space and the experiment space? Although region 2 provides direct and discriminating evidence for all hypotheses, it is most useful for discovering selector rules. Therefore, we expected that selector participants who had observed the outcome from one or more region 2 experiments would be more likely to discover the correct rule than those who never entered region 2.

In order to determine the effect of experiment space region on overall success rate, we calculated the frequency with which the correct rule was discovered as a function of the regions actually visited. When success rates are aggregated over all grades and conditions, there appears to be no benefit from having been in region 2. Sixty-four percent of the forty-four participants who had one or more region 2 experiments were successful, whereas 45 percent of the twenty who never entered region 2 were successful. However, as predicted, a closer analysis reveals a clear effect of region 2's utility for discovering Selectors. Table 5.6 shows the number of participants in each Actual condition and grade level who were successful or unsuccessful according to whether or not they ever went into region 2. As just noted, most participants in the Actual = Counter conditions are successful, regardless of whether or not they entered region 2. However, for all but one university participant in the Actual = Selector conditions, having at least one experiment in region 2 is a necessary but not sufficient condition for success.

Table 5.6
Number of successful and unsuccessful participants who did and did not have at least one experiment in region 2 for different actual conditions.

	Actual = Counter		Actual = Selector	
	Successful	Unsuccessful	Successful	Unsuccessful
in R2	18	3	10	13
not in R2	8	3	1	18

Study 4 Discussion
The idea behind study 4 was to manipulate participants' initial location in the hypothesis space in order to examine their search in the experiment-space. Thus, our discussion will focus primarily on developmental differences in experiment-space search. However, it is important to recall that in all conditions—including Counter-Counter and Selector-Selector conditions—the given hypothesis was always wrong. *Participants always had to search for the correct hypothesis.* Therefore, we also include a discussion of hypothesis-space search as necessary.

Experiment Generation Heuristics   Compared to the unbounded size of the experiment space faced by a scientist in a laboratory, the BT domain may appear to be an unrealistically simple context in which to investigate experimentation skills. In fact, the potential size of the BT experiment space is surprisingly large. When command-level differences between experiments are taken into account, the number of distinct experiments is in the billions (see chapter 3). Adult participants quickly realized that although the specific commands in a program might be used as useful markers of BT's behavior, the essential attributes of the experiment space were the values of λ and n. Nevertheless, even this "reduced" space has 225 cells and participants had to decide which of them to explore.

Both university and community college adults were effective at drastically pruning the experiment space. Over half of their experiments occurred within the $\lambda \leq 4$, $n \leq 3$ area of the experiment space, which represents only 5 percent of the full space. In contrast, less than one-third of the children's experiments were so constrained. Furthermore, the pattern of results described in the previous section revealed a developmental trend in the overall systematicity and effectiveness with which participants searched the experiment space. Our interpretation of this pattern is that it is a consequence of developmental differences in the application of a set of domain-general heuristics for searching the experiment space. The four principal heuristics follow.

1. USE THE PLAUSIBILITY OF A HYPOTHESIS TO CHOOSE EXPERIMENTAL STRATEGY   As noted earlier, one of the most robust findings in the literature on scientific reasoning in adults is that participants attempt to confirm, rather than disconfirm, their current hypothesis (Gorman, 1989; Klayman and Ha, 1987). Similarly, developmental studies show that even when explicitly instructed to generate evidence that could potentially falsify a rule, children at the sixth-grade level or below perform very poorly (Kuhn, 1989; Ward and Overton, 1990). However, in this study, we found a more flexible kind of response. That is, both children and adults varied their approach to confirmation and disconfirmation according to the plausibility of the currently held hypothesis.

More specifically, participants chose λ–n combinations that could either demonstrate or discriminate hypotheses according to their plausibility. When hypotheses were plausible, participants at all levels tended to set an experimental goal of demonstrating key features of the given hypothesis, rather than conducting experiments that could discriminate between rival hypotheses. (However, when given counters, the third graders did not emphasize the value of n to the extent that the other three groups did.)

For implausible hypotheses, adults and young children used different strategies. Adults' response to implausibility was to propose hypotheses from frames other than the Given frame and to conduct experiments that could discriminate between them. Our youngest children's response was to propose a hypothesis from a different but plausible frame, and then to ignore the initial, and implausible, hypothesis while attempting to demonstrate the correctness of the plausible one. Third graders were particularly susceptible to this strategy, but by sixth grade, participants appeared to understand the type of experiments that are informative.

2. FOCUS ON ONE DIMENSION OF AN EXPERIMENT OR HYPOTHESIS   Experiments and hypotheses are both complex entities having many aspects on which one could focus. In this study, experiments could vary at the λ–n level, at the command level, or even at the level of arguments for commands. Similarly, for hypotheses, there are auxiliary hypotheses, ancillary hypotheses, and additional assumptions that are never directly tested (cf. Lakatos and Musgrave, 1970). An incremental, conservative approach has been found to be effective in both concept attainment (Bruner, Goodnow, and Austin's "conservative focusing") and hypothesis testing (Tschirgi's, 1980, VOTAT strategy). This suggests that in moving from one experiment or hypothesis to the next or in moving between experiments and hypotheses, one should decide upon the most important features of each and focus on just those features.

Use of this focusing heuristic was manifested in different ways with respect to hypotheses and experiments. For hypotheses, it led all groups except the third graders to focus initially on *how many* times something was repeated when given counters, and *what* was repeated when given selectors. This produced the λ–n pattern depicted in figure 5.4. For experiments, it led to a characteristic pattern of between-experiment moves that minimized changes at the command level. Here, the university adults stood apart from the other three groups. They were much more likely than any of the three other groups to make conservative moves—that is, to minimize differences in program content between one program and the next. Although there are few sequential dependencies in the informativeness of experiment space regions, university adults may have used this heuristic to reduce the cognitive load imposed when comparing the outcomes of two programs.

Interestingly, only the third graders failed to use this heuristic when searching the hypothesis space, whereas only the university adults used it effectively when searching the experiment space. It is possible that, because the hypothesis search aspect of the discovery task is so familiar, all but the third graders were able to use the focusing heuristic. In contrast, when confronted with the relatively novel experimental design aspect of the task, even adults, if untrained in science, remained unaware of the utility of a conservative change strategy.

3. *MAINTAIN OBSERVABILITY*   As BT moves along the screen from one location to another, it leaves no permanent record of its behavior. Participants must remember what BT actually did. Thus, one heuristic is to write short programs in order to make it easy to remember what happened and to compare the results to those predicted by the current hypotheses. At the level of individual commands, this heuristic produces small arguments for the ↑ and ↓ commands, so that BT does not go off the screen. There were clear differences in the use of this heuristic. Adults almost always used it, whereas the youngest children often wrote programs that were very difficult to encode. This heuristic depends on knowledge of one's own information processing limitations as well as a knowledge of the device. Our finding that the third graders did not attempt to maintain observability, whereas the sixth graders and adults did, may be a manifestation of the more general findings about the development of self-awareness of cognitive limitations (Brown et al., 1983; Wellman, 1983).

4. *DESIGN EXPERIMENTS GIVING CHARACTERISTIC RESULTS*   Physicians look for "markers" for diseases, and physicists design experiments in which suspected particles will leave "signatures." In the BT domain, this heuristic is instantiated as "use many distinct commands." This heuristic maximizes the interpretability of experimental outcomes. It is extremely difficult to isolate the cause of a particular piece of BT behavior when many of the commands in a program are the same. All four groups were roughly equivalent in their use of this heuristic; on average, about half of all programs did not contain any repeated commands.

Overall, adults and children differed widely in their use of these heuristics. Adults not only appeared to use each of them but also appeared to be able to deal with their inherent contradictions. No participant ever used the 1,1 cell, even though it would yield the easiest to observe behavior, because it is so uninformative with respect to discriminating among rival hypotheses. Additionally, in a related study (Klahr, Dunbar, and Fay, 1990), adults' experiments were significantly overrepresented in the $\lambda = 3$, $n = 2$ cell of the experiment space. This cell represents the shortest possible region 2 experiment, and its overrepresentation suggests a compromise between informativeness and simplicity. Adults' tendency to cluster their experiments in the $\lambda \leq 4 \times n \leq 3$ region of the experiment space in the present study represents a similar compromise among competing heuristics.

In contrast, children either failed to use these heuristics at all or they let one of them dominate. For example, one approximation to the "characteristic result" heuristic would be to write long experiments that could generate unique behavior, although that would violate the "maintain observability" heuristic. Even on their first experiments, adults tended to write relatively short programs. Only one-third of them wrote first programs with $\lambda > 3$, whereas 80 percent of the children wrote first programs with $\lambda > 3$.

Search in the Hypothesis Space   In this study, as in all our previous studies, all participants in all four groups found counter hypotheses more plausible than selector hypotheses. Indeed, the relative plausibility of selectors was so low for third graders that when selectors were given they were disregarded and replaced by counters. We have already suggested several potential sources of domain-specific knowledge about what "repeat" might mean that could account for this bias, including linguistic knowledge, programming knowledge, and the particulars of the BT command syntax.

Although we found no age-related differences in the preference for counter hypotheses, there was a developmental difference in the implications of this preference, which was manifested in participants' ability to consider multiple hypotheses. One-third of the adults, but almost none of the children, began by considering more than one hypothesis. Although the results from our earlier studies did not reveal multiple hypothesis testing, such strategies were reported by Klayman and Ha (1989) in their investigation of the Wason rule discovery task. Indeed, Klayman and Ha found that successful participants were three times more likely to test multiple hypotheses than were unsuccessful participants. One possible explanation for why participants in our earlier studies did not use this strategy is that they had to generate their own initial hypotheses, whereas in the studies described here, they were given hypotheses to test. This procedural difference may have induced in participants a mild skepticism for a hypothesis not of their own making, even when it was from a plausible frame. Indeed, in a study with a more complex microworld, Schunn and Klahr (1993) found that presenting participants with someone else's hypothesis led to increased skepticism about, and more thorough testing of, all hypotheses, but not to any fundamental changes in the search process itself. In the present study, for adults this increased skepticism resulted in the testing of multiple hypotheses, whereas for most children it led to replacement of an implausible given hypothesis with a different hypothesis.

These results suggest that one developmental difference in hypothesis-space search is in how the strength of belief in a hypothesis determines whether multiple or single hypotheses will be considered. The cognitive demands imposed by the need to search the hypothesis space for a plausible hypothesis to oppose an implausible one, and then to search the experiment space for a discriminating test, may have exceeded the capacity of our youngest participants. This led them to avoid considering multiple hypotheses. If the initial hypothesis was plausible, then they accepted it; if it was implausible, their only recourse was to abandon it and replace it with one that was more plausible. In contrast, when adults were given a hypothesis, whether plausible or implausible, they had sufficient resources to contrast it with another one.

Toward a Resolution of the Child-as-Scientist Debate

We opened this chapter by revisiting the child-as-scientist debate and by pointing out that it might be resolved by distinguishing between developmental differences in domain-specific knowledge and developmental differences in the domain-general processes associated with making valid inferences. We believe that the results of studies 3 and 4, when interpreted within the SDDS framework, contribute toward a resolution of this debate. More specifically, we view the search constraint heuristics as domain-general, because they were applied in a context far removed from the situations in which they were acquired. However, the plausibility of specific hypotheses, which influences search in both the hypothesis space and the experiment space, is based on domain-specific knowledge. In the study reported here, it results from participants' strong biases about what "repeat" might mean.

Our study yielded a picture of both similarities and differences in the way that children and adults formulate hypotheses and design experiments to evaluate them. At the top level of the cycle of scientific reasoning—that is, the level of hypothesis formation, experimentation and outcome interpretation—older elementary schoolchildren approached the discovery task in an appropriate way. Most sixth graders and some third graders understood that their task was to produce evidence to be used in support of an argument about a hypothesis. Contrary to the claims of Kuhn, Amsel, and O'Loughlin (1988) that even adults tend to confuse theory and evidence, we found that children were able to distinguish between theory (hypotheses) and evidence. However, when placed in a context requiring the coordination of search in two spaces, children's performance was markedly inferior to that of adults (both with and without technical and scientific training).

An examination of the fine structure of the participants' sequences of experiments and hypotheses revealed that their overall performance differences could be attributed to characteristic differences in how they searched both the hypothesis space and the experiment space. The most important difference in hypothesis-space search was in the way that adults and children responded to plausible and implausible hypotheses. When adults were given an implausible hypothesis, they established a goal of designing an experiment that could discriminate between the given implausible hypothesis and a plausible hypothesis of their own creation (usually one of the standard counters).

When children were given hypotheses to evaluate, they were not insensitive to whether they were plausible or implausible, but they responded by generating a different goal than the adults. In the implausible case, rather than simultaneously consider two alternative hypotheses, children focused only on a plausible one of their own making (a counter), and attempted to generate what they believed would be extremely convincing evidence for it. This was not an unreasonable goal, but it produced uninformative experiments. More specifically, in order to generate a convincing case for a counter hypothesis, third graders chose large values of n, so that the effect of the number of repetitions would be unambiguous. Because their goal was demonstration, inconsistencies were interpreted not as disconfirmations, but rather as either errors or temporary failures to demonstrate the desired effect. When subsequent efforts to demonstrate the counter hypothesis were successful, they were accepted as sufficient. Because the third graders did not seek global consistency, they extracted only local information from experimental outcomes.

The BT context elicited behavior in our third graders that is characteristic of younger children in simpler contexts. Resistance to disconfirming evidence has been observed in studies of discrimination learning (Tumblin and Gholson, 1981), but it has been limited to much younger children. For example, Gholson, Levine, and Phillips (1972) found that kindergarten children maintained disconfirmed hypotheses on about half of the negative feedback trials, but by second grade the rate dropped to 10 percent. The complexity of the discovery context, in conjunction with strong plausibility biases, may have caused our third graders to function like kindergarten children in the simpler discrimination-learning task.

With respect to search heuristics in the experiment space, children were less able than adults to constrain their search, they tended not to consider pragmatic constraints, and they were unsystematic in the way that they designed experiments. These findings indicate that one of the problems for the younger children is to apply effective search constraints on their experiments. This viewpoint is consistent with research on the effects of constraints on problem solving in younger children. When presented with "standard" puzzles (involving search in a single problem space), young children perform much better when the order of subgoals is constrained by the structure of the materials than when they have to decide for themselves what to do first (Klahr, 1985; Klahr and Robinson, 1981). Here too, we find the third graders in our dual-search situation behaving analogously to younger children in single-search contexts. That is, in our study, when given a task in which they had to impose multiple constraints on hypotheses and experimental design, children did not conduct appropriate experiments. However, in studies where both hypotheses and experimental choices are highly constrained, young children can select appropriate experiments (Sodian, Zaitchik, and Carey, 1991).

Overall, the SDDS framework has helped us to begin to answer some enduring questions about the development of scientific discovery skills. The results of our analysis, when combined with the related work from other laboratories, clarify the conditions under which children's domain-general reasoning skills are adequate to successfully coordinate search for hypotheses and experiments: (1) hypotheses must be easily accessible (such as the highly plausible counters in our study) or few in number (as in the two-alternative situations used by Sodian, Zaitchik, and Carey), (2) the experimental alternatives must also be few in number (also as in Sodian, Zaitchik, and Carey), and (3) the domain must provide feedback relevant to discriminating among plausible hypotheses (as in region 2 experiments in BT studies). It is important to reiterate the point that the performance deficits we found were not simply the result of children's inadequate encoding or mnemonic skills. As shown earlier, when experimental outcomes were consistent with children's expectations, they were correctly encoded, even though they were three times as long as those incorrectly encoded, but discrepant from children's expectations. Instead, the adult superiority appears to come from a set of domain-general skills that go beyond the logic of confirmation and disconfirmation and deal with the coordination of search in two spaces.

Notes

1. For the other children in this study, the experimenter did not provide such scaffolding (see also comments following RJ's experiment 7).
2. One version of BT, written in LISP and run on a Xerox Dandelion workstation, was used

by the university students and the children, and the other, written in cT for the Apple MacII, was used by the community college students.

3. These subjects were a subset of a larger group from a related experiment reported in Klahr, Dunbar, and Fay (1990). That study used an extended set of problems that included two *different* Given-Actual pairs in each cell (e.g., for Counter-Counter, both C2 → C1 *and* C1 → C2).

4. DP was in the extended group described in the previous note, so this specific counter-selector combination does not appear in table 5.3. However, his protocol is typical of other adult protocols.

5. Chi-square tests were used for all analyses involving response category contingency tables, except for cases of very small n's, in which Fisher Exact tests were used instead.

6. But note that for any program with $\lambda > 5$, *some* command must be repeated, inasmuch as there are only five distinct commands.

7. More generally, the number of instructions executed for a given λ-n combination depends on the actual rule. For C1 (Repeat entire program n times), the number of instructions executed is $2 * \lambda$ in region 1 and $(n + 1) * \lambda$ in regions 2 and 3. For Rule S1 (Repeat last n steps once), the number of executed instructions is $\lambda + 1$, $\lambda + n$, and $2 * \lambda$, in regions 1, 2, and 3, respectively. (See discussion of table 3.4 for further explanation.)

8. Some subjects contribute mean values for both the correctly and incorrectly encoded programs, whereas subjects who either misencoded or correctly encoded all programs only contribute one mean to the analysis.

Appendix 5.1
Protocol for an eleven-year-old girl (RJ) attempting to discover how the RPT key works on BigTrak

Notation:		RJ's comments in normal font.
PROGRAM		
→		*Experimenter's comments in italics.*
BT'S BEHAVIOR		
Prediction: *Expected BT behavior under current hypothesis*		

		How do you think it might work?
	0:30	I think that if I push something like Fire and then I push Repeat 5 then it will repeat Fire five times.
		So if you have Fire 1 it would repeat. . . .
		Fire 1, five times. And like if I said go Forward 1 it would go forward five times.
		Right; so the thing is for you to find out how it works and keep on saying what's going on in your mind.
		OK.

Exp 1	1:00	It repeated what? . . .
↑ 1 FIRE 6 RPT 6		The whole program it repeated.
→		That makes sense, the RPT button . . . when
↑ 1 FIRE 6 ↑ 1 FIRE 6		I push. . . . when I put in the program then it tells the program to do it over again.
Prediction: *FIRE 6 FIRE 6 FIRE 6 FIRE 6 FIRE 6 FIRE 6*		OK, that makes sense.

Exp 2		
↑ 2 FIRE 1 ← 34 FIRE 6 RPT 3		
→		
↑ 2 FIRE 1 ← 34 FIRE 6 FIRE 1 ← 34 FIRE 6		
Prediction: *↑ 2 FIRE 1 ← 34 FIRE 6 ↑ 2 FIRE 1 ← 34 FIRE 6 ↑ 2 FIRE 1 ← 34 FIRE 6*	2:00	It repeated my program again, let's see.

Exp 3		I don't think I'm gonna use such large numbers the next time.
FIRE 3 ↓ 2 ↑ 4 RPT 2		
→		
FIRE 3 ↓ 2 ↑ 4 ↓ 2 ↑ 4		
Prediction: *FIRE 3 ↓ 2 ↑ 4 FIRE 3 ↓ 2 ↑ 4*	4:00	

Appendix 5.1 (continued)

	4:30	*So what are you thinking*
		What am I thinking?
		I'm thinking how come no matter how many times I push repeat.
		If it is 5 then it only goes as many times as I push the number.
	5:00	The Repeat key to me doesn't seem, you know. If you really wanted the program to go more than one time, it seems unnecessary.
		But you know, basically you just want your program, your—whatever this thing is called—to go . . .
	5:30	you just want it to go, like, Forward 8.
		Then it's not really necessary to even have that key.
		To have the Repeat key?
		Sometimes though, say I want it to go Left, and then I want it to go Forward, and then I want it to go Left again so that it will go into the next room maybe.
		That makes sense to have it then.
		But this way I don't have to press Left Forward, Left Forward, Left Forward. I could just push RPT.
	6:00	*So how do you think the repeat key works now?*
		Well if you push in your program, then you push in RPT.
		The number you push after repeat.
		That's how many times it will repeat your program.
		I see. Are you sure that's how it works?
		I think. I'm not sure.
		So why don't you see if that really is how it works?
		OK.

Exp 4
$\uparrow 4 \leftarrow 23 \downarrow 2$ RPT 3
$\rightarrow$
$\uparrow 4 \leftarrow 23 \downarrow 2 \uparrow 4 \leftarrow 23 \downarrow 2$

Prediction: $\uparrow 4 \leftarrow 23 \downarrow 2 \uparrow 4 \leftarrow 23$
$\downarrow 2 \uparrow 4 \leftarrow 23 \downarrow 2$

		You will have to rescue it—it was about to get stuck.
	7:00	I put in so many commands I can't remember exactly what I did.
		I think I'm gonna put in smaller commands. 'Cause I can't remember what I did.

Exp 5
$\uparrow 2$ RPT 3
$\rightarrow$
$\uparrow 4$

	7:30	Let's try this again. I'm gonna push on.
		It repeated my program three times.
		Are you sure?

Appendix 5.1 (continued)

Prediction: ↑2 ↑2 ↑2		Well, I'm not sure how long each of its steps are.
		It looked like one and then two.
	8:30	*So bring it back. Why don't you try the same thing with FIRE?*

Exp 6
FIRE 1 RPT 2
→
FIRE 2

That's what it did, it repeated Fire once twice.

So how does it work?

It repeats the program that you put in, but I'm gonna try it with two things and see if it

Prediction: FIRE 2   just repeats the first one.

Exp 7
↑ 1 FIRE 2 RPT 2
→
↑ 1 FIRE 2 ↑ 1 FIRE 2

	9:00	It just repeats my program twice.
		So that's how you think it works now, is it?
Prediction: ↑1 FIRE 2 ↑1 FIRE 2		Well, I think after you push it, after you do your program, and you push Repeat and you push how many numbers it's how many times it repeats.
	9:30	Because every time I try to do something like that that's what it does.
		But I don't think, you know it might be just easier if you like you do Forward 2, Backward 2, Forward 2, Backward 1, because most of the time I don't think someone's going to.
		If they really wanted to push Fire five times they would just push Fire 5.
	10:00	*So, you are absolutely sure how it works?*
		Well, that's what I think, because every time I do it that's what it does.
		What would happen If you had RPT 9 there? What would it do then?
		It would repeat it nine times.
		Why don't you try?

Exp 8
↑ 2 FIRE 1 RPT 9
→
↑ 2 FIRE 1 ↑ 2 FIRE 1

	10:30	It's gonna run into something. It didn't repeat it nine times, it just went nine steps.
Prediction: ↑2 FIRE 1 ↑2 FIRE 1		It didn't repeat it nine times. Let's see.
↑2 FIRE 1 ↑2 FIRE 1 ↑2 FIRE 1		Boy, this is confusing.
↑2 FIRE 1 ↑2 FIRE 1 ↑2 FIRE 1		I'm glad I don't have one of these at home.
↑2 FIRE 1		There's no way I would ever be able to play with this.

Appendix 5.1 (continued)

		I would probably get so fed up with this, I'd probably just just trash it.
		OK.

Exp 9
↑ 2 FIRE 1 RPT 9
→
↑ 2 FIRE 1 ↑ 2 FIRE 1

Prediction: ↑2 FIRE 1 ↑2 FIRE 1
↑2 FIRE 1 ↑2 FIRE 1 ↑2 FIRE 1
↑2 FIRE 1 ↑2 FIRE 1 ↑2 FIRE 1
↑2 FIRE 1

11:00	Let's try again.
	This thing makes no sense.
	Maybe. . . . I don't know.

11:30	Maybe it repeats, it will only repeat your program twice no matter how many times you push Repeat.
	It seems to me that every time I push Repeat it only goes twice.
	That's what it seems to me, 'cause every time I push Repeat it only goes twice.
	So what do you think the number stands for that goes with the Repeat?
	The number stands for . . . I haven't the slightest idea. I really don't.
	So why don't you try and find out what the number stands for?

Exp 10
↑ 1 ↓ 1 RPT 4
→
↑ 1 ↓ 1 ↑ 1 ↓ 1

Prediction: ↑1 ↓1 ↑1 ↓1 ↑1 ↓1
↑1 ↓1

12:00	I'm just using small numbers so I can remember.
	OK, I think I'm gonna try that again, just with a different number and see what happens.

Exp 11
↑ 1 ↓ 1 RPT 3
→
↑ 1 ↓ 1 ↑1 ↓ 1

Prediction: ↑1 ↓1 ↑1 ↓1 ↑1 ↓1

12:30	Nothing happened. Maybe the number just tells it that you are repeating.
	I haven't the slightest idea what the number is for.
	But I'm going, I'm very determined.

Exp 12
← 15 → 15 RPT 5
→
← 15 → 15 ← 15 → 15

13:00	(Slowly, and deliberately) I'm very calm.

Appendix 5.1 (continued)

	13:30	This machine is not making sense to me. I understand everything you told me. I just don't understand why no matter what I push with Repeat it just does it twice. One of these days I'm gonna figure out how this machine works.

Prediction: $\leftarrow 15 \rightarrow 15 \leftarrow 15 \rightarrow 15$ $\leftarrow 15 \rightarrow 15 \leftarrow 15 \rightarrow 15 \leftarrow 15 \rightarrow 15$

Exp 13
$\downarrow 1 \leftarrow 30$ RPT 1
$\rightarrow$
$\downarrow 1 \leftarrow 60$

	14:00	It did my second command twice.

Prediction: $\downarrow 1 \leftarrow 30 \downarrow 1 \leftarrow 30$

	14:30	'Cause I only said go Right 30, and it went all the way around. So it does the last command the number of times. Because it did my last command twice, and the first command once. Or I pushed a number that I didn't think I pushed, one or the other. I'm gonna try this again.

Exp 14
$\downarrow 1 \rightarrow 30$ RPT 1
$\rightarrow$
$\downarrow 1 \rightarrow 60$

Prediction: $\downarrow 1 \leftarrow 30 \downarrow 1 \leftarrow 30$

	15:00	It repeated my last command, not my first one. Which makes no sense to me whatsoever. But I'm gonna try it with a different number. The same command just with a different number this time.

Exp 15
$\downarrow 1 \rightarrow 30$ RPT 2
$\rightarrow$
$\downarrow 1 \rightarrow 30 \downarrow 1 \rightarrow 30$

Prediction: $\downarrow 1 \rightarrow 30 \rightarrow 30$ *or* $\downarrow 1$ $\rightarrow 30 \downarrow 1 \rightarrow 30$

	15:30	OK. If you push 1 it only repeats one of the commands. If you push 2 it repeats both. That's my guess.
	16:00	Because when I push 1 with the command to go Back 1 and sideways 30 it only did . . . and Repeat one, it makes, it made the machine go round 60. And when I pushed the same command just with Repeat 2 it repeated both commands. So I guess if you push 1 it only repeats the first one.
	16:30	The second second one if you press two or more, it repeats them both. That's what I guess.

Appendix 5.1 (continued)

		So what's the purpose of the number?
		What's the purpose of the number?
		To show which command . . .
		Ah, now it makes sense!
		It's however many commands.
		If I have 3 or more, and if I push Repeat 3 it would repeat all 3 commands.
		If I had 2 commands and only pushed one it would only repeat one of the commands.
		If I had 2 commands and pushed repeat twice, it would repeat both.
	17:00	So if you have so many commands, whichever number, however many commands you have, like if I had four commands and I pushed Repeat 3 it would repeat three of the four commands the last 3 commands.
		Not the first one.
		So why don't you . . .
		OK, I'm just gonna put easy commands so I can remember this.

Exp 16
↑ 1 ↓ 1 → 30 ← 30 RPT 3
➔
↑ 1 ↓ 1 → 30 ← 30 ↓ 1 → 30
← 30

17:30 — That's what it did, it only repeated the last three twice not the first one.
I figured this machine out, I think.

Prediction: ↑ 1 ↓ 1 → 30 ← 30 ↓ 1
→ 30 ← 30

18:00 — This is amazing. I would never get my cousins one of these.
Because they would probably get so worked up at trying to figure out how to do this.
Oh boy. Finally! I figured this out . . . I think.
So how sure are you that you figured it out?
Not very sure, but I'm gonna try again.

Exp 17
↑ 2 ↓ 2 ← 15 → 15 RPT 2
➔
↑ 2 ↓ 2 ← 15 → 15 ← 15 → 15

18:30 — I'm sure!
I'm pretty sure now.
Because when I pushed Repeat 2 it repeated the last two commands that I put in out of four.

Prediction: ↑ 2 ↓ 2 ← 15 → 15 ←
15 → 15

Note: Use of CLR and GO commands have been deleted for clarity.

Appendix 5.2
A complete protocol from a CM (adult) subject (DP). Given: *C1—Repeat entire program* n *times.* Actual: *S3—Repeat* nth *step once*

Notation:		
PROGRAM		DP's comments in normal font.
→		*Experimenter's comments in italics.*
BT'S BEHAVIOR		

	0:00	What I want to do is, um . . .
		I want to test to see if repeat repeats the statements before it, so I'll write just a little program that does something, say turns left ten, and then put the repeat statement in and we'll just repeat it twice 'cause it's not really important for the first program.
	0:30	And then just to check I'll put in a statement after the repeat to see if it has any effect on that,
		so it's just left ten, repeat it twice and then right ten.
Exp 1		*OK, so what are the commands?*
← 10 RPT 2 → 10	1:00	Left ten, repeat two, and right ten.
→		OK, it did what you would expect it would do, it did repeat the left ten twice so it turned left twenty and then back to the right ten,
← 20 → 10		so it appears that the repeat doesn't have any effect on any statements that come after it,
	1:30	so I guess now we'll try putting more than one statement in front of the repeat and see what happens we'll do left ten and forward two, repeat twice, and just to check it again at the end we'll just have it fire once and see
Exp 2		if it repeats it or not.
← 10 ↑ 2 RPT 2 FIRE 1	2:00	It's left ten, forward two, repeat twice, fire one.
→	2:30	OK, it only turned left once,
← 10 ↑ 4 FIRE 1		but it went forward four,
		so it looks like it only repeats the statement immediately in front
	3:00	of it. Oh . . . um . . .
		I guess for the last test we'll just try a more complicated program with the repeat in the middle of it
	3:30	and see what statements are repeated. Ahh, forward one and . . .
		So this is just a long program with a repeat in the middle of it to see what statements are repeated.
		OK, so what are the commands?

Appendix 5.2 (continued)

	4:00	Forward one, right fifteen, back one, repeat two, left ten, forward one.
Exp 3 ↑1 → 15 ↓1 RPT 2 ← 10 ↑1	4:30	Um, that's the old program. I don't think that you cleared.
		OK, forward one, right fifteen,
➡ ↑1 → 15 ↓1 → 15 ← 10 ↑1	5:00	back one, repeat two, left ten, forward one.
	5:30	OK , that time it repeated the uh . . . the right fifteen command.

		So do you know how it works, or would you like to write more programs?
		I'm not really sure how it works, because it seemed to act differently in number two, and number three.
		It would be best to write more.
		OK.
		Should I just go ahead?
		Yes, just write number four.

	6:00	Um . . . Let's just try the same program as before, except we'll put a three in, repeat three instead of a repeat two,
	6:30	and see if that has anything to do with it.
Exp 4 ↑1 → 15 ↓1 RPT 3 ← 10 ↑1 ➡		Forward one, right fifteen, back one, repeat three, left ten, forward one, and go.
	7:00	That time it repeated the statement here but it repeated it twice,
↑1 → 15 ↓2 ← 10 ↑1		the number four . . . the number three . . .
	7:30	it repeated the turning statement once . . .
	8:00	Um . . .
	8:30	*Would you like to try another program?*

		Um . . . I guess, I don't really have any idea of what it's doing
	9:00	because when I change the number not only did it change . . . it didn't change the uh . . . the number that it repeated
		but it did change the uh . . . the actual instruction it repeated . . .
	9:30	Um, I'm going to try . . .
		I guess my conjecture is, right now, that it says repeat two so it repeats the second instruction, and here it repeats three and it repeats the third instruction. So we'll try the same thing with repeat one, and see if it repeats the first instruction . . .
Exp 5	10:00	Forward one, right fifteen, back one, repeat one, left ten,
↑1 → 15 ↓1 RPT 1 ← 10 ↑1 ➡	10:30	forward one, go.
		OK, OK, I think I know what it does now.
↑1 → 15 ↓1 ↑1 ← 10 ↑1		*OK.*

Appendix 5.2 (continued)

		When it hits the repeat statement . . . when it says repeat one it means at this point repeat statement
	11:00	number one and in this case because it went forward and it turned and it went back and then it came forward again, which is the first statement. And it did something simi- lar, I mean it went forward one, turned right went back, and it hit repeat three and this is the third statement so it went back again
		OK, so how, in general, how does the Repeat key work?
		If you type, it looks, when it hits the repeat statement,
	11:30	if you look through the program and it's like repeat six, it takes the sixth statement and does that, then when it hits the repeat state- ment it'll repeat the sixth statement once.
	11:42	*OK, great.*

Appendix 5.3
Computer-based BigTrak Isomorphs

We moved our discovery environment to a computer microworld for several reasons. First, the computer facilitated the ease with which we could record subjects' experiments. Second, it was much more reliable than the mechanical BigTrak device, which had to function in a world of friction, battery failure, and mysterious glitches that one might expect from a fifty-dollar toy. Most importantly, by moving to a computer we were able to control the way that the RPT key actually functioned, and systematically vary that with respect to subjects' favored hypotheses about it.

Having moved to a computer microworld, we realized that we were able to easily construct slightly different semantic contexts for the cover story associated with the discovery challenge. The computer "microworlds" described in this appendix were all isomorphic to the BigTrak device. They displayed a "point and click" keypad on part of a workstation screen, and the behavior of the device as an animated movement on another section of the screen. The keypad and its relation to the basic actions of the focal device were isomorphic to the original BigTrak. (However, as noted above, in some cases we modified the function of "Repeat" so that we could control what the "correct" hypothesis was.)

The features of these BigTrak isomorphs are summarized in table 5A.1. (The studies using these microworlds are described in chapter 6.) The one that most closely resembled BigTrak was called *BT*. In one variant of BT, the key to be discovered was marked with a "?" instead of "RPT," but the cover story was still about programming the movements of a spaceship. Two isomorphs of BT are also described here. They have the identical algorithmic behavior, but the interface has a different cover story. In *Dancer*, the icon is an animated ballerina on a stage, and the task is to "choreograph" a sequence of movements (spin, leap, backflip, etc.). In *FaceMover*, the task is to animate a clown's face with a series of commands (blink, wiggle tongue, wiggle ears, etc.). The keypads in these variants are isomorphic to the BT keypad, and the functions of the RPT key are identical. Each of these microworlds will be described in subsequent chapters.

These microworlds can be downloaded from the MIT Press web site, along with operating instructions, at <http://mitpress.mit.edu>.

Although these variants reduce, to some degree, the possibility that our results and conclusions result from some idiosyncrasies of the original BT context, it is important to note that these variations were not intended to be systematic explorations of a space of possible microworlds. In chapter 7 we introduce yet another microworld that has very different properties from those of the BT world.

Table 5A.1
Computer microworld isomorphs of BigTrak.

	Microworld name			
	BT (RPT)	BT (?)	Dancer	FaceMover
Cover story	Spaceship moving about in a two-dimensional space	Spaceship moving about in a two-dimensional space	Dancer moving about on a stage	Face that can move its components
Commands that take a numerical argument	• Forward n units • Back n units • Rotate clockwise n units • Rotate counter-clockwise n units • Fire laser canon n times	• Forward n units • Back n units • Rotate clockwise n units • Rotate counter-clockwise n units • Fire laser canon n times	• Left Leap n times • Right Leap n times • Left Flip n times • Right Flip n times • Spin n times	• Grow Hair n times • Protrude Tongue n times • Wink Left Eye n times • Wink Right Eye n times • Wiggle Nose n times
Command to be discovered	RPT	?	RPT	RPT

Chapter 6

Further Explorations of the BT Experiment Space

with Anne L. Fay, Kevin Dunbar, and David Penner

One important consideration that emerges from this analysis is that models of scientific discovery need to pay attention to the need for organizing multiple experiments. Faraday never discovered anything with a single experiment, and neither, I suspect, did anyone else.
(Tweney, 1990, p. 475)

For those of us who investigate the science of science, there inevitably comes a time when the best characterization of what we are doing involves a reflexive application of our own theoretical constructs. In terms of our model, the SDDS framework that guides our work is a complex hypothesis frame having many slots whose values need to be further specified. Thus, the series of studies described in this chapter represents part of our attempt to refine some of those slot values. That is, much remains to be discovered about how different aspects of the discovery context influence the discovery process, and the purpose of this chapter is to learn more about some of these aspects. Several questions motivated the four studies described in this chapter.

One important question raised by our discovery of theorist and experimenter strategies (first described in study 1) concerns the factors that lead participants to choose between these two approaches. Although people's individual proclivities may play a role here, we believe that prior knowledge is a much more important factor: one that is sufficiently strong to overwhelm individual differences. Our paradigm enables us to explore this question by varying constraints on search in either the hypothesis space or the experiment space.

Recall that we are viewing scientific discovery as a type of complex problem solving, and that problem solving, in turn, consists of constrained search in one or more problem spaces. We can influence hypothesis-space search by manipulating the degree to which participants can bring prior knowledge to bear, and one way to influence that, in turn, is to modify the clues in the microworld about the nature of the thing to be discovered. More specifically, we reasoned that if the relevance of participants' prior knowledge is reduced, then they would find it more difficult to generate hypotheses via the *Evoke Frame* path (see figure 2.9). This, in turn, would cause them to use the *Induce Frame* path instead. As a result, participants attempting to make discoveries in contexts having low relevance of prior knowledge would be more likely to behave like experimenters than like theorists. Study 5 focuses on this issue.

Another way to influence participants' approach to the discovery task is to constrain their experiment-space search in specific ways. One particularly interesting manipulation is to constrain permissible experiments to the most informative parts of the experiment space, and then to examine the way that this constraint interacts with high or low constraints on the search in the hypothesis space. Study 6 illustrates how we approached this problem.

A second question addressed in this chapter relates to an aspect of our microworld paradigm: its generality. In several places in this volume we have argued the merits of using microworlds to study the process of scientific discovery. Nevertheless, until now we have based our conclusions about participants' discovery processes on their behaviors in only one such microworld: BT. It is important, therefore, to show that our results are not limited to this specific device and cover story. At the least, we need to demonstrate that an isomorphic task—that is, one that has exactly the same underlying structure for the programming conventions and the function of the RPT key, but a different cover story—will not produce markedly different behavior. To this end, in study 7 we made a change in the cover story and visual display that make up the microworld context in order to explore, in a small way, its generality.

At the same time, we used this change in context to explore another aspect of scientific discovery that is widely acknowledged to be important, but that is absent from our model of the discovery process: motivation. Thus, in study 7 we used not only the standard BT (spaceship) context, but also one that, on the face of it, might be expected to be particularly engaging to our participants. The questions of interest were (1) whether the new context would increase participants' motivation to make a discovery and (2) how this increased motivation might influence the discovery process. Moreover, our developmental orientation led us to examine the extent to which such potential effects were age-related.

The third aim in study 7 was to revisit the "forced search" condition (used in study 2) in order to determine the extent to which there were developmental differences in the effects of generating several hypotheses prior to experimentation. All of these issues were combined in the design of study 7, in which we asked girls from the third to the twelfth grades to "program a rocketship" or "choreograph a dancer" while figuring out how the rocketship or dancer interpreted the RPT key, and in which we contrasted the forced search condition with the standard condition.

Another issue that we have not yet confronted concerns the way in which our current paradigm fails to provide participants with anything analogous to the historical context in which real science is carried out. That is, although scientists are always well versed in both the theoretical and experimental history of their domains, in our standard paradigm participants do not receive any information about how others have formulated hypotheses or designed experiments. But it is easy to contextualize our microworld approach by providing participants with some suggestive experiments, hypotheses, or both, and in study 8 we provided such information. Additionally, in order to further demonstrate the generality of the basic paradigm, in study 8 we introduced yet another microworld context—this time in the form of an animated clown's face,—and we made a direct comparison between this context and the original BT context.

The search we ourselves exhibit in this chapter can be seen as traversing the *Search E-Space* nodes shown in the lower left and center of the SDDS framework (figure 2.9) because when we conducted the studies to be described here, we were at the early phases of hypothesis formulation. In designing these studies, we were not immune to the general preference for testing positive instances. We reasoned that if our hypotheses about dual search were correct, and if we made specific modifications to our basic paradigm, then we would be able to predict certain outcomes. The four studies presented in this chapter describe our search in more detail.

Study 5: Mystery Key I—Manipulating Search in the Two Spaces

In this study and the next we explored the constraints that operate on the *Induce Frame* process shown in the left-hand side of figure 2.9. In study 5 we investigated the way in which differences in domain-specific knowledge can influence strategies used in the discovery process. We manipulated the relationship between prior knowledge and the thing to be discovered by making a simple change in the information we presented about the to-be-discovered key. One group of participants was informed that the key was a "mystery" key, and the other group was given the standard story about a "repeat" key. We expected this manipulation to have an effect on how participants approached the discovery task—that is, in their tendency to use either theorist or experimenter induction strategies—as well as on their overall success rates.

We reasoned that the manipulation would have two consequences. First, mystery participants should propose a more wide-ranging set of initial hypotheses, because the mystery key—unlike the RPT key—gives them no clue whatsoever as to its function. Second, this lack of constraint would be accompanied by a lack of confidence in initial hypotheses, so mystery participants would base their initial hypotheses primarily on experimental outcomes. In contrast, more of the participants in the standard repeat condition should behave like theorists and generate their initial hypotheses via *Evoke Frame*. Because they know that the key is a repeat key, they can formulate various hypotheses about "repeat" without conducting experiments. In terms of our model, then, we expected that participants in the mystery condition would—via the *Induce Frame* path in figure 2.9—tend to use an experiment-space search strategy because initial memory search (in *Evoke Frame*) would yield no compelling hypotheses regarding the function of the mystery key.

Method
We used the same BT interface and training procedure described in chapter 5. Forty McGill University undergraduates participated, twenty in each condition. Participants in the repeat condition were given the standard instructions and saw the standard interface shown in figure 5.2. Participants in the mystery conditions received the same instructions except that what had been the RPT key was now shown with a "?" and was called the "mystery key." All participants were told to figure out how the key worked, and that they could write as many programs as they liked. In both conditions, the function of the unknown key was our standard selector: repeat the last n steps in a program.

Results
Although we thought that the mystery condition would be more difficult, there was no significant effect of condition on solution rates (thirteen out of twenty for the mystery condition, and twelve out of twenty for the repeat condition). However, there were striking differences in the initial hypotheses generated by participants in the two conditions. As indicated in table 6.1, only two participants in the mystery condition thought that the mystery key was a repeat key. All the others thought that the key performed an action and that n determined the number of times that the action would be executed. In contrast, and not surprisingly, most participants (sixteen of twenty) in the repeat condition proposed counter hypotheses.

But as soon as the mystery-condition participants had conducted their initial experiment there was a radical change in the types of hypotheses that they held; eighteen of the twenty participants proposed a

Table 6.1
Number of participants in each condition holding specific initial hypotheses.

	Condition	
Initial Hypothesis	Mystery [?]	Repeat [RPT]
Counter		
Repeats n times	2	0
Repeats prior command n times	0	10
Repeats prior program n times	0	5
Repeats Fire command n times	0	1
Selector		
Repeats from nth step	0	3
Other		
Does some novel action n times	8	0
Goes diagonally	5	0
New function	4	0
Does a combination	1	0
Adds to prior step	0	1

counter hypothesis, that is, that the mystery key repeats something in the program. Participants in the repeat condition continued to hold some form of counter hypothesis. Thus, by the second experiment participants in both conditions were working under the assumption that unknown function was a "repeat" key of some sort. It is clear that, for the mystery-condition participants, just a little bit of evidence was sufficient to impose substantial constraint on their search in the hypothesis space.

Successful participants in the mystery condition were predominantly (ten of thirteen) experimenters, whereas successful participants in the repeat condition were more evenly split between experimenters (seven) and theorists (five). This difference, although weak, is consistent with our earlier prediction that mystery participants would be more likely than RPT participants to require empirical results to constrain their hypothesis-space search.

The effects of the manipulation are particularly evident in the intermediate hypotheses of participants who *failed* to discover the correct selector rule. In the repeat condition, unsuccessful participants proposed intermediate hypotheses where n was a counter or repeated something once. Unsuccessful mystery participants also proposed these types of hypotheses. However, mystery participants also proposed several additional hypotheses in which "? n" performed a variety of mathematical functions, including, among others: (1) multiplies the argument of the prior step by n, (2) multiplies by 2; (3) doubles prior step; (4) odd n repeats prior step, even n repeats prior program; (5) repeats $\sqrt{n}$ times; and (6) repeats prior step $n - 1$ times. All of these suggest that mystery participants were drawing analogies to a calculator. Given that by the second experiment most of the mystery participants hypothesized that they were dealing with *some* kind of repeat function, the fact that they still proposed a much more varied (and ingenious) set of hypotheses than did the repeat participants suggests that the effect of the RPT versus ? manipulation was long-lasting. Even by the time they proposed their final (incorrect) hypotheses, unsuccessful participants in the two conditions had different distributions of types of hypotheses (see table 6.2), although the pattern evidenced in table 6.2 barely approaches statistical significance because of the small sample size. Thus, the prior knowledge manipulation had its greatest effect on performance at the beginning and middle of the task, with a hint that it might have lingered on to the very end of participants' discovery attempts.

Discussion of Study 5
The results of this study provide additional support for two of the major assumptions underlying SDDS: (1) if there is little prior knowledge associated with the focus of the current discovery attempt, then initial H-space search will be very wide ranging; (2) however, this search can be rapidly constrained by experimental outcomes. The finding that so

Table 6.2
Distribution of unsuccessful participants in each condition holding different final hypotheses.

Final Hypothesis	Repeat	Mystery
Counter n role		
C1: n repeats of the last step	2	0
C1': $n - 1$ repeats of the last step	1	0
Unspecified n-role		
U1: One repeat of entire program	1	1
U2: One repeat of the last step	3	2
Other types of hypotheses		
If $n > 1$ then repeat entire program, else repeat prior step once	1	1
Multiplies prior command by 2	0	2
Random repeat	0	1

many mystery participants favored E-space search (recall that ten of the thirteen successful mystery participants were experimenters) even when they had hypothesized that the mystery key was a repeat key is, at first glance, surprising. When the mystery group proposed that the key is a repeat key they were in the same position as the repeat participants, yet they did not use this knowledge to search memory for a specific hypothesis. Instead, they continued their attempts to induce their hypotheses from experimental outcomes.

This finding suggests that participants in the mystery condition construed the problem as one of generating experimental results and then attempted to propose hypotheses that could account for the data. Even when they had gathered sufficient information to consider that the mystery key was some kind of repeating function, they continued to use this strategy. Participants in the repeat condition were equally likely to search either the experiment space or the hypothesis space. Overall, the results of study 5 suggest that when given little prior knowledge of a domain, participants will prefer to induce hypotheses by examining features of experimental outcomes, rather than by searching the hypothesis space.

Study 6: Mystery Key II—Constraining Search in the Experiment Space

The aim of this study was to investigate the way in which domain knowledge interacts with the types of experimental data to which participants have access. By limiting the types of experiments that participants could run, we constrained them to the most informative regions of the experiment space. The question was how this constraint on experiment-space search would differentially affect participants in the mystery and repeat conditions. It might be the case that participants in the mystery condition who use an experiment-space search strategy (attending to key features of the data) would benefit most from this manipulation, inasmuch as it would avoid uninformative experimental outcomes and thus provide better evidence from which to induce hypotheses. Another possible effect of the manipulation might be that the increased likelihood of producing informative experiments would influence participants to attend to the particular features of the experiment and adopt an experiment-space search strategy. In this case, even participants in the repeat condition might prefer an experiment-space search strategy.

Method and Procedure

The BT interface was programmed so that it would not accept programs in region 3 of the experiment space (i.e., where $n > \lambda$). That is, only experiments in regions 1 and 2 were accepted by the interface. The manipulation decreased the number of unique n-λ combinations that participants could generate by about half and it increased the proportion of region 2 cells from 40 percent of the full experiment space to nearly 90 percent of the reduced E-Space. (For a visual image of this effect, look at figure 3.3 and imagine that region 3 has been eliminated.) This constraint increased substantially the likelihood that participants would design experiments that were particularly informative about the way the key works. Forty McGill University undergraduates participated for course credit. There were twenty participants in each condition (Repeat and Mystery).

Results
Participants in study 6 were about as successful as their counterparts in study 5. (In study 5 the success rates for the mystery and RPT conditions were 13/20 and 12/20, respectively, and in study 6 they were 15/20 and 11/20 respectively.) For study 6, there was no significant effect of condition on success rate. However, if we relax the success criterion and classify final hypotheses by frame, instead of whether the correct version of the selector frame was discovered, then mystery participants outperformed repeat participants (see table 6.3). Using this measure, there was also an improvement in performance in the mystery condition relative to study 5.

The finding that more mystery participants than repeat participants proposed final selector hypotheses indicates that the added experiment-space search constraint was particularly useful to participants whose initial hypotheses (as we know from study 5) were very wide ranging. The combination of initially diverse hypotheses and highly informative experiments resulted in all but two of the twenty mystery participants proposing a selector hypothesis at the end. Conversely, the E-space search constraint had no effect on performance of participants in the repeat condition, presumably because the name of the key itself provided such a strong tendency to propose counters.

Table 6.3
Distribution of final hypotheses by condition (study 6).

	Counter	Selector (Incorrect)	Selector (Correct)
Repeat	8	1	11
Mystery	2	3	15

Summary of Mystery Key Studies (Studies 5 and 6)
Studies 5 and 6 indicate that the strategies that participants adopt to induce new hypotheses from experimental data are influenced by (1) prior knowledge of the domain, and (2) the constraints on the data that participants collect. Participants will adopt a theory-driven induction strategy if it is easy for them to generate such hypotheses, and this ease is determined in large part by the fit between the current context and participants' prior knowledge. However, this strategy does not necessarily lead to better performance. As study 6 demonstrates, participants who have little prior knowledge of a domain perform better when the data from which they induce hypotheses are constrained, whereas participants who are theory-driven may not benefit from receiving constrained data. At a more general level, the results of these two studies indicate that (1) the specific order in which the SDDS subgoal hierarchy is traversed depends on the interaction between participants' prior knowledge and external constraints imposed by the discovery context and (2) that these constraints can occur in either the hypothesis space or the experiment space.

Study 7: Dancer—Developmental Differences in Context Effects

This study had several aims. First, we wanted to demonstrate that our results were not so paradigm-limited as to fail to generalize to a different "cover story" associated with the discovery of the RPT key. Concurrently, we wanted to see if children's performance on a discovery task could be enhanced if we made the cover story more inherently interesting and thereby increased children's motivation to make a discovery about the domain. We decided to address both the generality and the motivation issues by testing a commonly held view that young girls would exhibit more interest and better performance if we used a more "gender appropriate" task than asking them to program a laser-firing rocketship. To this end, we created a new microworld called "Dancer" that involved the choreographing of a ballerina, and we contrasted girls' performance in the BT and Dancer environments. The question of interest was whether they would be more successful in discovering how the RPT key worked when it controlled a ballerina rather than a spaceship.

A further aim of this study was to explore developmental differences in participants' reaction to the forced hypothesis-space search condition that we used earlier with adults. Recall that in study 2, before participants began the experimentation phase they were repeatedly prompted to generate several hypotheses about how RPT worked. Two questions motivated the forced search procedure used in that study: (1) Is it possible to generate the correct selector hypothesis without any experimental results? (2) Would this more extensive initial search of the hypothesis space affect performance on the subsequent dual search process? The results of study 2 indicated that, for adults at least, the answer to both questions is "yes." When prompted repeatedly, many participants managed to generate the correct selector hypothesis before they ran any experiments, even though it was unlikely to be their first hypothesis. With respect to the second question, the effect of forced memory search was to reduce substantially the mean number of experiments needed to discover the correct rule (from fifteen in the standard condition to less than six in the forced search condition). In study 7, we examined both of these questions across a wide age range, but with a fairly homogeneous population.

Method and Procedure

These multiple questions led to the design of study 7. We used a two context (BT versus Dancer) × two hypothesis-space search (forced versus standard) × four grade (fourth, fifth, eighth, and twelfth) between-participants design. Participants included twenty-one fourth graders, nineteen fifth graders, seventeen eighth graders, and fourteen twelfth graders from a private girls' school.

The experimental session consisted of our standard training phase, during which participants learned the basic commands, followed by the test phase, during which they attempted to discover how the RPT key worked. For participants in the forced search condition, the test phase was preceded by the hypothesis-space search phase in which we used the same three probes as in study 2: (1) "How do you think the RPT key might work?" (2) "We've done this experiment with many people, and they have proposed a wide variety of hypotheses for how RPT might work. What do you think they may have proposed?" (3) "When BT (or Dancer, depending on the context condition) was being programmed, the designers thought of many different ways RPT could be made to work. What ways do you think they may have considered?" After each question, participants responded with as many hypotheses as they could. Then the next probe was used. After participants had completed their response to the third probe, the experimental phase began. Participants were encouraged to conduct as many experiments as they wanted to while attempting to discover how the RPT key works.

Dancer

Dancer is an isomorph of the BT microworld described in appendix 5.3. Rather than program a spaceship, participants use the keypad to control the movements of an animated ballerina who moves across a stage (see figure 6.1). The basic execution cycle is the same as in the other BT iso-

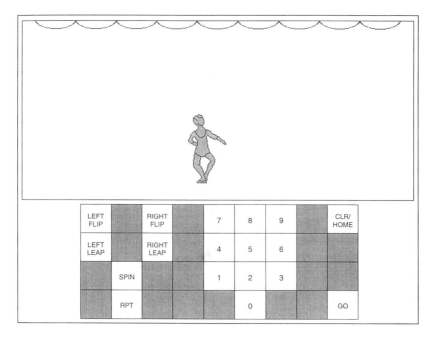

Figure 6.1
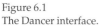

The Dancer interface.

morphs. The first step is to clear memory with the CLR/HOME key. This lowers the "curtain" and places the dancer at the center of the stage where she awaits instructions. Then participants enter a series of instructions, each consisting of a command and a one- or two-digit number (the argument). Dancer commands include LEFT LEAP, RIGHT LEAP, LEFT FLIP, RIGHT FLIP, and SPIN. Up to fifteen such command–argument pairs may be entered. When the GO key is clicked, the curtain is raised to the position shown in figure 6.1, and the animated dancer carries out the sequence of instructions.

The Dancer RPT key functions in the same way as in the original Big-Trak: it repeats the last n instructions once. Dancer's commands are similar to BT's with respect to symmetry (left and right leaps and flips are similar to forward and backward movement and left and right rotations), and distinctiveness (SPIN is similar to FIRE in that it has no symmetric counterpart). Moreover, like BT, as the dancer moves across the stage, its final position provides at least some indication of the program that got it there, although not a complete trace. However, there are some obvious differences between the two microworlds. For one thing, the cover story is quite different. In one case, participants are writing programs to control a military vehicle—a laser-firing rocketship—whereas in the other they are choreographing a ballerina's movements across a stage. For another, the rocketship moves in two-dimensional space, whereas the dancer, except for a slight vertical motion associated with her leaps and flips, is primarily confined to left and right motion across the stage.

Results

Search in the Hypothesis Space   Participants in the forced search condition generated a mean of 1.5 hypotheses. This was only about one-third as many as were generated by adults in study 2. Of these, about one-third were selectors. Neither grade nor context had an effect on number of hypotheses generated, or on the proportion of participants who generated a selector during this phase. Even though only one of eleven fourth graders but nine of twenty-four older children generated selectors, this difference did not reach statistical significance, due in part to the small sample size.

Success rates   A 4 (Grade) × 2 (Condition) × 2 (Context) ANOVA on success rates revealed a main effect for grade, but no other main effects or interactions. In particular, there was no context effect: success rates for Dancer were the same as for BT. Success rates ranged from only 5 percent for the fourth graders to 36 percent for the twelfth graders (see figure 6.2). The results for the two younger grades are roughly similar to

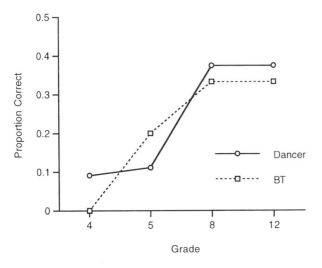

Figure 6.2
Success rates for each grade and context in study 7.

the success rates in study 3, where a mixed class of third to sixth graders had about a 10 percent success rate. However, the twelfth graders were no more successful than the eighth graders. This is surprising, because these (mainly college-bound) twelfth graders were only a year or two younger than the Carnegie Mellon undergraduate participants in studies 1 and 2, of whom 97 percent successfully discovered how RPT worked. One possible explanation for this relatively poor performance by the twelfth graders is simply that they were less interested in the task—in either context—than any of the participant populations we used in this and other studies. We reasoned that performance during the initial training phase might reveal such a lack of interest. This led us to analyze, for the first time in this series of studies, how participants performed during the training phase.

Training Time   One good indicator of interest is training time, that is, the time it takes to master the basic set of commands, prior to the challenge to discover how the RPT command works. A grade by context ANOVA on training time revealed two effects—one of them related to the initial design of the study, and the other related to the unexpectedly low success rate of the twelfth graders. With respect to the first issue, there was a main effect of context: mean training time for BT was about 18 percent longer than for Dancer. Moreover, as shown in figure 6.3, this effect is about the same magnitude for three of the four grade levels.

Because the scripts and the examples used for teaching participants about how each key worked were identical in the two contexts, the

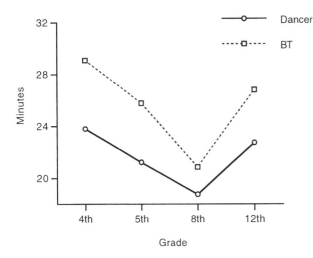

Figure 6.3
Mean training time for each grade and context.

training-time differences cannot be attributed to procedural differences. Nor is there anything in the execution time of the two interfaces that could account for the five or six minute difference in mean training times.[1] Thus, at the procedural level, there is no inherent bias one way or the other with respect to training time differences in the two contexts. Moreover, once the discovery phase started (when participants attempted to discover how RPT worked) there was no context effect in the mean time to design, run, and execute an experiment (i.e., minutes per experiment). All of this leads us to conclude that differences in participants' interest in the two contexts, rather than technical aspects, were the primary cause of the training time differences. Thus, at the outset at least, participants found the Dancer context sufficiently more interesting or motivating than BT, and this in turn led them to master its basic commands in substantially less time.

With respect to the lack of motivation among the twelfth graders, we found that they were unexpectedly slow during training in both contexts. Although training time was significantly shorter for fifth graders than for fourth graders, and for eighth graders than for fifth graders, it was significantly *longer* for twelfth graders than for eighth graders. In fact, the oldest girls were no faster than their fourth and fifth grade counterparts. This pattern held for both the BT and the Dancer contexts. It appears that these twelfth graders were performing well below the level that one would predict on the basis of a simple extrapolation from the performance of their younger classmates. We conclude, therefore, that these participants had an unusual lack of interest in our study (for both contexts).[2]

Number of Experiments   Another possible index of differential interest in the two contexts is the number of experiments run before participants decided to terminate their explorations. A context by grade ANOVA revealed a main effect for grade, and a context by grade interaction (see figure 6.4). With respect to the effect of grade, although the twelfth graders ran slightly more experiments than the eighth graders (6.8 vs. 5.4), the difference was not significant, whereas the difference between the twelfth graders and both the fourth and fifth graders was significant. With respect to context, although there was no main effect, the interaction between grade and context comes from the fact that fourth graders wrote more Dancer experiments than BT experiments. It seems that the initial context effect that was evidenced in the shorter training times for Dancer continued to influence only the youngest children once they had moved into the discovery phase.

The contrast in the absolute number of experiments between this study and previous studies is striking: the mean number of experiments

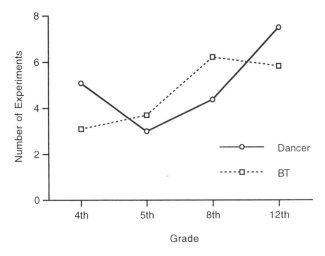

Figure 6.4
Mean number of experiments for each grade and context.

in the present study was between one-third and one-half the number of experiments run by adults in study 1 and children (third to sixth graders) in study 3. These numbers are comparable to the mean number of experiments (5.7) in the forced search manipulation used in study 2, even though in the present study there was no condition effect, that is, there was no difference between the forced search (4.7 experiments) and normal (4.8 experiments) conditions in this study. Given the low success rates reported earlier, we conclude that participants in all conditions tended to give up prematurely. This premature termination led to low success rates, and it also undermined the possibility of detecting a relationship between number of experiments and success. More specifically, although successful participants ran—on average—about one more experiment than unsuccessful participants (5.7 versus 4.5), the overall success rates were so low that the difference was not significant.

Experiment-Space Search and Success   Across all four grade levels, only one participant started out with only a selector hypothesis. Eleven started with *both* a counter and a selector and the rest proposed a counter. There was no effect of grade on these initial hypotheses. Given that most participants started with counter hypotheses, we expected that first experiments in region 2 would be particularly informative, and would be correlated with success.[3] However, the effect turned out to be marginal. An analysis by grade revealed that there was an effect only for fifth graders. Each of the three successful fifth graders started with a region 2 experiment, while only two of the twelve unsuccessful fifth graders started in region 2.

Dancer: Conclusions

The primary aim of study 7 was to see whether a more gender appropriate microworld would lead to improved performance as participants attempt to discover how the RPT key works. The results indicate that the Dancer context did lead to more rapid acquisition of the basic aspects of the domain—suggesting that it was more interesting than BT (especially for younger children and unmotivated twelfth-graders). However, once participants' focus was on the more abstract goal of discovering how the RPT key worked, this context effect disappeared. Indeed, children at all grade levels tended to terminate the discovery process prematurely, having explored the experiment space inadequately. This suggests that "tuning" a task domain to enhance interest can indeed elicit more attention and motivation and thereby improve performance at the outset and during the "easy" phases of familiarization. However, the effects of this increased interest do not maintain their influence once participants enter the more important and abstract phases of the discovery process. The secondary aim of this study was to see how a wider age range would respond to the forced search condition. Except for the youngest group, it appears that many children, when prompted to search the hypothesis space prior to experimentation, can move beyond counter hypotheses and propose selectors, although not at the same rate as adults.

Study 8: FaceMover—Enriching Background Knowledge

The primary goal of study 8 was to explore the effects of providing participants with additional background knowledge, in the form of "suggested" experiments or hypotheses. Such information corresponds to the fact that scientists do not work in a vacuum, but rather in a context of prior experiments and existing hypotheses. In terms of SDDS, such additional information can be viewed as assisting participants' search by providing, at the outset, fully specified examples from each space. We assisted search by providing both a "good" and a "bad" exemplar from each space. From the hypothesis space we provided an example of a counter and a selector, thereby exposing participants to exemplars of each of the two major frames that had been generated in earlier studies. Unlike study 4, where we never provided the correct rule (only the correct frame, at best), in this study, the specific selector that we provided was, in fact, the correct rule. From the experiment space, we provided a sample of three n–λ combinations: two from region 1 and one from region 2.

Our expectation was straightforward: providing both a counter and a selector hypothesis should help participants in two ways. First, it could help those participants who, like most of our other participants, would have otherwise devoted most of their search of the hypothesis space to counters. Second, providing a pair of contrasting hypotheses would help participants search the experiment space because the contrast between the hypotheses might suggest discriminating experiments. Similarly, providing three experiments might help participants search the experiment space by revealing the critical features of that space (i.e., λ and n). Finally, providing both hypotheses *and* experiments should help more than providing either alone. For all of these predictions, the most obvious manifestation of "help" would be an increase in solution rates, as well as a reduction in the number of hypotheses and experiments. A secondary aim of study 8 was to explore the effects of yet another context and cover story for the discovery microworld, in order to extend its generality. The new microworld is described in the next section.

Method

FaceMover   FaceMover is an isomorph of the BT and Dancer microworlds described earlier. The interface is shown in figure 6.5. Rather than program a "spaceship" as with the BT interface, participants specify a sequence of animated face movements in the left-hand panel by

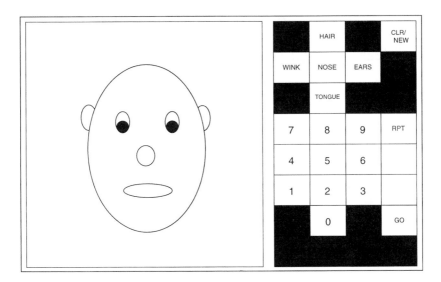

Figure 6.5
The FaceMover interface.

pressing buttons ("pointing and clicking") in the keypad panel on the right. The basic execution cycle involves first clearing the memory with the CLR/NEW key. This places a frame around the face, indicating that the memory has been cleared. Then participants enter a series of instructions, each consisting of a function key (the command) and a one- or two-digit number (the argument).

FaceMover commands include: HAIR—hair appears and disappears; WINK—winking an eye; NOSE—wiggling the nose; EARS—wiggling the ears; TONGUE—protruding and retracting the tongue. The numerical argument for each command indicates how many times that action will occur. For example, clicking HAIR 2, TONGUE 4, and then GO would cause the hair to appear and then disappear twice followed by four tongue protrusions and retractions on the cartoon face. Up to fifteen such command–argument pairs may be entered. When the GO key is clicked, the programmed actions are displayed on the screen serially in the order entered. Each separate face action is accompanied by a unique tone. The role of the FaceMover RPT key is identical to the BigTrak RPT key: it repeats the last n instructions once.

Thus, as a programmable device, FaceMover is isomorphic to BT. For any particular setting for the RPT key, the two microworlds execute identical mappings between the programs that participants write and the behavior of the "device." However, there are also some obvious differences. For one thing, the cover story is entirely different. In one case, participants are writing programs to control a "spaceship," while in the other they are controlling the behavior of a clown's face. For another, unlike BT and Dancer, the FaceMover action commands have no symmetry, and there is no distinctive command. Moreover, because BT moves around the action panel, its final position provides at least some indication of the program that got it there. In contrast, FaceMover leaves no such trace, as each face command is "done and undone" (e.g., the winked eye reopens after each wink). On the other hand, although excessive forward or backward motion of BT can cause it to get jammed against the boundaries of the frame, FaceMover has no such constraint.

Design and Participants   We used a 2×2 between-participants design in which participants were provided with either two suggested hypotheses, three suggested experiments, neither, or both (see table 6.4). In addition to the four FaceMover conditions, we included a fifth condition in which we used the BT microworld. Forty-six Carnegie Mellon undergraduates participated in this study: six in the BT condition and ten in each of the other four conditions.[4]

We used the same basic method as in our previous studies. Participants in the NIL condition were given no information beyond our nor-

Table 6.4
Design of study 7.

	No hypotheses provided	Two hypotheses provided
No experiments and outcomes provided	*NIL* and *BT*	*H*
Three experiments and outcomes provided	*E*	*H-E*

Note: Cell entries indicate the name of the condition.

Table 6.5
Programs and outcome provided in conditions E and H-E (study 7).

Program	Outcome
E1: HAIR-1, TONGUE-1, HAIR-1, RPT-1	HAIR-1, TONGUE-1, HAIR-2
E2: WINK-1, EARS-1, RPT-1	WINK-1, EARS-2
E3: NOSE-2, TONGUE-1, TONGUE-1, RPT 2	NOSE-2, TONGUE-4

mal instructions. Participants in condition H were given two hypotheses about how RPT worked, and they were told (correctly) that one of them was correct. Participants in condition E were provided with three experiments and their outcomes utilizing the RPT key. Participants in condition H-E were given both kinds of information provided in conditions H and E. The BT condition was the same as the NIL condition, except for using the BT interface. Context effects were assessed by comparing performance in conditions BT and NIL.

Procedure   The experimental session consisted of our standard training phase, during which participants learned the basic commands, followed by the test phase, during which they attempted to discover how the RPT key worked. Depending on the condition, when participants entered the test phase, they were given additional instructions. In condition H, participants were provided with two hypotheses about how RPT might work. One was a counter: "Repeat the last step *n* times." The other was a selector: "Repeat the last *n* steps," which was the correct rule. Both hypotheses were printed on a sheet that participants could refer to during the study. In condition E, participants were shown three programs (two from region 1 and one from region 2) that utilized the RPT key and the programs were run on the computer. The programs and their resulting outcomes are listed in table 6.5. Note that although region 2 is generally informative, the region 2 example that we provided (E3) included a specific set of commands that did not distinguish between counters and selectors. We did this in order to ensure that none of the outcomes would immediately rule out either of the hypotheses we provided. However, the E3 example does suggest that an experiment can have $n > \lambda$. Participants were given a summary sheet indicating what occurred when each of the provided programs was run. In condition H-E, participants were provided with the two hypotheses from condition H, and the three experiments (programs) from condition E. In conditions NIL and BT, participants were given no extra information.

Participants in conditions NIL and H were asked to write at least four experiments that would help them determine how the RPT key functioned. Participants in conditions E and H-E were asked to write at least one such experiment. (Because conditions E and H-E initially provided participants with three experiments, this change in procedure guaranteed that the minimum number of experimental outcomes observed would be the same for all conditions.) Participants could conclude the study at any time after completing their minimum number of experiments. To terminate, participants were required to state how they thought the RPT key functioned. If their statement was ambiguous they were asked for clarification.

Before each experiment was entered into the computer, participants were asked "What do you think will happen?" The experiment was then entered and run. Following its execution, participants were asked "Did it do what you thought it would?" The procedure was then repeated until the participant terminated the session. Participants had access to a summary sheet on which they could record the experiments they had entered.

Results

We first describe the analyses that compare FaceMover to BT. Following these analyses, the results from four FaceMover conditions will be described.

Context Effects: BT versus FaceMover NIL   There were no significant differences between BT and NIL participants on a variety of measures, including success rates (4/6 and 4/9), mean number of experiments (5.8 vs. 5.7), and different n-λ combinations (4.9 vs. 4.7). Another potential difference between the interfaces might be in the E-space search strategies. Participants using a VOTAT strategy (Tschirgi, 1980) would change either n or λ, or neither. In contrast, simultaneous changes to both n and λ reflect a nonconservative strategy. On average, 40 percent of the experiment-space transitions in both conditions were nonconservative.

Analyses of search in the hypothesis space also failed to indicate any differences in the two contexts. Recall that participants were asked to predict the outcome of their experiments prior to entering the commands into the computer. Thus, in both BT and NIL nearly every experiment was preceded by an explicit prediction. However, few hypotheses were explicitly stated in either condition. There were no differences between the two conditions in either the number of hypotheses or predictions generated or in the number of confirming/disconfirming statements made. Based on all of these analyses, we conclude that there is little difference in either experiment-space or hypothesis-space search between the two interfaces.

Effects of Assisted Search in the Experiment Space and Hypothesis Space Having established that the change in interface had no effect on participants' attempts to discover how RPT works, we can now turn to an assessment of the effects of the main manipulations in study 8. Thus, the following analysis focuses on performance comparisons between the four FaceMover conditions, NIL, H, E, and H-E. Table 6.6 presents a summary of the general performance measures.

USE OF PROVIDED INFORMATION   To what extent did participants in the three information conditions (H, E, and H-E) actually use that information? One measure of such use is the frequency with which participants consulted the information sheets during the session. Across the three conditions, the mean number of references during the full discovery session ranged from 1.6 to 1.8, with no effect of condition. Interestingly, in each condition, three of the nine participants made *no* reference to the provided information. (Although it is possible that, during the initial phase, they had encoded the provided information sufficiently accurately that they required no further explicit reference to it.) However,

Table 6.6
Performance summary for FaceMover conditions.

	Condition			
	NIL	H	E	H-E
Proportion successful	4/9	8/9	6/10	6/9
Experiments generated (mean)	5.9	5.4	7.0	4.1
(s.d.)	(1.9)	(2.2)	(6.0)	(2.7)
Experiments observed (mean)	5.8	5.4	10.0	7.1
(s.d.)	(1.9)	(2.2)	(6.0)	(2.7)
Distinct n–λ combinations generated (mean)	4.9	4.2	4.4	2.7
(s.d.)	(1.6)	(1.4)	(3.6)	(1.1)
Distinct n–λ combinations observed (mean)	4.9	4.2	7.4	5.7
(s.d.)	(1.6)	(1.4)	(3.6)	(1.1)

across conditions, there were considerably more referrals by successful participants than by unsuccessful participants.

EFFECT OF INFORMATION CONDITION ON SUCCESS RATES   First, we consider differences in success rates. Contrary to our expectation, the provision of hypotheses and/or experiments did not significantly improve success rates. Even when the three information conditions are combined and contrasted with the NIL condition, the difference in the number of successful participants in NIL versus the other conditions remains statistically insignificant.[5]

AMOUNT OF E-SPACE SEARCH   Table 6.6 makes two distinctions: between experiments *observed* and experiments *generated*, and between experiments and distinct n–λ combinations. We will first analyze experiments and then n–λ combinations. Recall that participants in conditions E and H-E were three experimental outcomes before they were asked to determine how the RPT key worked. Thus, for these two conditions, the number of experiments observed is—by definition—three more than the number generated by the participants, whereas for conditions NIL and H the number of observed experiments equals the number of generated experiments. When no experiments were provided, there was no effect of providing hypotheses on the number of experiments generated (NIL vs. H). However, when experiments (and their outcomes) *were* provided, then there was an effect of also providing hypotheses. Participants in condition E (when no hypotheses accompanied the experiments) tended to write more additional experiments than did participants in condition H-E (when hypotheses *did* accompany the experiments). That is, when experiments are provided at the outset, then providing hypotheses in addition tended to suppress the amount of E-space search, although it had little effect on success rates. However, these trends were weak.

Analysis of distinct n–λ combinations revealed a pattern similar to that of experiments observed and written. Moreover, the difference of exactly three between distinct n–λ combinations generated and observed for E and H-E indicates that participants never repeated the three n–λ combinations that were provided at the outset.

EFFECTS OF INFORMATION CONDITIONS ON REGIONS VISITED AND SUCCESS RATES   Are participants able to extrapolate the full value of the provided information in designing their first experiment? As in study 4, we interpret the distribution of participants' first experiments as an indicator of their responsiveness to the information provided. Note that for conditions H and H-E, regions 2 and 3 are equally informative in distinguishing between the provided hypotheses. If providing a pair of competing hypotheses biases people to write discriminating experiments, then participants in conditions H and H-E should be more likely to write their first experiment in region 2, or possibly region 3, than other participants. This was indeed the case. All of the H participants and seven of the nine H-E participants avoided region 1 for their first experiments, whereas eight of the eighteen NIL and E participants wrote their first experiment in that nondiscriminating region. This is important, because in this study, as in all previous studies, there was a clear effect of region searched on success rates. Averaged over all information conditions, successful participants were half as likely to write experiments in region 1 and three times as likely to write experiments in region 2 than were unsuccessful participants (table 6.7).

We continue this analysis at a finer grain by looking at how success was related to which regions of the experiment space were searched in each of the four conditions. First we look at the effect of providing hypotheses. One possible effect of having hypotheses on experiment-space search is that participants (in conditions H and H-E) would continue to favor search in regions 2 and 3 beyond their first experiment. This would not be the case for NIL participants because there is no information to constrain search in this condition. Table 6.8 shows that suc-

Table 6.7
Proportion of experiments written by region and task performance.

	Region		
	1	2	3
Successful	.17	.33	.50
Unsuccessful	.32	.10	.58

Table 6.8
Proportion of experiments by condition, region, and task performance.

		Region		
Condition	Outcome	1	2	3
NIL	Successful	.42	.35	.23
	Unsuccessful	.07	.08	.85
H	Successful	.10	.34	.56
	Unsuccessful	0	.25	.75
E	Successful	0	.39	.61
	Unsuccessful	.50	.06	.44
H-E	Successful	.21	.25	.54
	Unsuccessful	.56	.11	.33

cessful participants in condition H-E and H ran between 80 and 90 percent of their experiments in regions 2 and 3, whereas successful control (NIL) participants wrote only about 60 percent of their experiments in regions 2 and 3 (and unsuccessful NILs were almost entirely in region 3).

Condition E might affect search in two ways. First, the provided experiments might suggest important dimensions of variation in the experiment space. Second, the outcomes from those three experiments might suggest hypotheses to test. Successful E participants did not write *any* region 1 experiments, whereas their unsuccessful counterparts wrote one-half of their experiments in region 1 and almost none in region 2. This suggests that successful participants, in all information conditions, used the provided information to constrain their search of the experiment space. In contrast, successful participants in the NIL condition were more likely to write region 1 experiments and less likely to write region 3 experiments than were the participants in any of the three Information conditions. That is, successful participants without prior information explored more uninformative regions than did successful participants in the information conditions.

HYPOTHESIS-SPACE SEARCH   Analysis of number of the hypotheses generated is based on participants' verbal protocols.[6] Because participants in conditions H and H-E were provided with hypotheses at the outset, it is difficult to determine which of their statements refer to those hypotheses and which refer to participant-generated hypotheses. Therefore, we decided to analyze the number of hypotheses only for conditions NIL and E. Approximately the same number of hypotheses were generated in each of the two conditions. That is, merely having some initial experimental results did not effectively reduce search through the hypothesis space.

The interaction of hypotheses and experiments was investigated by comparing the effect of experimental results on the stated hypothesis. As we noted in chapter 4, following each experiment, participants have four options: (1) Reject the hypothesis following a confirming result; (2) Retain the hypothesis following a confirming result; (3) Reject the hypothesis following a disconfirming result; (4) Retain the hypothesis following a disconfirming result.

Participants in condition H were particularly interesting. Four of the nine participants generated a prediction for each of the two provided hypotheses before their first experiment. The remaining five all made a counter-based prediction for their first experiment. Following the first experiment, two of the five explicitly mentioned that the "Repeat the last *n* steps" hypothesis must be the correct one. All five switched from counter-based predictions to correct selector-based predictions on their second experiment. Although three of the participants did not explicitly mention the correct hypothesis at that time, their behavior strongly suggests that they were entertaining it. Each of these three participants correctly predicted the device behavior for all of their remaining experiments, and they stated the correct rule at the end of the session.

Condition H-E also presented participants with two hypotheses, but in conjunction with three experimental outcomes. Two of the nine participants explicitly mentioned contrasting predictions prior to the first experiment. Of the remaining seven participants, four switched from their initial counter hypothesis to the correct selector on their second experiment. Of the final three, one participant explicitly mentioned that he was going to test the provided selector hypothesis. However, he wrote a region 1 experiment and erroneously rejected the selector hypothesis. The other two participants never mentioned the provided hypotheses.

The results from conditions H and H-E indicate that even if participants do not explicitly mention a simultaneous test of two competing hypotheses, the experiments that they write suggest that this is their intent. Moreover, they are able to interpret experimental outcomes in relation to the two hypotheses. Consequently, most of the participants in the two groups were able to correctly predict the outcome by their second experiment. Participants used the strategy of a single critical experiment, in combination with the information provided, to drastically reduce their search through the experiment space.

Although all participants in conditions H and H-E were explicitly told that one of the two provided hypotheses was the correct one, they were not all successful (one participant in H and three in H-E failed to discover the correct rule). What accounts for these failures? We can see three possible explanations. One possibility is that too much information, having both hypotheses and experimental outcomes, impairs success if one does not have a clear means of organizing it all. That is, trying to integrate hypotheses and outcomes together is a difficult job. This may result in some participants being unable to abstract the important details of the provided information, or losing track of what they have been told.

A second possibility is that some participants are unable to use one or the other types of information. In particular, if participants cannot use hypotheses they may have some difficulty with the task. Because the given experiments do not clearly distinguish between the two hypotheses, a false conclusion can be easily reached. If a participant initially holds a counter hypothesis, the provided outcomes can be interpreted as providing confirming evidence for this position. Thus even having two mutually exclusive hypotheses does not guarantee success if participants fail to recognize that they come from different frames.

A final possibility is suggested by the sole failure, JJ, in the H condition. JJ initially proposed the correct rule following her first experiment. However, she then wrote a region 3 experiment and interpreted the result as supporting the rule "Repeat the entire program twice, regardless of the value of n." This led her to suspect that she had misinterpreted the outcome of her first experiment. She reran her first experiment and concluded that she had misinterpreted it. However, this first experiment—in which $\lambda = 10$ and $n = 9$—generates behavior that is very difficult to remember. Indeed, JJ misencoded FaceMover's actions when the program was repeated. This error was exacerbated by JJ's false belief that she had incorrectly encoded the first execution of her complex program. Nevertheless, it is surprising is that JJ never realized that her final rule was not one of the two hypotheses with which she had been initially provided.

FaceMover: Conclusions

This study presents a mixed set of results. One clear finding is that the introduction of yet another context for the microworld did not substantially change the nature of participants' approach to the discovery task. The discovery processes used by participants as they attempt to find out how the RPT key works on a programmable device appear to be unaffected by the cover story or the superficial aspects of the device's actions.

The effects of providing information about hypotheses and experiments were complex. Recall that our goal was to increase the external validity of our microworld paradigm by providing an analog to the historical context in which scientists ply their trade. We expected that this "up front" information would give participants some guidance on the essential features of experiments and hypotheses that would, in turn, be reflected in higher success rates. To our surprise, there were no clear effects of providing information on success, even though, in conditions H and H-E, one of the hypotheses that we provided was correct! Participants varied widely in how effectively they were able to use the provided information: although in each condition the average number of references to the information we provided was about 1.5, one-third of the participants in each condition made *no* explicit reference to that information, and this adversely affected their performance.

However, the information conditions did reveal an interesting interaction between providing hypotheses, providing experiments, and amount of additional search in the experiment space. In particular, when participants were given an initial set of experimental outcomes, then the provision of two competing hypotheses tended to produce more E-space search than when no hypotheses were provided. As we noted, there was no evidence that this extra search improved success

rates, but it may indicate that presentation of two competing and mutually exclusive hypotheses influences participants to adopt an experimenter, rather than a theorist, approach to the discovery task. Further
analysis of the regions searched, by condition, suggested that participants did attempt to create discriminating experiments when presented
with two hypotheses.

Conclusion: Searching Our Own Experiment Space

In concluding this chapter, we return to the reflexive mode with which
we opened it, and attempt to evaluate the nature of our own experiment-
space search and what we have learned from it. Studies 5 and 6 (mystery
key), represent a conservative step away from what we had done in the
previous four studies. In study 5 we made a small modification to the interface and simply replaced the RPT key with a "?" key, in order to reduce the constraint on the initial search of the hypothesis space, and in
study 6 we made another small modification and increased the constraint on E-space search. The results of both studies indicated that we
had a sufficiently firm grasp of the discovery process that we could
tweak it and get the results we expected. This approach is not unlike the
general tendency for demonstrating understanding of a domain by
adopting an "engineering" approach and attempting to get specific outcomes from specific experimental arrangements (Schauble, Klopfer, and
Raghavan, 1991).

In study 7 we varied another aspect of our paradigm by introducing
an entirely different cover story and interface layout. In one sense, this
was a large step in our E-space because the context was so different, but
at a deeper level of the underlying isomorphism, it was hardly a step at
all. Indeed, the basic research issue here is the extent to which this was
a large or small step. In other words, did the superficial aspects really
matter or were they just that—superficial? The results were clear: the
deep structure was what mattered in this kind of microworld, not the
context. Another goal of study 7 was to provide a rough replication of
the developmental differences found in earlier studies. Here we were
also conservative, and chose participants who covered the earlier
ranges. The main surprise here was the relatively uninspired performance of the twelfth-grade children.

Study 8 represents the largest move in our experiment space. We
changed our procedure substantially by providing participants with explicit descriptions of possible hypotheses, experiments or both. The
analogy to "real science" was supposed to be that scientists work in a
context of prior experiments and prior hypotheses that have been "provided" by the discipline. We thought that this would be a good way to

add another bit of external validity to our general paradigm, and we expected big effects. But we did not get them. This may have resulted from reaching too far: it is not clear how participants interpret the intent of us providing them with information, or how their interpretation was manifested in the way that they established their own goals. In retrospect, it seems that participants may have been confused about what they were supposed to extract from the information we provided, and the extent to which they were supposed to replicate or ignore what we gave them.

Perhaps the most important contribution of the studies reported in this chapter is that they indicate the potential fruitfulness of different kinds of extensions to our basic microworld paradigm. They suggest different dimensions of our own experiment space and ways in which they can be explored to further inform our model of the discovery process.

Notes

1. In fact, Dancer has a short preliminary animation (raising the "curtain") that takes *longer* than its analog in the BT interface (jettisoning the "launch platform").
2. There may be a mundane, pragmatic explanation for this: We tested the twelfth graders in the week following deadlines for college applications, and they seemed somewhat distracted and uninterested in participating in our study.
3. Recall a similar analysis of first experiments that we presented in study 4 (figure 5.4).
4. Procedural error or equipment failure eliminated one participant from three of the four FaceMover conditions, leaving ten in E and nine in the other three conditions.
5. The differences are in the expected direction. Perhaps a larger sample size would have yielded the effect we predicted, but at this point we will not take refuge in wishful thinking.
6. In condition E, one subject's protocol was lost, leaving a total of nine subjects in that condition for the following analyses.

Chapter 7

Multiple-Space Search in a More Complex Discovery Microworld

Christian D. Schunn and David Klahr

I argued that it was important not to place too much reliance on any single piece of experimental evidence. It might turn out to be misleading. Jim (Watson) was a little more brash, stating that no good model ever accounted for all the facts, since some data was bound to be misleading if not plain wrong. A theory that did fit all the data would have been "carpentered" to do this and would thus be open to suspicion.
(Crick, 1988, pp. 59–60, emphasis in original)

Most practicing scientists would agree with James Watson's claim and acknowledge that, for any theory, there always remain the annoying anomalies, the data that would require undesirable carpentering of the theory in order to be brought into its scope. Indeed, both scientists and nonscientists have a wide variety of potential responses to apparent anomalies. These range from outright rejection of the data, to explaining it away, to fully accepting it and revising their theory (Chinn and Brewer, 1992, 1998). Although our studies—based on BigTrak and its isomorphs—suggest that sticking to hypotheses in the face of inconsistencies is not unusual, we wanted to explore further the effects of repeated cycles of consistent and inconsistent data. Our challenge was to craft a discovery context that causes people to tentatively abandon lines of inquiry and that forces them to reconsider the very features of the data that they are attending to.

This was one of the motivations for the study reported in this chapter. Although the BT microworlds are much more complex than the types of problems typically used by cognitive psychologists interested in problem solving and reasoning, they represent only a small step on the continuum of complexity from "typical" cognitive studies to the real-world complexity of scientific discovery. Recall that both adults and children tended to spend no more than about thirty minutes on the task whether or not they discovered the correct rule. In contrast, real scientists work on their scientific discoveries for years—and with much lower success rates. What—in addition to the acquisition of vast amounts of domain-specific knowledge—accounts for this difference in difficulty? Is it simply a matter of more of the same activities, or are qualitatively different strategies and heuristics involved?

To investigate these questions, we designed a new discovery microworld that was considerably more complex than BigTrak. We "scaled up" the discovery task from one that required, in effect, a single insight (i.e., the shift from a counter frame to a selector frame) during about thirty minutes of problem solving to one that required a series of inter-related discoveries over more than an hour or so. We were particularly interested in the extent to which analysis of participants' behavior in a more complex microworld would provide evidence of different strategies and processes from those we had already identified. That is, the new task had the potential for revealing new heuristics and strategies that people use to deal with increased task complexity.

Several specific objectives motivated the design of this new discovery microworld. First, we wanted to make it sufficiently interesting to sustain participants' interest for more than an hour of focused problem solving. Second, in order to make the task more realistic, we wanted to provide an external memory for participants' experiments and their outcomes. Just as scientists can analyze and reanalyze outcomes from multiple experiments, we wanted our participants to be able to do so without having to rely exclusively on their own memories, as they did with BigTrak. Third, as in the BT microworld, we wanted prior knowledge to render some hypotheses more plausible than others. Fourth, we wanted to continue to use a task requiring a complex mapping between the experiment space and the hypothesis space.

The MilkTruck Microworld

The task we designed to meet these constraints is called MilkTruck.[1] As with BT, participants conducted experiments by using a computer microworld in which they controlled the actions of an animated device. Here, too, their goal was to discover the effect of a complex mystery function, but the MilkTruck cover story is different and the interface has many new features. Because it is difficult to understand our analysis of participants' behavior on the task without fully understanding the Milk-Truck microworld, we will describe it in detail.

An Overview of the MilkTruck Environment

Participants were introduced to the MilkTruck task with a cover story. They were told that they were milk truck drivers and that their company had received a fleet of computerized milk trucks. Unfortunately, the in-

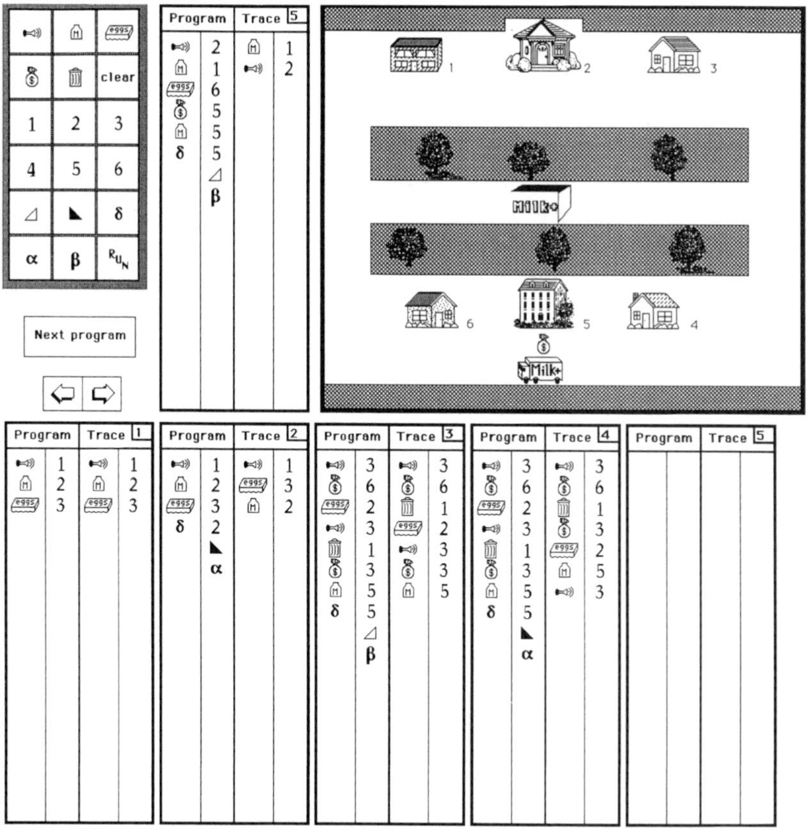

Program	Trace 5
◀)) 2	⌂ 1
⌂ 1	◀)) 2
⌨ 6	
$ 5	
⌂ 5	
δ 5	
△	
β	

Keypad:
◀)) ⌂ ⌨
$ 🗑 clear
1 2 3
4 5 6
△ ▶ δ
α β Run

Next program

⇦ ⇨

Program	Trace 1	Program	Trace 2	Program	Trace 3	Program	Trace 4	Program	Trace 5
◀)) 1	◀)) 1	◀)) 1	◀)) 1	◀)) 3	◀)) 3	◀)) 3	◀)) 3		
⌂ 2	⌂ 2	⌂ 2	⌨ 3	$ 6	$ 6	$ 6	🗑 6		
⌨ 3	⌨ 3	⌨ 3	⌂ 2	⌨ 2	🗑 1	⌨ 2	$ 1		
		δ 2		◀)) 3	⌨ 2	◀)) 3	⌨ 2		
		▶		🗑 1	◀)) 3	🗑 1	⌂ 5		
		α		$ 3	$ 3	$ 3	◀)) 3		
				⌂ 5	⌂ 5	⌂ 5			
				δ 5		δ 5			
				△		▶			
				β		α			

Figure 7.1
"Snapshot" of the MilkTruck microworld interface, showing the keypad (upper left), current program and trace (upper middle), run window (upper right), and history window (bottom). The current program—the fifth in the series—has completed the delivery of milk to house 1 and beeped its horn at house 2. Now it is retrieving money from house 5; that action has not yet been added to the current trace window. (The current program and its trace are located between the keypad and the run window.)

structions accompanying the new trucks are all in a foreign language unknown to the participants. Thus, they must figure out on their own how to control the milk trucks. However, all but one of the commands is very straightforward, and the participants were given step-by-step instructions on how to use those commands.

Figure 7.1 depicts the full display that participants encountered as they worked with MilkTruck. The milk truck is programmed using a keypad (upper left of figure 7.1). Each program step is entered by clicking on an "action" key (located at the top of the keypad) followed by a number key (located in the middle of the keypad). The action keys control the five actions that the milk truck "driver" can perform. (It turns out that the *sequence* in which these action keys are arranged on the keypad is important, although this point was not emphasized during the familiarization phase.) As indicated by their icons on the keypad, these actions are: beep the horn, deliver milk, deliver eggs, receive money, and receive empties (garbage). The number keys correspond to the six houses on the delivery route (depicted in the upper right of figure 7.1).[2] The CLEAR key is used to delete all the steps from a prior program. Any action can be performed at any house, and both actions and locations can be repeated in a program. A program consists of a sequence of up to fourteen action-location pairs.

To help participants remember the programs that they entered, their current program was displayed in the program window. For example, the leftmost program shown at the bottom of figure 7.1 is the following sequence: beep the horn at house one, deliver milk to house two, and then eggs to house three. Once participants had entered a program, they would click on the RUN key, and the program would be executed. During program execution, an animated milk truck traced out the programmed route in the run window (upper right of figure 7.1). The truck first exited the garage in the center of the screen, and then moved to each location in the program route in the order dictated by the program. Animated icons were used to indicate what transpired at each location. In figure 7.1, we see the milk truck picking up money from house 5. At the end of the route, the driver would exit the truck and jump up and down several times. This signaled the end of the route (and helped to keep the participants interested). While programming the route the participants could use the CLEAR button to clear out the current program to start over from scratch. However, once the RUN button was hit, the program would run to completion.

Immediately to the right of each program window is the trace window. Before the program is executed, the trace window is empty. As each step in the program is executed, the trace window displays the executed step. During the training phase—that is, before the introduction of the mystery key—the milk truck executes the steps in the program exactly in the order that they were programmed, and by the end of the program, the content and order of the items in the trace window is identical to the listing in the program window (cf. program 1 at the bottom left of figure 7.1). However, with the addition of the mystery command, the trace could be different from the program.

Below the number keys on the keypad are the δ keys and its associated parameters. The δ ("delta") command is the mystery command whose function must be discovered. Recall that in the BigTrak task the mystery key (RPT) is a function with only one parameter (a number). In Milk-Truck, things are much more complicated, because δ is a function with *three* parameters. The first parameter following δ must be one of six numbers (1–6). The second parameter is one of two triangles (either ◁ or ◣). The third parameter is one of two Greek letters (either α or β). When the δ command is used in a program, it must always be followed by its three parameters (see programs 2, 3, and 4 in the lower panels of figure 7.1). For example, the fifth (and current) program displayed at the top of figure 7.1 shows the legal sequence δ, 5, ◁, β. This sequence of four special keys must be at the end of the program (i.e., once δ is selected, no other commands may be added).

To appreciate the difficulty of this task, try to figure out the function of the δ command from the example programs and their outcomes displayed in figure 7.1. Spend a few minutes to come up with at least one hypothesis for the function of each the parameters. What does the number signify? What do the triangles signify? What do α and β signify?

Consider first the second program and its trace, shown at the bottom of figure 7.1. Early in the task, participants typically describe this kind of outcome as "it switched the second and third steps" or "the delivery to house 2 was put last." Thus, based on program outcomes such as this one, participants typically propose that δ switches steps, with n being the house number of the item that is moved (house 2 in this case), and ◣ signifying that deliveries to that house number should be put last. The implication is that with ◁, the action would be put first in the list. However, as can be seen from the traces of programs 3 and 4, the actual function of δ is much more complex. At this point, try to propose a hypothesis about δ that could account for the three examples in figure 7.1.

How Does δ Work?
The global function of δ n is to reorder—or sort—the last n steps in the program. The particular direction of the sort depends on the triangles: ◁ sorts in ascending order and ◣ sorts in descending order. The "sort key" (i.e., the thing that determines the sort) is controlled by the selection of either α or β. For α it is the order of the actions on the keypad, and for β it is the house number of the command. The two triangles and the two Greek letters can be combined into four different specific sorting functions, as shown in table 7.1.

For example, in program 4 of figure 7.1, δ5◣α caused the last five steps in the initial program to be executed in decreasing action order. Note that when a step is already in the correct order, its position is left unchanged. For example, in program 3, only three of the last five steps are moved—the last two steps were already in the correct order (increasing house number) and thus are unaffected.

Table 7.1
Summary of the function of the δ command, in conjunction with parameters α, β, $\triangle$, and $\blacktriangle$.

δn re-orders the last n steps in the program according to:		
	$\triangle$ (increasing)	$\blacktriangle$ (decreasing)
α (action)	. . . action in increasing keypad order: Beep, Milk, Eggs, Money, Garbage	. . . action in decreasing keypad order: Garbage, Money, Eggs, Milk, Beep
β (house)	. . . house in increasing number order: 1, 2 , 3, 4, 5, 6	. . . house in decreasing number order: 6, 5, 4, 3, 2, 1

Like many scientific discoveries, the function of δ is easy to describe and very difficult to induce from evidence. Successful discovery requires at least two insights. The first insight is that only part of the program is affected (i.e., the last n steps) by the δ command. In other words, like the original BigTrak RPT function, δ functions as a selector, not a counter. Without this insight, it is nearly impossible to discover a pattern to the ordering. Moreover, as in the BT microworld, for programs where $\lambda \leq n$, this selection effect is undetectable. The second insight is that the particular items and houses that are in the program determine the specific effects of the δ command. Participants typically initially assume that the particular values do not matter. For example, they might believe that δ simply reverses the last n items, regardless of which commands or house numbers are included in that set of commands. Several features of the to-be-discovered rule add to this difficulty. First, the rule itself is a compound conditional. That is, it is of the form "if (*specific triangle*) and (*specific Greek letter*) then (*specific sort function*) over the last n items." Second, the sort key for β is "natural" in that it uses the number attached to the command, but the sort key for α is arbitrary and local to the context of the MilkTruck keypad. Discovery of these features requires a very high degree of attention to experimental outcomes.

To aid the participants in this complex task, the interface contained several supportive features. Not only was the content of the current program and its outcome displayed in the program and trace windows, but also the programs and outcomes of all previous programs were available for inspection. The seven most recent program and trace listings were displayed concurrently below the run window, and participants could scroll this "history window" to view any and all previous programs (see the bottom of figure 7.1). When a new program was being entered, the program and outcome of the previous program was added automatically to the history window. Another supportive feature of the interface

involved the syntax of program entry: the keys that could be legally selected at a given point in time were highlighted. Moreover, illegal selections were ignored.

Study 9: MilkTruck

Participants and Procedure
Twenty-two university undergraduates attempted to solve the task in
two sessions on two consecutive days. The first day consisted of an introduction phase and a discovery phase. The introduction phase included detailed instruction about the basics of the MilkTruck domain,
followed by a description of the syntax of the δ command, and the presentation of the goal of discovering the effect of δ. In the discovery phase,
participants designed, conducted, and analyzed experiments in order
to discover the role of δ and its arguments. On the first day, following the
introduction phase, participants were given thirty minutes in the discovery phase to work at the task until they felt they had solved it or they
wished to give up. If they had not finished after thirty minutes on the
first day (nineteen of twenty-two did not finish), then they returned the
next day to continue.

All programs were automatically recorded on the computer, and all
participants' verbal protocols were audio recorded. These twenty-two
participants generated over thirty-three hours of discovery behavior
data, including more than 1,000 programs and more than 110,000 words
of verbal protocols. The analyses presented in this chapter are based on
several forms of aggregation of these data: (1) the content of the programs generated; (2) statements made in generating programs; (3) statements made in analyzing program outcomes; and (4) the participants'
final solutions.

Results
Participants were grouped into three categories: those who discovered
how the δ key and its parameters worked (solvers); those who mistakenly thought they had made such a discovery (false solvers); and those
who gave up without any solution (nonsolvers). Table 7.2 presents the
mean number of experiments and time on task for each group. The task
was difficult but not impossible: half of the participants were solvers,
and solution times ranged from 30 to 179 minutes. Note that the nonsolvers did not fail from simple lack of effort: they ran slightly more experiments over a longer period of time than the solvers. As expected, the
MilkTruck task was significantly more difficult than the BigTrak studies
described earlier: MilkTruck participants ran three times as many programs over four times as much time.

Table 7.2
Mean number of experiments and time on task for each solution group (and standard deviation).

Group	n	Experiments (sd)	Time on task (sd)
Solver	11	49.5 (18.6)	78.6 (40.9)
False solver	5	33.6 (19.6)	61.6 (42.8)
Nonsolver	6	54.5 (17.6)	118.8 (17.8)
All groups	22	47.2 (19.4)	85.7 (41.2)

A Typical MilkTruck Protocol   Appendix 7.1 presents the full protocol of a solver (MA). MA is a third-year physics major who solved the task in 41.5 minutes and forty-two experiments. Each of MA's experiments and their executions are listed in appendix 7.2. Recall that this history is available at all times to MA. (Only seven experiments at a time are visible, but MA can scroll through the entire history window whenever he wants to.) His experiments and hypotheses are representative of solvers, but he is atypical in one respect: he induces patterns quickly and solves the task fairly quickly. In this section we provide an overview of MA's protocol. Although the protocols from this task are quite long, they reveal an unusually rich set of strategies that accompany the discovery process. In subsequent sections, we will return to the protocol to discuss various aspects of the discovery process in further detail.

Like most participants, MA does not have a detailed initial hypothesis. This leads him, like many of the successful participants, to begin with a fairly simple experiment. In his first several experiments, MA's primary goal is to find any effect of δ, and this goal is not reached until experiment 4. MA's first hypotheses are in terms of particular steps being "delayed," and these hypotheses are quickly disconfirmed.

In experiments 7, 8, and 9 MA tries again to produce any change with δ. Difficulties in reproducing an effect lead MA to examine how experiment 4 is different from subsequent programs. This leads MA to propose that perhaps the items matter and that δ may place certain items first. Although the next several experiments produce no confirmation of this hypothesis, MA begins a careful search of the experiment space (experiments 12–17) with this general hypothesis in mind.

The outcome of experiment 17 leads to the hypothesis that n relates to the number of steps in the program, which is apparently confirmed in experiment 18. Note, however, that MA is still entertaining the hypothesis that δ switches a particular pair of steps rather than working on a larger group of steps ("see if it reverses the first two commands").

After experiment 21, MA first proposes that the items may be placed in house number order, a very important step toward the final solution. However, this hypothesis is quickly disconfirmed, and MA does not return to it until much later.

Following experiment 22, MA reaches an impasse and lapses into silence—a typical pattern in these participants. In response to this impasse, MA switches from investigating Δ to investigating $\blacktriangle$, and, with one exception, does not return to Δ until the following day.

Beginning with experiment 24, MA embarks on a more systematic experiment space search, contrasting α with β, and $\blacktriangle$ with Δ. This sequence of experiments enables MA, for the first time (following experiment 26), to propose a complete hypothesis for all the δ parameters: that Δ affects the trash command and $\blacktriangle$ affects the horn command; that β is picking that item second, and α for picking that item first; and that n refers to the number of steps (implicit from previous comments and experiment selections).

This complex hypothesis is immediately disconfirmed by experiment 27. However, in experiment 28, MA carefully varies only n with respect to experiment 27. His choice of program content is particularly serendipitous not only because $1 < n < \lambda$, but also because all four of the selected items are rearranged with this $\blacktriangle$ α combination, making the role of n quite salient. Thus, MA is now able to propose the correct role of n—that n refers to the number of items from the end that are changed.

In experiments 29 and 30, MA attempts to induce the function of α and β by varying only that aspect of the program. Because the outcomes are the same, these experiments completely disconfirm the notion that α and β simply refer to opposing orders.

Experiment 31 is conducted with the goal of determining the ordering among the items. The outcome leads to two alternative hypotheses: that $\blacktriangle$ α sorts either in decreasing command order or in decreasing house number order. At this point, MA has all the important components of the correct solution. Experiment 32 then confirms that $\blacktriangle$ α is decreasing command order. In the immediately following experiment, MA proposes that $\blacktriangle$ β refers to decreasing house number order.

At this point, the first's day session ends. MA's final guess for that day is completely correct although not yet adequately tested. Interestingly, during the interval between sessions, MA appears to forget some aspects of this final hypothesis, as indicated by his comments—on the second day—during experiments 34 and 35. By experiment 36, MA reestablishes that n refers to the number of steps, and that Δ is increasing order—however, the role of α is not yet correct.

In experiment 37, MA reestablishes the fact that β places the steps in house number order and a fully correct hypothesis is reproposed following experiment 38. The remaining experiments are then used to insure that the hypotheses for all α/β $\triangle/\blacktriangle$ combinations are correct, to rule out any alternative orderings.

As this protocol demonstrates, even with a fairly sophisticated experimenter, the path to discovery is complex and fraught with many blind alleys. How representative is this protocol? Because the MilkTruck task is a complex, multiple-insight problem, the duration and order of occurrence of the various events are idiosyncratic within each participant. However, the set of processes and strategies found within this protocol are highly representative of those found in the other protocols. We shall now consider various processes illustrated in this protocol in further detail, applying the SDDS framework.

Experiment-Space Search   One of the most striking differences between these experiments and the earlier BigTrak experiments is the frequency with which MilkTruck experiments were conducted without hypotheses. Recall that in study 1, more than 70 percent of BigTrak experiments were conducted while participants had a particular hypothesis in mind. In contrast, only 39 percent of MilkTruck experiments were conducted with an active hypothesis.[3] Table 7.3 presents the mean proportion of experiments conducted with explicit active hypotheses for each solution group. Although solvers have the highest proportion and nonsolvers the lowest, even the solvers have hypotheses for only 51 percent of their experiments. The distinction between H-space search and E-space search corresponds to participants asking themselves "what's going on here?" versus "what can I do next?" It is clear that the complexity of the Milk-Truck domain led to an emphasis on the latter.

What factors might contribute to this tendency to spend more time considering what experiment to run next than to thinking about specific hypotheses? We suggest several candidates. First, as we discovered in the mystery key study, when the label on the unknown key conveys no semantic hints about its function—as in the case of δ—then it is difficult to have much confidence in any hypothesis generated via pure hypothesis-space search, in the absence of data. Indeed, there is an extremely

Table 7.3
Mean proportion of experiments (and standard deviation) for which participants had a current hypothesis, for each solution group.

Group	n	Proportion of experiments having explicit hypotheses
Solvers	7	.51 (.06)
False solvers	5	.33 (.18)
Nonsolvers	3	.20 (.14)
All groups	15	.39 (.17)

wide range of *initial* hypotheses about how δ works, with little overlap in these initial guesses. A second possible contributing factor is that the conditional sorting invoked by the δ key is much more complex than the RPT's single repetition of the final program segment. This makes it much more difficult to come up with even one hypothesis that can account for a current outcome. A third contributing factor is that program content plays a role in the effect of δ. Consequently, for many programs (such as those in which items are already sorted in the order mandated by the δ key and its parameters), there may be no discrepancy at all between program and execution trace. This may produce what appears, at first, to be quite erratic behavior. Finally, the external memory support provided in MilkTruck—that is, the display of a full set of previous experiments and their outcomes—provides an unanticipated extra hurdle for hypotheses. Hypotheses must account not only for the current experimental outcome but also for the past experiment outcomes, which are not easily ignored inasmuch as they are displayed prominently in the history window.[4] Thus, MilkTruck participants frequently devote their experimentation efforts to uncovering data that might suggest new hypotheses. This corresponds to the Induce Frame process within the SDDS model (figure 2.9), the very process that was so difficult in the BigTrak context.

If we suppress the detail about the contents of specific commands, then the MilkTruck experiment space is about 50 percent larger than the 225 cells of the BT experiment space: there are $14 * 6 * 2 * 2 = 336$ cells[5] and the two additional parameters in addition to λ and n (i.e., the choice of α or β and $\varDelta$ or ◣) make it more structurally complex. We will begin with an expanded version of the λ–n analysis used previously with Big-Trak and its isomorphs, and then we will introduce new aspects that result from the increased complexity.

For our initial analysis, we divided the experiment space into five mutually exclusive regions, as shown in figure 7.2: region 1: $n = 1$; region 2: $\lambda = 1, n > 1$; region 3: $\lambda > n > 1$; region 4: $\lambda = n > 1$; region 5: $1 < \lambda < n$. Then we looked at how participants from the three solution groups searched the experiment space. All three groups showed a similar profile: a very large proportion of region 3 experiments (which are the most informative because $\lambda > n$), very few region 2 experiments (where, because $\lambda = 1$, outcomes are the least informative), and an intermediate proportion of experiments in the other regions. However, as shown in figure 7.3, there were some differences across the solution groups. False solvers had the largest proportion of experiments in region 1, in which having $n = 1$ makes them the easiest to interpret but least informative. Solvers had the largest proportion of region 4 experiments—in which having $\lambda = n$ makes the sorting action more obvious because the entire program is affected—and the smallest proportion of region 5 experiments in which

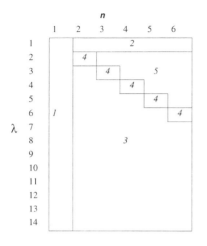

Region	Boundaries	Example
1	$n = 1$	B1 M2 δ1 ▲ β
2	$\lambda = 1, n > 1$	B1 δ3 ▲ β
3	$\lambda > n > 1$	B1 M2 E3 $4 δ2 ▲ β
4	$\lambda = n > 1$	B1 M2 E3 δ3 ▲ β
5	$1 < \lambda < n$	B1 M2 E3 δ5 ▲ β

Figure 7.2
Regions of MilkTruck experiment space, with examples.

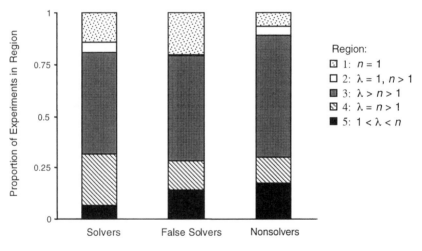

Figure 7.3
The mean proportion of experiments in each λ-n E-space region for each solution group.

having $\lambda < n$ masks the function of n. Thus, there appears to be a similar relationship between the λ–regions and solution rate as in the BigTrak tasks. We will return to this relationship subsequently, in our analysis of hypothesis-space search.

In addition to analyzing λ–n regions, we also investigated search through the triangle-Greek letter regions. Over all programs, participants were more likely to use α than β (64% versus 46%) and equally likely to use either of the triangles. Temporally, participants typically began with α, and α was more difficult to understand and thus was used in more experiments. In contrast, although participants typically began with ⊿, it usually did not produce any changes (because the steps were commonly already in order), and thus participants switched to investigating ▲. Interestingly, there were no relations between use of these parameters and solution group,[6] suggesting that this aspect of the experiment-space search was not as important as correctly navigating the λ-n regions.

New Heuristics in a Complex Experiment Space   What strategies did participants use to search the complex MilkTruck experiment space? Some of these strategies related to aspects of λ–n regions as with BigTrak. However, other strategies related to the expanded MilkTruck regions, which included the Greek letters and the triangles. In terms of λ–n regions, there was one very popular strategy: A majority of the participants used a strategy of starting simple and building up toward more complex experiments. Use of this strategy is indexed by analyzing changes in program length over the discovery session. The mean length of first programs was 2.7 steps. By the end of the task, participants were using programs between six and fourteen steps long. Figure 7.4 illustrates this gradual increase in mean program length over task quartiles.

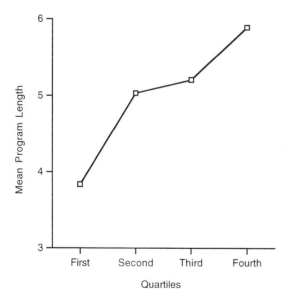

Figure 7.4
The mean length per program within each task quartile.

All three solution groups had this same gradual increase across quartiles, although solvers began with slightly smaller programs and finished with slightly longer programs than the other two groups.

Another strategy for searching the MilkTruck experiment space is one we call the Put Upon Stack Heuristic (PUSH). We define PUSH as follows: (1) When confronted with an impasse while investigating a particular region of the experiment space (e.g., $\blacktriangle\alpha$), explicitly switch to investigating a different region of the experiment space (e.g., $\blacktriangle\beta$) with the goal of returning to the confusing region later. (2) Upon successfully completing the investigation of the new region, return directly to the old region, rather than a third region (e.g., $\triangle\beta$). In other words, when participants use PUSH, they do not entirely abandon the confusing experiment-space region; instead they momentarily defer investigation of it. The time spent away from the problematic region proved useful as participants not only solve the problem in the new region, but also, upon returning, quickly resolve the confusion underlying the impasse in the old region. We observed the used of PUSH in several of the solvers' protocols, but in none of the false solvers' or nonsolvers' protocols.

PUSH can be useful in three different ways. First, by enabling participants to work on a different problem, PUSH allows new ideas to become activated and the activation of old ideas to decay, thereby reducing set effects and affecting the hypothesis-space search in the old situation. Second, the investigation of a different problem can suggest new operators that may be applied to the old situation, thereby improving the experiment-space search. MA's protocol (experiments 22–23) provides evidence for this use of PUSH:

> "Yeah. I'm just baffled right now. OK, let's take a different tack. See if we can figure something out from a different angle. Let's go at it, looking at these other, what this other triangle does."

Then, for the first time, MA ran two programs that directly contrasted α with β, that is, varied only α/β between two programs (experiments 24–25). This approach produced useful information and led MA to say (experiment 26):

> "Let's try the same combination with other triangle again. I have a feeling that this might be what I need to be doing all along. The white triangle. We'll start with alpha."

MA then went on using this type of newly discovered contrast, among others, to successfully solve the task.

The third way that PUSH is useful is that in inducing a complex concept involving interactions (such as those underlying the δ command), discoveries about one part of the concept facilitate discoveries about another part of the concept. Thus, as the predictive power of hypotheses improve, the easier it is to resolve the remaining ambiguities.

A related strategy identified in previous research is the Investigate Surprising Phenomena (ISP) strategy (Kulkarni and Simon, 1990), in which people focus their attention on surprising experimental results and set a subgoal to determine what caused the surprising results. On the surface, the two strategies would seem to be incompatible: in the face of difficulty, one strategy (PUSH) advises switching to a different experiment-space region, whereas the other strategy (ISP) advises redoubling effort in this exact experiment-space region. However, the two apply to slightly different situations. When the surprising phenomenon has some unique, salient characteristics or features that can be tested in follow-up experiments, then ISP applies. On the other hand, when all the salient possible reasons for the surprising phenomenon have been exhausted, then PUSH applies. In this case, the strategy is to defer further investigation until new information has been gathered.

What Constitutes an Experiment?   Two additional aspects of search in the MilkTruck experiment space deserve mention. The first is the role of confirmation in experimentation. The SDDS model suggests that individuals go through a natural cycle of using experiments to generate hypotheses followed by experiments to test the generated hypotheses. The structure of the MilkTruck task enables us to see whether this simple cycle generalizes to a situation in which there are multiple components to discover. That is, do people try to induce a complete hypothesis and then test it, or do they test the partial hypotheses as they are generated?

We found that MilkTruck participants tended to follow both approaches. In the example protocol, MA usually conducted a hypothesis-testing experiment to evaluate newly generated hypotheses. For example, based on the outcome of experiment 4, MA proposes that n refers to the step that is placed last, and then tests this hypothesis in experiment 5. However, at the end of the second session, MA conducts an additional series of complex experiments (experiments 38–42) all designed to confirm his current hypothesis. This was a common pattern among the MilkTruck participants.

The final aspect of search in the MilkTruck experiment space that we will discuss relates to our own operational definitions. Thus far we have been defining an experiment as a single program and its outcome.[7] However, because participants have access to the results of all previous programs, an experiment could also be defined as an aggregate of more than one program. For example, some participants ran a series of programs in which they held the base program constant and varied the δ parameters systematically (e.g., $2 \triangle \beta$, $2 \blacktriangle \beta$, $3 \triangle \beta$, $3 \blacktriangle \beta$, etc.). These participants spent little time examining the intermediate outcomes. Instead, they waited until the end of the series before attempting to induce some regularities over the set of outcomes. A related strategy is to add or remove a feature with respect to the previous program and see how the outcome differs. In both of these approaches, each program is a "cell" in a larger factorial experiment.

In generating such experiments, one must decide how many features to vary from one program to the next. Figure 7.5 presents the mean number of features varied by the different solution groups across quartiles of the task. There were four features defined for this analysis—one for each of the δ parameters and one for remaining content of the program. Overall, participants tended to vary two or three features at a time between successive programs, and the overall effect of solution group was not significant. However, there was an interaction between quartile and solution group: solvers varied the fewest features early in the process. In the later quartiles, nonsolvers and false solvers also varied fewer features. False solvers varied the fewest features, and this may have prevented them from visiting E-space regions that would have disconfirmed their incorrect hypotheses.

Valid inferences from experimental contrasts demand that only one feature can be varied at a time. Under this strict view, few participants

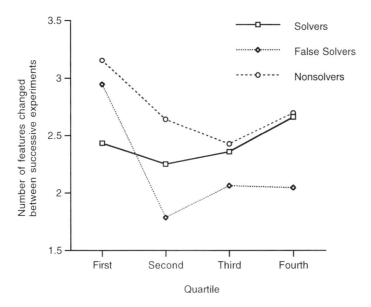

Figure 7.5
Mean number of program feature changes between successive programs for each solution group for each quartile of total experiments.

could be described as having created unconfounded experiments because most of them varied two or three features from one experiment to the next. However, there are two reasons why our index—the number of feature changes in between successive programs—may overestimate participants' penchant for confounded experimental comparisons. First, although our measure is based on comparisons between adjacent programs, participants may be basing their experimental contrast for a given experiment on one that occurred earlier than its immediate predecessor. Second, the structure of the changes within a single program provides a large portion of the information. For example, the exact coincidence of $n = 4$ and the last four items of a program being changed suggests that n is the number of items from the end that are changed. In this second case, a single program can serve as a full experiment. In such experiments, which can be thought of as case studies, the participant looks for identity relationships between aspects of the program and the outcome (e.g., noticing that the δ number is 2 and the delivery to house 2 was moved last).

Hypothesis-Space Search   We begin our discussion of search in the hypothesis space by focusing on aspects that are similar to BigTrak and then move on to novel features resulting from the increased complexity of MilkTruck. Developing the correct hypotheses in MilkTruck required three primary discoveries: (1) that n acts as a selector on the last n items in the program; (2) that—in contrast to BigTrak—the items in the program (i.e., house numbers and actions) matter; and (3) that action of the δ command is to sort the steps. These three insights were approximately equally difficult (achieved by sixteen, eighteen, and seventeen of the twenty-two participants respectively). Moreover, none of them was more likely to occur before the others.

How independent were these three discoveries? Although there was no relation between discovering the selector function of n and the other two insights, there was a significant relation between success and the other two discoveries. Of the seventeen participants discovering that δ sorts the steps, 94 percent discovered that the items matter, whereas only 40 percent of the remaining five participants discovered that items matter. It is not entirely surprising that there is some relationship between the sort and item discoveries, in that the sort discovery implies that something about the step matters. However, the two are separate discoveries, with neither insight being necessary nor sufficient to induce the other. Moreover, of the sixteen participants who made both discoveries, only three made both discoveries on the same experiment.

What was the impact of experiment-space search activities on these insights? Discovering the selector role of n was associated with proportionally fewer $n > \lambda$ experiments (.07 versus .24), more $n < \lambda$ experiments (.55 versus .44), and more experiments involving β (.39 versus .22). Thus, the importance of $n < \lambda$ experiments is the same as it was in BT. Discovering that items matter was associated with proportionally more $\lambda = n$ experiments (.22 versus .08), fewer $n < \lambda$ experiments (.48 versus .68), and more α experiments (.66 versus .53). The reason for the association with α experiments is obvious—items did not matter for β experiments. The importance of $\lambda = n$ experiments is also intuitive—having the full program sorted made the sort function more apparent. Discovering the sort function was unrelated to these gross-level λ–n and Greek letter-triangle E-space regions. However, it was related to the more specific conjunction of $\lambda > 4$ and $n > 4$ experiments (.26 versus .15), whose results are sufficiently complex to push the participants away from simple item-swap hypotheses (e.g., "it swaps the last item with the nth item from the end"). Thus, as with BigTrak, MilkTruck displays an important correspondence between E-space and H-space search—certain hypotheses are less likely to be entertained without visiting the appropriate E-space regions. In the next sections we turn to some of the novel features of hypothesis-space search in the MilkTruck domain.

PIECEMEAL INDUCTION   One of the most striking features of participants' search in the MilkTruck hypothesis space is the incremental fashion in which hypotheses were constructed. Rather than develop monolithic hypotheses about the function of δ, the participants developed smaller hypotheses about each of the parameters, typically one parameter at a time. We call this process *piecemeal induction*. Because it constructs only partial hypotheses, piecemeal induction tends to produce a large number of hypotheses. MilkTruck participants produced on average thirty-two hypotheses each,[8] and one participant produced sixty-three unique hypotheses.

In piecemeal induction, new hypotheses frequently add to, rather than replace, existing hypotheses. For example, in experiment 19, MA has the hypothesis that n represents the number of items in the program (from experiment 17). From the outcome of experiment 19, MA adds the hypothesis that $\Delta\alpha$ places the horn command first. Here, the hypothesis for the function of n is retained, and the hypothesis regarding the $\Delta\alpha$ combination is added.

Another form of hypothesis change involves the combination of component hypotheses to form more general hypotheses. For example, a participant might generalize the hypotheses that $n = 2$ changes the last two steps and $n = 3$ changes the last three steps to the more general hypothesis that n changes the last n steps. A variation of this generalization process involves segmenting hypotheses about parameter combinations into separate, more general hypotheses about each parameter. For example, from the hypotheses that ▲ α sorts items in decreasing action order and ▲ β sorts them in decreasing house number order, participants frequently generalize to the hypothesis that ▲ refers to decreasing order.

HYPOTHESIS GENERALITY   MilkTruck hypotheses vary not only in terms of their referents (objects, boundary conditions, or both), but also with respect to the generality versus specificity of those referents. For example, in the hypothesis, "with black triangle alpha, n refers to the number of steps from the end of the program that are reversed," the object is n. The generality-specificity of boundary conditions refers to the limitations on applicability of the hypothesis. In this example, the boundary conditions are ▲ α. That is, the hypothesis regarding the object n is true only when the boundary conditions ▲ and α are met. Table 7.4 presents examples of hypotheses with general and specific objects and boundary conditions.

Boundary conditions occur frequently in both the physical and social sciences. For example, the laws of Newtonian physics are assumed to apply only at speeds significantly below the speed of light. In the social sciences, hypotheses regarding group structure are often specific to boundary conditions such as sex, age, ethnicity, and so on. In this domain, the generality of both object and boundary conditions varies from combination hypotheses to specific parameter hypotheses to general parameter hypotheses. We have already seen several examples of combination hypotheses (e.g., "▲ α sorts decreasing function," "▲ β reverses the steps"). Some combination hypotheses are very specific: "2▲ β with an even number of items swaps the last two steps." Specific parameter hypotheses refer to specific values of a parameter (e.g., $n = 2$, ▲, β). At the most general end of the generality-specificity continuum are general

Table 7.4
Examples of general and specific objects (in boldface) and boundary conditions (in italics).

	Boundary condition	
Object	General	Specific
General	LS Exp 12: The **triangle** is just on and off.	MW Exp 44: The **number** is simply the number of deliveries that it will organize for alpha, er, for *white alpha.*
Specific	MA Exp 6: **White triangle alpha** was the milk got delayed.	MW Exp 26: Delta **five**, seems like it reverses them. *Except where they are the same command.*

Table 7.5
Mean of participant ($n = 9$) proportions (and SD) for each type of object hypothesis.

Object	Example	Frequency	MA Exp#
Specific triangle	White triangle	.21 (.06)	26
Specific letter	Beta	.21 (.09)	33
Specific combination	White alpha	.20 (.16)	19
General n	n	.17 (.09)	18
Specific n	$n = 3$	.12 (.09)	—
General letter	Alpha/Beta	.05 (.06)	30
General triangle	White/Black	.03 (.05)	—
General combination	n and triangles	.01 (.03)	—

parameter hypotheses that refer to one of the three general parameters—n, the triangles, or the Greek letters.

Table 7.5 presents the relative frequency of object hypotheses at various levels of generality. The most common hypotheses involve specific triangles, specific Greek letters, specific combinations, and the general n. Interestingly, for the triangles and Greek letter parameters, specific value hypotheses were more common than general value hypotheses, whereas for the n parameter the reverse was true. This difference may reflect participants' general belief that n, being an interval scale, should involve a general function. This presumption would preclude proposing hypotheses for which the value of n could not be generalized immediately. In support of this assumption, specific n hypotheses are considerably less frequent than specific triangle and specific Greek letter hypotheses. However, the difference could also reflect the ease with which general hypotheses for n are proposed—general hypotheses for n are three to six times as frequent as with the triangles and the Greek letters.

How did the generality of hypotheses vary over time? Typically, the participants began by trying to propose very general hypotheses. For example, MA's first hypothesis (developed following experiment 4) was that n refers to the house number that is placed at the end (in his terms, which action it "delays"). In this complex task, these first general hypotheses failed miserably. Following these early failures, participants attempted to build more specific hypotheses, accounting for regularities of more limited scope. For example, following experiment 5, MA proposes that the specific combination $\Delta\alpha$ "delays" milk commands. Over the course of the discovery processes, participants attempted to generalize these specific hypotheses to more general hypotheses. Of course, this process was iterative, inasmuch as the second, third, and fourth attempts at general hypotheses often failed. However, by the end of the task, all of the solvers and false solvers proposed general hypotheses. It seems that the participants considered a single general hypothesis as considerably more desirable than many specific hypotheses.

One final aspect of hypothesis-space search deserves mention: when are new hypotheses proposed? The SDDS model (see figure 2.9) assumes that new hypotheses are proposed either during the evidence evaluation phase (in Review Outcomes, where the outcomes of one or more experiments are examined) or during the Induce Frame process. For the MilkTruck task, hypotheses were proposed primarily (79% of the time) while the participants were encoding the outcome of the most recent experiment rather than while they were examining outcomes of previous experiments (5% of the time). It appears that new data are used to suggest new hypotheses and previous data are used to confirm or verify them. Surprisingly, a substantial proportion (15%) of hypotheses were also proposed during the design of an experiment.

Consider several examples from MA's protocol. On five occasions, hypotheses were first mentioned during the design of an experiment. In four of these cases—experiments 5, 10, 18, and 41—the most plausible assumption is that the hypothesis motivated the design of the experiment rather than vice versa, because there are usually direct precursors to the hypothesis to be found in the outcome interpretation of the immediately preceding experiment. For example, the hypothesis "let's see if the delta changes the priority in which they are done" that occurs in the design of experiment 10 is preceded by the statement "I wonder if it is like a priority thing" in the interpretation of the outcome of experiment 9.

The fifth case, experiment 6, does not seem to follow this pattern. The quest for a new approach to designing experiments (varying the triangles and Greek letters) led MA to examine how the previous experiments fit in this scheme, which in turn led to the proposal that $\varDelta \alpha$ delays the delivery of milk. This example shows how experiment-space search can have a direct influence on hypothesis-space search (by producing a new way to interpret previous outcomes) in addition to the more typical sequence in which experiments generate data that are then analyzed to produce hypotheses.

Data Representation-Space Search   Our analysis thus far has been couched in the now-familiar terms of the dual space framework, that is, in terms of search in the experiment space and the hypothesis space. However, analysis of the MilkTruck protocols led us to formulate an entirely new space: the data representation space. First we will indicate the kind of data that led to this formulation, and then we will define the new space by contrasting it with the now-familiar hypothesis space.

Consider the four excerpts from participant MW listed in table 7.6. Of particular importance are the different aspects of MilkTruck's behavior to which MW attends. In the first excerpt, MW counts *the number of times the milk truck driver jumps up and down* at the end of the program. He makes no mention at all of the content of the program. In the second excerpt, MW attends to the *path of the milk truck* in the run window, in particular whether the milk truck took the most efficient route from house 1 to house 6. In the third excerpt, MW continues to attend to the path of the milk truck, but now he characterizes it in terms of *different features of the path:* "top row," "pass at four," "path evidently was back." In the final excerpt, MW refers to *the commands used and their ordering as a group.* Note that only the commands ("Milk. Milk. Eggs. Eggs.") and not the house numbers are mentioned. In these four excerpts there is little overlap among the features that are considered as data from one excerpt to the next. During the course of his session, MW's conception of what counts as data (i.e., his *representation* of the data) changes radically. That is, in addition to changing hypotheses, MW changes what aspects of the data are worth encoding and how to characterize the phenomenon that is to be explained.

Because data representations are usually not distinguished from hypotheses (cf. Schunn and Klahr, 1996), we will first review the features of the hypothesis space, and then get to the data representation space. Recall that the hypothesis space involves propositions about the world, potentially at varying levels of abstraction and of varying levels of generality. For example, one might have the following hypotheses—varying in scope and abstraction—about the results of an experiment on reading comprehension: "there was no effect of manipulating motivation in this experiment (on comprehension of some history text)," "there is generally no effect of monetary reward on comprehension of history texts," or "there is generally no effect of motivation on reading skills." In our earlier discussion of hypothesis-space search we provided several examples of MilkTruck hypotheses at these different levels of scope and specificity.

By contrast, the data representation space involves the objects and object features of the data. For example, one might graph different relationships between different variables, one might use different kinds of graphs, and one might recode, collapse, or expand the same data. In the MilkTruck domain, objects include the jumps of the driver at the end of the route, the way in which the milk truck exits the garage at the beginning of the route, the path taken in the run window during the delivery route, the individual steps in the program and trace listings, groups of steps in program and trace listings, and the δ parameters. Each of these objects has multiple features. For example, the individual steps in the

Table 7.6
Excerpts from MW (Biomedical engineering sophomore).

Excerpt 1:

OK. I'm going to try this one more time. I'm going to beep a house one. Use the delta command. This time I'm going to do three times with the white triangle and alpha. And run.

Exp. 3
B1 δ3 △α
→
B1

That blew that hypothesis. I thought after the delta that, uh, these numbers related something to the person jumping and the number of times. I guess it didn't work. He jumped like six times with output three. Next one. I'm going to change a little bit. By using delta again. I'll do delta three again. I'm using the black triangle this time with alpha.

Excerpt 2:

Uh, well. Let's try commands going to different blocks. From one house one to house six. Delta. (BEEP) Whoops. Sorry. Um. Six. White triangle and alpha. It doesn't allow you to go back to commands does it? Hmm. Delta has to have something to do with the finishing of the route. Cause you can't put any more commands after you put in a delta.... But. Let's see what is going to happen.

Exp. 12 (11:42)
B1 M6 δ6 △α
→
B1 M6

It took the long route for some reason.... Hmm. Uh. I'm just going to write down something. Just what happened there. So it went to . . .
Keep talking.
I'm just writing down the path, and what the last, the delta value that I put in. See if there is any, uh. If I can get any differences in the path.

Excerpt 3:

Wait a second. Something different happened this time. Ahhh! For some reason, it did the commands in opposite. Let me test some-thing. Uh. I'm going to do the same commands, except I'm going to use the bottom row. Just to see what it does. Hopefully, if I use a num-ber up in the top row, it will reverse it....

Exp. 21 (21:47)
B4 M5 E6 δ2◣ β
→
B4 E6 M5

Ah, let's see. It should pass at four. Maybe not.... What. This is totally messed up now. Whoa. Wait a second.... I'm going to write down what it did for these last two programs. Do anything different. So the path evidently was back. This was delta five black beta. And the last one went to 4 to 6 and back to 5. And I have no idea why. Um....

Excerpt 4:

It seems if I put a value of n for delta that's less than the number of commands, it doesn't follow that grouping deliveries by home....

Exp. 40 (20:55)
B1 M2 E3 E2 M1
B3 δ6 △α
→
B1 B3 M1 M2 E3 E2

I won't worry about that. I'll just. I'll do something that I am sure of right now. And see what alpha does to the program. I'll come back to the numbers later.

. . . Milk. Milk. Eggs. Eggs. Well, that's real cool. White triangle and alpha groups deliveries by the commands. I mean by what the deliv-eries are. It just groups them together....

program and trace listings have the following features (all of which were spontaneously mentioned by at least some of the participants): house color, house number, house number parity (even/odd), top row houses versus bottom row houses, nth step (first, second, third, . . .), nth from the end, action, and action type (deliveries versus pickups).

The two spaces also differ in terms of their goals. The goal in searching the hypothesis space is to produce parsimonious explanations or descriptions of objects and relations in the world. By contrast, the goal in searching the data representation space is to find regularities. A data representation is abandoned if it does not lead to regularities or interpretable patterns, whereas it is maintained when it does. In other words, people search in the data representation space in order to find regularities, and search in the hypothesis space in order to explain them.

We coded participants' data representations by using their descriptions of experiments as they designed them and interpreted their outcomes. Thus, data representations could be revealed by experiment design statements (e.g., "Let's try commands going to different blocks"), outcome prediction statements (e.g., "See if there is any, uh. If I can get any differences in the path"), data description statements (e.g., "So the path evidently was back"), and hypothesis statements (e.g., "White triangle and alpha groups deliveries by the commands").[9]

For each experiment (design and outcome interpretation combined) we coded for the presence of seven objects and thirty total object features. Although at least one feature was typically coded with the presence of each object, this was not necessarily true—it is possible the participant did not specify any particular feature of an object. We did not code the frequency of mention of a given feature within each experiment; but rather simply its presence or absence—because the verbal protocols are not always complete, it was assumed that a finer level of analysis would be unreliable. Initial and final hypotheses were also coded but counted separately from the experiments.

How did the data representations typically change over the course of each participant's discovery process? At the gross level, there were shifts in the types of objects that the participants included in their data representations. Figure 7.6 presents the mean frequency of each object within each quartile of the task. Although there was no overall increase in the number of objects across quartiles, the main effect of object type and the interaction of object frequency by quartile were significant. Man jumps, garage exits, and delivery path were objects that appeared primarily in the beginning of the task—the participants quickly learned to exclude those features from their data representations.

Both program step and δ objects remained quite frequent throughout the task. The program steps and δ objects were the level at which the

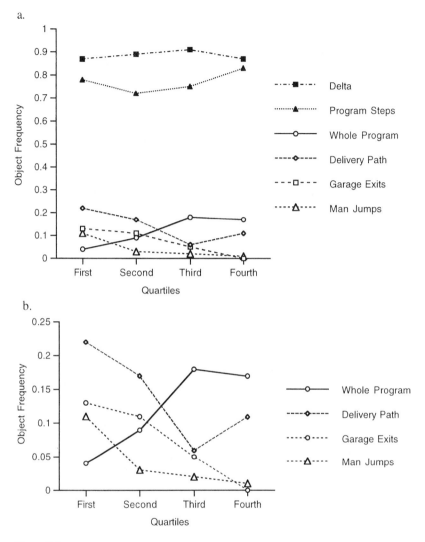

Figure 7.6
Mean frequency of data representation objects within each task quartile. (a) All objects.
(b) "Zoomed" display of 7.6a with delta and program steps not included.

programs were entered (i.e., one step at a time), and this aspect of the computer interface may explain the high frequency of use for steps and δ. Thus, if programs could have been entered in some other way (e.g., cutting and pasting larger program segments from previous programs) then the frequency of discussion of individual program steps might have changed over the course of the task. The reason for the constant, frequent presence of the δ object is obvious—it is the target of the discovery task.

The use of program segment and whole program objects increased steadily over the course of the task, with the largest increases occurring in the use of house number order, command order, and number of steps in a segment—these features corresponded to the actual function of the δ command. Thus, the gross level changes in data representations reflected the influence of the target function of δ—those features that were not relevant were weeded out, and those features that were relevant were gradually added. Moreover, although participants changed their focus from one set of objects to another, they usually had several objects and features in each experiment. The mean number of objects (2.7) and features (5.4) did not change over the course of the task, nor were they related to success.

At the micro-level, the changes in data representation from one experiment to the next were quite striking—for all of the participants, frequent change was the norm. More than 97 percent of transitions from one experiment to the next involved at least one data representation change and over 71 percent of experiments involved a change in which objects were included. Adding features, deleting features, and replacing features (i.e., adding and deleting) were all common activities (see table 7.7).

In sum, the search through the space of data representations in the MilkTruck task was a frequent activity. From one experiment to the next, the objects and object features used to describe the data changed more often than not. And, by definition, only by converging on the correct data representation could participants discover how the δ key worked.

Table 7.7
Mean frequency of each data representation change type from one experiment to the next for objects and object features.

Entity	Addition	Only Addition	Deletion	Only Deletion	Addition and Deletion
Objects	.45	.27	.44	.26	.18
Features	.81	.21	.76	.16	.60

The Effects of a More Complex Discovery Microworld

In this chapter we have addressed one overarching question: How do the discovery processes described in the preceding chapters change as the discovery task becomes more complex? The data from the MilkTruck task suggest that although some important new features of the discovery process are introduced, the earlier features remain. Most importantly, behavior in MilkTruck can be described using the constructs from dual space search: experiments constrain search in the hypothesis space, and hypotheses constrain search in the experiment space.

What features of the discovery process changed as the discovery task became more complex? First, we found evidence of several new experiment-space search heuristics that are useful in managing the increased complexity of the task. For example, the participants started with relatively simple experiments and gradually switched to more complex experiments, and they also made use of the PUSH heuristic.

Second, we found more complex kinds of hypotheses and patterns of hypothesis change. Hypotheses involved many components that could vary in generality along several dimensions. Moreover, hypotheses were found to be built up in a piecemeal fashion rather than from whole cloth.

Third, behavior in the MilkTruck task led us to propose the existence of a new space: the data representation space. We believe that this new space is not unique to the MilkTruck task. Whenever the discovery task is difficult and there are many features to which one could pay attention, we expect that people will explore the data representation space. As a common real-world example, scientists must frequently decide what dependent measures to gather in their studies or how to code and plot their data. These are examples of search in the data representation space. Yet, previous research on scientific reasoning did not propose a data representation space. Why is this? We believe that data representation change has frequently been assimilated into the hypothesis space. In other words, researchers have assumed that changes in descriptions of the data directly reflected changes in hypotheses. Also, in some very simple scientific reasoning tasks, it may have been that the important features were immediately identifiable.

The addition of such theoretical entities raises an important meta-theoretical question: will entirely new theoretical entities be needed to account for the much more complex discovery tasks found in real science? Moreover, the decision to add theoretical entities such as new spaces must be carefully justified (cf. Schunn and Klahr, 1996). Although our experience with increasing complexity in a small way suggests that new entities are likely to be needed, we expect that the features that we have described thus far will remain important in the more complex situations, just as the hypothesis space and experiment space used to describe behavior in the BigTrak task were useful in describing behavior in the MilkTruck task. In the next chapter, we will examine how these new theoretical entities might be included in the SDDS framework.

Notes

1. The MilkTruck task has been used to address a variety of questions about scientific discovery (e.g., Schunn and Klahr, 1992, 1993, 1995, 1996). In this chapter we describe only the first in our series of MilkTruck studies, and we focus on the basic impact of the more complex interface on discovery processes.
2. Note that this is unlike BT, where the numerical part of each command corresponded to the number of times that an action was executed (e.g., "Fire 5" led to the cannon's being fired five times). In BT, this tended to reinforce subjects' propensity to view the n associated with RPT as a counter rather than as a selector.
3. These numbers were derived from a detailed encoding of the verbal protocols from the first fifteen participants.
4. Crick's opening caveat to the contrary notwithstanding.
5. There are from one to fourteen program steps, six possible houses associated with each action, two values for the Greek letter, and two kinds of triangles.
6. However, there was a weak trend for solvers to have the smallest proportion of α experiments (the more difficult Greek letter) and nonsolvers the highest proportion (.61 versus .70).
7. Or, in a few cases in study 1, as a pair of programs: a "control" experiment without a δ followed by the same program *with* a δ.
8. The data regarding the hypothesis-space search is based on careful protocol analysis of the first ten participants. Data from one of the participants were removed because that participant typically did not verbalize his current hypothesis. Thus, the n for these analyses is 9.
9. These examples are all taken from the four excerpts shown in table 7.6.

Appendix 7.1
Protocol of a University Student (MA) Attempting to Discover the Function
of the δ Command in the MilkTruck Task

B = beep M = milk E = eggs $\$$ = money G = garbage
$(x{:}xx)$ = time since beginning of session

	δn: Re-order the last n steps according to:	
	$\triangle$ (increasing)	◣ (decreasing)
α (action)	. . . action in increasing keypad order: B, M, E, $, G	. . . action in decreasing keypad order: G, $, E, M, B
β (house)	. . . house in increasing number order: 1, 2, 3, 4, 5, 6	. . . house in decreasing number order: 6, 5, 4, 3, 2, 1

Do you have any initial hypotheses? Any guesses at what delta might be doing?
I have no idea.
Just a guess.
If I were to guess. Let's see. Um. If I were to guess. Probably go back and verify that, uh. Go back to each of the original, uh, the items on the command list. As a, I don't know, a verification that those things were done.
OK, that's fine. Go ahead. And keep talking.

Exp 1 (0:24) M1 M3 δ1 $\triangle$α ➔ M1 M3	Well, let's start out with this simple program. We'll deliver some milk to, uh, a couple of houses. Then, we use delta one. *White*[1] triangle, alpha. We'll see what this does. . . . Milk. . . . Milk to that one. . . . OK. It didn't seem to do anything, for the delta. . . .
Exp 2 (1:17) B1 M4 E1 δ1 $\triangle$α ➔ B1 M4 E1	OK. Let's try something with each one of these. Beep at there. Uh, let's put in another one on the other side. Milk. Some eggs. Back at one. Two at one. And the delta one *white* triangle alpha. . . . Milk. . . . It's back around to one for the eggs. And then he gets out and jumps up and down.
Exp 3 (2:18) $1 G3 $5 δ1 $\triangle$α ➔ $1 G3 $5	OK. . . . Let's try a different, a different combination of delta. Let's try it with money at one. Pick up some trash at three. Let's see if it does something if we, mumble, a little bit more money, delta. . . . . . . Money. . . . Empty containers, I guess. Yeah. Money. And he's done. Hmm.

Appendix 7.1 (continued)

Exp 4 (3:06) M2 B3 $\delta 2 \triangle \alpha$ → B3 M2	OK. Let's try a different form of delta. Let's go back with the original milk. And beep. Try delta two. *White* triangle alpha. . . . Hmm. Ok. That delayed two.
Exp 5 (4:03) M3 E5 \$1 $\delta 5 \triangle \alpha$ → M3 E5 \$1	Let's try something similar. Say, we'll send milk to three. Eggs five. Money one. Delta five, *white* triangle, alpha. Let's see if it delays this. . . . Hmm. One two three four. . . .
Exp 6 (5:15) E1 M3 \$5 $\delta 1 \triangle \beta$ → E1 M3 \$5	OK. Let's see if there is a correlation between these combinations with the triangles and the alpha and the beta and what it does at each one of these. *White* triangle alpha was the milk got delayed. So, let's see if, uh, eggs to one, milk to three. Money at five. Delta, and let's see, if eggs is like (beep), oops. Alpha beta. . . . . . . Well. Go to the eggs first. . . . OK. . . . So, it is not going to jump out and bite me.
Exp 7 (5:55) B1 M2 $\delta 1 \triangle \alpha$ → B1 M2	Let's go with two cases. Beep one. Milk two. Delta one. Let's get through this. . . . Hmm. . . . OK. . . .
Exp 8 (6:35) M1 M2 M3 M4 M5 M6 $\delta 2 \triangle \alpha$ → M1 M2 M3 M4 M5 M6	We'll try all the milks now, and see if they will go out of order with this in mumble. . . . OK. That had no effect on that.
Exp 9 (8:00) M1 M2 M3 E1 E2 E3 $\delta 1 \triangle \alpha$ → M1 M2 M3 E1 E2 E3	So, let's see if a different version of the. . . . Hmm. Send milk to, milk and eggs to the first three. Oh no. . . . Put in delta one. Try it and see if the milk and the eggs mumble on this. . . . Hmm. . . . Well. So far, only this milk and beep have been reversed by this. . . . I wonder if it is like a priority thing. . . .
Exp 10 (9:05) B1 M1 E1 \$1 G1 $\delta 1 \triangle \alpha$ → B1 M1 E1 \$1 G1	OK. Send one of each of these to the same house. . . . Let's see if the delta changes the priority in which they are done. . . . . . . Well, it beeped. It's doing the milk. It is probably doing the eggs now. Get the money. And the trash. . . . It didn't have that effect. . . .

Appendix 7.1 (continued)

Exp 11 (10:05) B2 M3 δ1 △α ➜ B2 M3	OK. Let's see if the thing I did is number dependent. Milk to three. Let's see if I do delta. This same combination will still reverse them, or is it some other. Something else. OK. The number definitely has something to do with which one is done first. Or delayed actually. . . .
Exp 12 (11:00) B1 M2 δ1 △β ➜ B1 M2	Hmm. . . . OK. Beep at one. Deliver milk at two. . . . See if changing that has any effect. . . . OK. It still didn't have any effect. . . .
Exp 13 (11:30) B1 M2 δ2 △β ➜ B1 M2	I'm going to try this delta with a beta now. . . . OK. It reversed it. . . . Beta did that. It didn't reverse like it did here. . . .
Exp 14 (12:30) M2 E3 δ2 △α ➜ M2 E3	OK. . . . Let's try milk to two. Eggs to three. Delta. . . . Delta. Let's see if it delivers the eggs first. . . . No, it doesn't deliver the eggs first. . . .
Exp 15 (13:25) M3 M1 δ1 △α ➜ M3 M1	OK. Let's try and do something with the black triangle. See if we can get different results. . . . Ya know. Maybe I want to that. Maybe I want to put these in, like, a different order, and try this. The milks in different order. . . . . . . OK. That didn't do anything. . . .
Exp 16 (13:55) M2 B1 δ2 △α ➜ B1 M2	Let's do milk at two. One. Now, this reversed when that beep was at three. Let's see if it has any effect this time. . . . Yes. It does. OK. . . .
Exp 17 (14:39) M2 B1 E3 δ2 △α ➜ M2 B1 E3	Well, let's add something to this. Milk to two. Beep at one. Deliver some eggs at three. . . . No. Milk to two. Beep at one. Eggs at three. Delta. . . . Now, let's see if this shifts it past the beep or past the eggs. . . . OK. It goes ahead and it delivers milk. Then it beeps. Drops off the eggs. That had no effect on it. None whatsoever.
Exp 18 (15:30) M2 B1 E3 δ3 △α ➜ B1 M2 E3	OK. Let's see if that number there represents the number of items. . . . . . . Beeps first. Delivers the milk. Then drops off the eggs. OK. This probably has to be the number of items.

Appendix 7.1 (continued)

Exp 19 (16:15) M2 E1 B3 $1 δ4 $\triangle$α → B3 M2 E1 $1	Well, let's test and see if that is right. Milk two, eggs one. Beep three, money for one again. Delta four. See if this reverses the first two commands. . . . OK. . . . OK. With this number is the number of items in the program. And. Then the delta. The white triangle alpha seems to put the horn first. . . .
Exp 20 (17:20) G2 $1 B3 δ3 $\triangle$α → B3 $1 G2	OK. (beep) Oops. Next program. Let's try putting the horn last, in three list, three items. . . . See if the horn is pushed to the front. . . . Horn is pushed to the front. OK. It goes from the horn back up. OK. Let's test that once. If it goes from the horn back up.
Exp 21 (18:10) E3 M2 $6 B5 δ4 $\triangle$α → B5 M2 E3 $6	If I put eggs at three, milk at two, money at six. Horn at five. Delta four white triangle alpha. It should go beep money milk eggs. Let's see if it does that. . . . Beep. Pick up the money now? No, it doesn't. . . . It goes and delivers the milk. Then it will probably drop off the eggs. Then the money. . . . OK. It does them ascending house number? Perhaps.
Exp 22 (19:07) $2 M3 E2 G4 B2 δ5 $\triangle$α → B2 M3 E2 $2 G4	Let's see. Money at two, milk at three. Eggs, at two. Trash at four, beep two. . . . It should beep at two. Drop off eggs at two. No. Milk at three. Eggs at two. The money at two. And deliver at four. Uh, that didn't help any. . . . *So, keep talking.* Yeah. I'm just baffled right now. OK, let's take a different tack. See if we can figure something out from a different angle.
Exp 23 (20:31) $3 M5 B5 δ3 $\blacktriangle$ α → $3 M5 B5	Let's go at it, looking at these other, this other triangle does. (beep). . . . OK. Try the black triangle now. And, . . . It didn't seem to have any effect on the order with this setup. . . .
Exp 24 (21:05) E2 $4 G3 δ3 $\blacktriangle$ β → $4 G3 E2	Let's try to see if it is related to some of these other items. See if it is related to. . . . No, we don't want to start out with that. Deliver some eggs. Pick up some money. Pick up some trash. . . . . . . Picks the money up first. . . . Picked up the trash. Then it delivered the eggs. OK.

Appendix 7.1 (continued)

Exp 25 (22:00) E2 $4 G3 δ3◣α ➔ G3 $4 E2	Let's see what the difference between that with alpha, with the beta and the alpha is. . . . So, we'll just change this last letter. And see if it affects it in any way. . . . It goes and picks up the trash first. . . . And it picks up the money. . . . Then it delivers the eggs.
Exp 26 (22:55) E2 $4 G3 δ3△α ➔ E2 $4 G3	OK. . . . Let's try the same combination with the other triangle again. I have a feeling that this might be what I need to be doing all along. The white triangle. We'll start with alpha. . . . The eggs first. Then the money. OK. . . . Let's see. The black triangle affected this trash. Yes. And the white triangle affected the horn. They don't seem to be affecting anything else. Except. . . . On the beta, it is picking it up second. And the alpha, it is doing it first.
Exp 27 (24:21) $1 M2 G3 E1 M2 δ5◣β ➔ G3 M2 M2 E1 $1	OK. On that premise. Let's give it this. Money first. Milk second. Trash third. Then it's back to one. Milk at two. . . . And, let's see. We want the trash picked up second. Let's see what order it does that in. . . . Of course it goes and picks up the trash first. Delivers the milk. Delivers the milk again. . . . Drops off the eggs. Picks up the cash. OK. . . . Hmm.
Exp 28 (25:24) $1 M2 G3 E1 M2 δ4◣β ➔ $1 G3 M2 M2 E1	If I change that number, if it does that differently? If it changes the, uh, milk pickup from the last one. If the delta is only four. . . . . . . Let's see what it does first here. It grabs the money first. . . . Then it picks up the trash. . . . Delivers the milk to two. Delivers the milk to two. Then it will deliver the eggs to one. OK. Obviously, it is the numbers back from the delta. So, that number is the number of commands it looks back from the delta. . . .
Exp 29 (27:00) $2 G3 δ2◣α ➔ G3 $2	OK. If we go with that, we get a next program. Let's give it two things. Let's give it money at two. Trash at three. Delta two. So it looks back two. Black triangle. Uh. . . . What am I looking for? I'm looking for . . . I want this alpha or beta. Um. Let's say alpha. . . . Let's try both. It should pick up the trash at three. Pick up the money at two.
Exp 30 (27:35) $2 G3 δ2◣β ➔ G3 $2	If I do this with beta it should do it in reverse. . . . It should go ahead and pick up the money first. And then pick up the trash. . . . Aha. Alpha and beta don't have anything to do what order they are done in. . . .

Appendix 7.1 (continued)

Exp 31 (28:05) M2 $3 G4 δ3◣ α → G4 $3 M2	Let's try throwing in something like milk here. Money here. Trash. Let's see what order it picks these two up after it picks up the trash.
	. . . Let's see. It will probably will pick up. . . . If it picks up the money, then it is going descending order. If it delivers the milk. . . . OK. This is descending order. And it is either descending order. Or descending order this way. With this one with the products, or this way with the house number. So, it's reversed those house numbers. . . .
Exp 32 (28:55) M3 $2 G4 δ3◣ α → G4 $2 M3	Money two. Trash four. . . .
	. . . Picks up the trash. That's good. Let's see if goes for the money or the milk. . . . It gets the money. OK. So, it is descending this way. . . . .
Exp 33 (29:40) M2 $3 G4 δ3◣ β → G4 $3 M2	OK. Let's test out beta with these two cases, and see what it does. Milk two. Money three, trash four. Star beta I think it is going to pick up the trash, deliver the milk, pick up the money. . . . That is what I think it is going to do. . . .
	But, it is not. It is going to pick up the money and then deliver the milk. OK. Could it be that beta is house dependent? . . . OK. Let's try. . . .

(30:20)

OK. Hang on. Time's up. So, what's your final guess?

My final guess? The delta function says look at the previous number of program steps. Um, then the triangle says, um, go do them in the following order: uh, either start with the, um, start with the trash with the black triangle, start with the beep in the white triangle. And then go in, the alpha and the beta, I haven't figured out which order, what it is related to. But, I think it is related to, um, go to the following places in, uh, descending, for the alpha it goes descending product order, trash can back down this way. And for beta it is descending house number, from six down to one.

(31:30)   END OF FIRST SESSION

BEGINNING OF SECOND SESSION

Before we get on to that, let me ask you some questions. So, did you do any thinking about yesterday's experiment?

A little bit.

Did you come up with any new ideas or any conclusions?

Well. I just thought about what had been the theory that I'd been thinking of. And I'm just going to test it out. Basically to see if it is right.

So what do you think about the programs that you chose before?

Appendix 7.1 (continued)

The programs that I chose. The first twenty or so were just random programs looking for a pattern of some sort. Seeing if it did anything actually. And the last I guess fourteen or twelve were actually working on little bits and pieces of what it did once I had an idea to work with.

How do you think you are going to do things today?

How am I going to do things today? Um, well, I thought of a few test cases. To test out two of the things. And then actually to test out all three. And I'm just going to try those. And if they work then I think my theory holds. And if they don't then I'll have to start over again.

(0:00)	*Hop to it, and keep talking.*
	I guess first of all, we'll test out this one theory about. . . . It won't let me select a number. How cute.
Exp 34 (0:45) M2 $3 B2 B6 δ3 △α ➜ M2 B2 B6 $3	OK. We'll try a couple of things stuck up here in front. We'll put a horn and another horn. Six. And then we'll say, uh, delta three, uh, white triangle alpha. And I think this should do both the horns first, the two and then the six.
	Aha. It doesn't. Oh wait. I set this on three, so it should do the milk first. Go down here and beep at six. And pick up the money.
Exp 35 () M2 $3 B2 B6 δ3 △β ➜ M2 B2 $3 B6	. . . Now. If I do this same thing again, and change it from an alpha to a beta. It will either do the same thing again, or it will reverse the horns. If it reverses the horns, then the alpha and beta refers to this program number on the horns. And if it doesn't then I will have to. . . .
	Aha. OK. Just beeped once. OK. Well. Maybe the alpha and the beta is just how many. . . . Alpha will do it for all the horns, and beta will just grab. . . . The horns? Uh, no, I doubt that.
Exp 36 (3:04) M2 $3 E3 B2 B6 δ4 △α ➜ M2 B2 B6 E3 $3	Let's try it with some other things thrown in there. Still put the milk in front. Put some cash again. Then we will put eggs at, uh, the same place. Then we'll go back, oops. Mumble the horns in. Money at three. Eggs at the same place. Horns at two. And a horn at six. Uh, go back four now. OK. This should do milk, the two horns, and I think it will do the eggs and then the cash. . . . If it does the eggs and then the cash then alpha just runs down this list, products. . . .
	Let's see. Eggs and then the cash. OK. So, alpha puts, four is the number of steps, and white triangle is horn to trash priority. And the alpha says, uh, you do that many.

Exp 37 (4:13) M2 $3 E3 B2 B6 δ4△β → M2 B2 E3 $3 B6	OK. Let's try it with beta now. Two. Cash at three. Eggs at three. Horn at two. Horn at six. Delta four white triangle beta. Um. This, I think, is a number priority. And it will do this two here. Horn two. Then these three. And then the six. And we shall see. Milk. It should beep. . . . And then go to three. And eggs, cash. . . . Then go to six and beep.
Exp 38 (5:25) M2 $3 E3 B6 B2 δ4△β → M2 B2 E3 $3 B6	Hmm. . . . Let's see if that's doing that by that order, or if it is just taking the first horn it finds. . . . I'm reversing the two and the six on the horns. . . . Eggs money horn six. And then horn two. . . . Go deliver the milk. . . . Beeps at two. Eggs, cash. Then it will go to six and beep. . . .
Exp 39 (6:35) M2 $2 E5 B3 B6 δ4△β → M2 $2 B3 E5 B6	OK. Let's reverse some of these numbers here. And see if it's, if you go to beta if it's the actual horn, or the number that is important. . . . Let's keep milk at two just to. . . . Uh, let's put cash at three, the eggs at two. One horn. . . . No, I want the eggs and the cash further apart. Put the cash at two. The eggs at five. The horn at three. And horn at six. . . . OK. If the beta still keeps the priority, then it will do this one horn at three first. Aha. It did the cash. Now, it will beep. Then the eggs. And then another beep. . . . Ah. . . . Beta is a number priority then. . . . OK. The alpha puts the priority on this order, I think.
Exp 40 (7:55) M2 $2 E5 B3 B6 δ4△α → M2 B3 B6 E5 $2	Let's see if alpha puts the priority on this order, or on the numbers in a different way. . . . Let's see. How do I want to test that? If I use the same setup with alpha, and I should expect, if it is a priority with the products, then it will beep here, and then beep here. And then do the eggs and the cash. . . . Two. Eggs at five. Horn at three. Horn at six. . . . . . . OK. Milk. Two. Beep at three. Beep at six. . . . Deliver eggs at five, and then pick up the cash. . . . OK. So, that is what the white triangle and the alpha and the beta do.
Exp 41 (9:15) M2 $2 E5 G3 G6 δ4▲α → M2 G3 G6 $2 E5	Let's see if it is similar for the black triangle, alpha and beta just to make sure. . . . Let's take a similar program. Cash at two. Eggs at five. We'll use trash, even though it really doesn't matter, 'cause I think it is just a priority going from trash back to horn. Delta, back four, black triangle, alpha. OK. This should pick up both the trashes, first at three then at six. Then it will pick up the money at two. And then deliver the eggs at five. . . . Pick up the money at two. And deliver the eggs at five. . . .

Appendix 7.1 (continued)

Exp 42 (10:23)	OK. Now, if we try this with beta. A constant milk, just as a
M2 $2 E5 G3 G6 δ4◣ β	. . . Five Trash three. Trash at six. . . . OK. What should
→	this do? Trash at six. Eggs at five. Trash at three. Money
M2 G6 E5 G3 $2	at two. That's what it should do. . . .
	House number two just needs a lot of milk. . . . OK. Pick up
	the trash at six. Go back and deliver the eggs to five. . . . Go
	around and pick up the trash at three. Pick up the money
	from two. OK. I've got it.

(11:10)

OK, give me an explanation.

OK. The delta is a priority function. Uh, the white triangle is . . . well, the number is the number of program steps you go back from the delta. Four meaning you take the four program steps before it. The white triangle is an ascending priority. Well, alpha, you start with horn, and then move to trash. Beta, you start with house one, and move to house six. Uh, the black triangle is descending program. If you start with alpha, it starts with trash and goes down to horn. If you use beta, it starts with house six and goes down to house one.

(12:10)

1. MA referred to the white triangle as the "left" triangle for the first several experiments. However, we have replaced all such references with "*white*" for ease of interpretation. Subsequent references in which MA actually said "white" are not italicized.

Appendix 7.2
Full Set of Programs and Their Execution Traces for Participant MA

Chapter 8
Discovery Discoveries

All progress is precarious, and the solution of one problem brings us face to face with another problem.
(Martin Luther King, Jr., 1963)

In this book, my colleagues and I have described our efforts to contribute to knowledge about the thinking processes involved in scientific discovery. Our approach is an elaboration and amplification of an idea first proposed more than thirty years ago (Simon, 1966): that the psychology of scientific discovery is neither impenetrable nor ineffable. We have attempted to demonstrate that an understanding of the discovery process can be advanced by applying the same types of analyses to scientific thinking as have been successfully applied to other kinds of "higher order" mental processes.

The problem we set for ourselves was how to answer three related questions: (1) What is scientific thinking? (2) How can it be studied? And (3) What is its developmental course? The work described in this book offers a partial solution to this problem, and in this chapter I review the various components of that solution. But in science, as in most other areas of human endeavor—as Martin Luther King asserts in the quotation above—with the solution of one problem comes another. Thus, this chapter concludes with a discussion of some of the new problems, new questions, and new issues that our work has raised.

The Discovery Process

We have characterized the scientific discovery processes in terms of a widely accepted view of problem solving: of constrained search in problem spaces (Newell and Simon, 1972). In the case of scientific discovery, this search takes place primarily—but not exclusively—in two spaces: a space of experiments and a space of hypotheses. This dual search process is complex, and the relations among its major components were elucidated in the presentation of the SDDS framework in chapter 2. The framework consists of three main components: (1) *Searching the hypothesis space.* The hypothesis space contains structured frames representing the important elements of hypotheses. Search in the space involves the initial generation of a partially specified frame, and then gradual refinement of all of its essential elements. (2) *Searching the experiment space.* The experiment space consists of a set of objects and operations related to, but rarely identical to, the elements of the hypothesis space. Here also, different search methods determine movement through the space. (3) *Evaluating evidence.* This process provides the primary coordination between search in the two spaces. As indicated by the SDDS framework depicted in figure 2.9, I have not unpacked the components of this process as fully as the other two, although it remains high on the agenda for further development of the model. Such an elaboration would be informed by the results of several of our earlier studies (to be reviewed later in this chapter) showing how participants respond to experimental results in deciding to accept, reject, or modify hypotheses or to continue to search in the discovery spaces.

This framework enables us to ask many questions about scientific discovery processes and their development. In this chapter I will indicate how our research has contributed partial answers to the following seven questions: (1) Are there characteristic strategies for approaching the discovery process, and for coordinating search in the two spaces? (2) How do these strategies change as a function of the types of prior information available to the problem solver? (3) What are the factors that influence the way in which evidence is acquired and processed? (4) What are the similarities and differences in the way these questions are answered for children and for adults? (5) To what extent do the results of the microworld studies presented in this book compliment and converge with other approaches to the study of scientific discovery? (6) What important additions to the dual search model are suggested by our own evidence and by other studies of discovery? (7) What are the practical implications of this work, especially with respect to early science education?

My answers to these questions will be organized as follows. First, I will review the studies described earlier and discuss the extent to which they support or challenge the SDDS framework. I will reexamine the distinction between experimenters and theorists, the seeking and using of evidence, and the management and coordination of dual search by children. In addition, I will address the issue of the number of problem spaces involved in the discovery process. Throughout this discussion I will suggest convergences between the approach to studying discovery taken in this volume and other complementary, but distinct, approaches to science. Finally, I will use the SDDS framework as a point of departure for dealing with two important developmental issues—one old and one new. The old issue is the "child-as-scientist" controversy that we have visited several times already. The new issue has to do with the extent to which a better understanding of children's scientific thinking might contribute to improving early science education.

Summary of Microworld Studies

As the discerning reader may have already realized, the first few chapters in this book represent an anachronistic account of our early explorations. The truth is that when we ran our first BigTrak study (reported in chapter 4), we had not yet formulated the SDDS model first presented in chapter 3. Instead, it was our analysis of participants' attempts to discover how the RPT key worked on the BigTrak device that led to our formulation of SDDS and to our characterization of the theorist versus experimenter strategies for managing the dual search.

That first study led to many others, eight of which have been described in this book. More than three hundred adults and children participated in those studies of the discovery process, and in the next few sections, I will summarize the main findings from this series of investigations (see table 8.1). The summary will proceed in the approximate order in which the studies were reported, but it will be organized around several issues that emerged as our research program evolved. The first issue addresses the idea of dual search. The second issue deals with how evidence is generated and interpreted. The third issue focuses on developmental differences that we have found in how children deal with our discovery tasks, and the fourth issue deals with our effort to increase the external validity of our paradigm by scaling up the complexity and hence the number of problem spaces involved in the discovery process.

Theorists and Experimenters

Our first study revealed two characteristic strategies for approaching discovery tasks, strategies that can be distinguished by whether they give primary emphasis to the space of hypotheses or the space of experiments during the discovery process. We found that some participants (theorists) used the hypothesis space to generate theories in the absence of much evidence, drawing instead on prior knowledge to evoke the main components of their hypothesis frame, which is subsequently refined by further experimentation. Others (experimenters) tended to "stick to the data" and generate most of their experiments not in the service of testing hypotheses, but instead with the goal of generating a

Table 8.1
Study summary.

	Goal	Context	Participants	Main findings
Chapter 4				
Study 1: Theorists and experimenters	Establish paradigm	BigTrak device	20 university students	Two main strategies for managing dual search: experimenters and theorists Non-normative evidence evaluation processes
Study 2: Forced search in the hypothesis space	Determine whether or not prior search of H-space impacts on dual search, and ultimate success.	BigTrak device	10 university students	Correct hypotheses can be generated without E-space search. Having generated several hypotheses at outset makes participants more willing to respond "correctly" to disconfirmation.
Chapter 5				
Study 3: Dual search by children	Extend paradigm for use with children	BigTrak dragon	22 3rd–6th grade children	Children fail mainly, but gerry-mander hypotheses, look for slot values that will keep frame alive
Study 4: Designing good experiments to test bad hypotheses	Developmental differences in experimental heuristics	BT computer microworld	54 3rd graders, 6th graders, community college students, university students	Engineering vs. scientist stance

Chapter 6

Study		Model	Participants	Findings
Study 5: Mystery Key I. Manipulating search in the two spaces	? vs. RPT less constraint on H-space	BT Mystery key	40 university students	Lack of constraint on hypotheses forced fast convergence with evidence
Study 6: Mystery Key II.	No region 3 experiments	BT RPT vs.	40 university students	Constrained evidence helps when prior knowledge is low
Constraining search in the experiment space	allowed	Mystery, E-space constraint		
Study 7: Dancer. Develomental differences in context effects	BT vs. Dancer	BT/Dancer	71 5th–12th grade girls	Motivational context effects only at start, not for deep structure
Study 8: FaceMover. Enriching background knowledge	Provide H or E or both, calibrate FaceMover with BT	BT/FaceMover	46 university students	Participants did not use provided experiments or hypotheses effectively. Perhaps confused by what they were supposed to do with them.

Chapter 7

Study		Model	Participants	Findings
Study 9: MilkTruck	Adults on more complex microworld	MilkTruck	22 university students	PUSH heuristics Additional spaces(s)

pattern of data from which hypotheses can be induced. The operational definition of these two strategies was based on the type of evidence available to participants at the time they proposed the correct theory of how the RPT key worked. Associated with this single defining property were several important correlated properties, such as the number of experiments run and the tendency to run experiments without explicit hypotheses.

Similar differences in preference between experiment-driven and theory-driven strategies have been noticed in other laboratory studies (Okada, 1994; Okada and Simon, 1995). Studies based on historical approaches can be interpreted in terms of the balance between hypothesis-space search and experiment-space search. For example, in most histories of Faraday's discovery of induction of electricity by magnets, much emphasis has been placed on the influence of Ampère's theory of magnetism on Faraday's thought, but a strong case can be made (Gooding, 1990) that Faraday's primary search strategy was to focus on experiment-space search, yielding a discovery path that was driven largely by phenomena rather than theory. (See Klahr and Simon, 1999, for further comparisons between laboratory and historical studies of the discovery process.)

In study 2 we induced participants to put additional effort into searching the hypothesis space before running any experiments. This led to much faster convergence on the correct hypothesis, but it still generated two types of strategies (experimenters and theorists). In this case, the distinction seemed to be related to prior knowledge because people lacking potentially relevant prior knowledge were more likely to be experimenters. However the main difference between study 1 and study 2 showed up in the *Evidence Evaluation* phase, and I turn to that next.

Evidence: Seeking It and Using It
Both study 1 and study 2 revealed two characteristic patterns of evidence generation and evaluation. With respect to generation, people tended to search the experiment space by following the "positive test strategy" discussed at length in chapter 4. That is, they reasoned, in effect, "my theory is that RPT does X. If I am right, and I write program Y, then BigTrak will do Z." As I noted earlier, this was a sensible approach, because even though participants were looking for confirming evidence, their hypotheses were frequently falsified. More generally, a positive test strategy may help scientists in two ways. First, it may enable them to avoid perseveration on incorrect frames by abandoning *Evoke Frame* altogether in favor of *Induce Frame*. Second, it may influence them to conduct different types of experiments for whatever hypotheses they do hold. Deepak Kulkarni and Herbert Simon (1988) have argued that

Hans Krebs's discovery of urea was prompted by an exploration of the experiment space. Thus, a positive test strategy may be a useful heuristic in the early stages of investigation, as it allows the participant to determine those types of instances that are worthy of further experimentation. In studies 1 and 2, we found that search of the experiment space was initially guided by a positive test strategy, but because so few regions of the experiment space were consistent with initial hypotheses, this strategy provided useful information as to which parts of the experiment space to search next.

With respect to evidence evaluation, participants showed substantial departures from the dictates of formal logic: confirmed hypotheses were often abandoned, and, more importantly, disconfirmed hypotheses were frequently maintained. This tendency could be attenuated if, as in study 2, participants were forced to spend more time at the outset generating alternative hypotheses. It is possible that a more extensive prior search of the hypothesis space increases the expected value of additional hypothesis-space search and, correspondingly, makes it easier to abandon the current (disconfirmed) hypothesis.

Nevertheless, the tendency to diminish the strictly "logical" implication of anomalous data is a fairly pervasive phenomenon in both the history of science and in laboratory studies of people's evidence interpretation proclivities. It appears that people are loath to replace something with nothing, even when the "something" is a hypothesis that is inconsistent with the most recent experimental outcome. As noted in chapter 4, Chinn and Brewer (1998) have documented a wide variety of people's responses to such anomalies, ranging from outright rejection of the data without justification to various levels of partial acceptance without substantial theory revision to, finally, acceptance of the anomalous data and its "inevitable" consequence: theory revision.

Developmental Differences in Scientific Discovery Processes
Elementary schoolchildren's approach to scientific discovery in terms of dual search was first investigated in study 3. Two questions motivated that study. First, could children do the task at all? Second, how would children's negotiation of the two spaces compare to adults'? Because only two out of twenty-two children discovered how the RPT key worked, it is tempting to conclude that children found the task much more difficult than did adults. However, more than half of them self-terminated their explorations confident that their incorrect theory was, in fact, the correct one. In addition, these children approached the task with an appropriate scientific bent. They were eager to find the "truth" about the RPT key, and they knew that they could discover it by running experiments and observing the results.

Incomplete Hypotheses   But we discovered several characteristic differences between the children in study 3 and the adults in studies 1 and 2. For one thing, children tended to generate incomplete hypotheses in which only some of the slot values in a frame were specified. Because these partially specified hypotheses (such as "it repeats something over again") were consistent with a wide variety of outcomes, it was easy for children to interpret experimental outcomes as consistent with their current hypotheses. This lack of specificity also made children less likely to design informative experiments, because the imprecision of their hypotheses imposed lower constraint on their search of the experiment space. Also, children appeared to be fairly myopic in comparing evidence to theory: if the current outcome (often from an experiment of low discriminating power) was consistent with their hypothesis, then they blithely ignored earlier evidence that was inconsistent with that hypothesis.

Positive Capture in Children and Adults   The behavior of grade-school children in this regard was reminiscent of other studies that examined preschoolers' ability to distinguish between patterns of determinate and indeterminate evidence. Fay and Klahr (1996) found that although young children can distinguish among highly salient patterns of determinate and indeterminate evidence, they are usually misled by an evidence pattern in which (1) one item is clearly a potential cause of a target outcome, (2) another visible item is clearly *not* a plausible cause, and (3) a third item, which might also be a cause, has not yet been examined. Preschoolers nearly always incorrectly judge this pattern to be determinate even though the lack of information about the unexamined alternative renders the situation logically indeterminate. Fay and Klahr used the term positive capture to describe children's tendency to respond incorrectly to this evidence pattern. Subsequent studies have shown that this *positive capture* effect is quite robust, even when the situations are grounded in everyday contexts, even with children as old as six or seven, and even when children are given substantial hints about the possibility of alternative evidence sources.

Are adult scientists vulnerable to positive capture? If presented with the simple situations devised by Fay and Klahr for preschoolers, it is unlikely that adults would be unable to distinguish determinate from indeterminate evidence. But what happens in more complicated situations when both the hypothesis space and the experiment space begin to increase in complexity and search in both becomes correspondingly more challenging?

We are usually very good at knowing when we know nothing. We recognize when we have no evidence to distinguish among possible interpretations or hypotheses. We are equally good at knowing when a particular piece of evidence is inconclusive with respect to two competing hypotheses. However, I believe that we often find ourselves captured by evidence that supports one or the other of two mutually exclusive hypotheses. Perhaps the source of the difficulty is that we believe the alternative hypotheses to be not only mutually exclusive, but also exhaustive, even though we know better. Newell (1973) offers a critical summary of the tendency of many scientific fields to fall prey to just such a premature decision that the evidence supports a particular hypothesis. In terms of our model, scientists in well-established research areas often find it difficult to search the space of hypotheses for the possibility that there are more than two ways that the current pattern of evidence could have been produced.

Plausibility and Prior Knowledge   Another potential source of developmental differences here is that children and adults are likely to differ in their prior knowledge about what "repeat" might mean in different contexts. Such a prior knowledge difference would affect the plausibility of different hypotheses, and this in turn could play an important role in the dual search. In order to directly investigate plausibility effects, we decided to directly contrast performance of children and adults as a function of the plausibility of the hypothesis governing the way that RPT really worked.

In study 4 we introduced BT, the first computer-based version of Big-Trak. The primary purpose of this move to a computer microworld was to control the RPT function in such a way that we could study the effect of plausibility on dual search. Recall that we provided all participants with a hypothesis that was always incorrect, but we varied the degree of incorrectness in terms of our characterization of the hypothesis space. For some conditions the true hypothesis was only slightly different from the suggested one (within-frame modifications could find the correct rule), whereas in others the true hypothesis was from a different frame than the provided hypothesis. This discrepancy was crossed with plausibility: counters were plausible and selectors were implausible. Thus, the design enabled us to observe the effects of hypothesis plausibility on search in the experiment space. One important question was whether people would generate characteristically different experiments when considering plausible or implausible hypotheses.

This design also enabled us to look at the effects of two types of theory change. Changing from one hypothesis to another *within* a frame—requiring only the change of a few slot values, but no change in the overall structure of the hypothesis—corresponds to *theory refinement*. In contrast, a change in frames requires a simultaneous change in more than one attribute, because the values of some attributes are linked to the values of others. Thus, changing from a hypothesis from one frame to an hypothesis from a *different* frame (e.g., from a counter to a selector) is much more difficult, and corresponds to *theory replacement*. This distinction between refinement and replacement has been identified by some as important both in the history of science and in the development of children's theories of specific physical domains (Carey, 1985). The design of study 4 enabled us to examine this experimentally. In addition to the Given-Actual hypothesis conditions, we also used four levels of age and scientific training of our participants: third graders, sixth graders, community college students, and university students (mainly technical majors). Thus, all of the issues listed above could be examined at different developmental levels.

We found characteristic differences in the way that children and adults searched the hypothesis space and the experiment space. When adults were given an implausible hypothesis (i.e., selectors), they searched the hypothesis space for a plausible alternative hypothesis (i.e., a counter) and then searched the experiment space for an experiment that could discriminate between the given implausible hypothesis and plausible hypothesis of their own creation. However, when children were given implausible hypotheses they effectively ignored them, replaced them with plausible counters, and then attempted to generate evidence consistent with them. When *any* such efforts were successful, they were accepted as sufficient, even if there was unexplained inconsistent evidence from earlier or subsequent experiments. Once again, this reflects the positive capture problem noted earlier. Another interpretation of this kind of response is that, in complex hypothesis testing situations, children may be more likely than adults to adopt an engineering stance, in which they could get the effect they wanted most of the time, rather than a science stance, in which they could formulate a rule that could explain all of the evidence (cf. Schauble, Klopfer, and Raghavan, 1991).

Manipulating Constraints in the Hypothesis Space and Experiment Space
Our own shift from the science to the engineering stance was evidenced in the next two studies, where we adopted a positive test strategy in attempting to demonstrate that we could predict the effects of either decreasing the constraints on search in the hypothesis space (study 5) or increasing the constraints on search in the experiment space (study 6). In study 5, when we replaced the RPT key with a key simply marked as "?" (mystery key condition), there was a substantial increase in the variety of hypotheses generated. However, participants appeared to realize that this was indeed a vast space, and most of them adopted the experi-

menter strategy, so that their search was rapidly constrained by experimental outcomes. In study 6 we crossed the reduced H-space constraint with an increased E-space constraint (by allowing only informative experiments). We found that the E-space constraint was particularly useful to participants in the mystery condition. This makes sense: when the size of the hypothesis space is increased, then the payoff from particularly informative experiments is correspondingly increased compared to a less constrained E-space search.

Motivational constraints are not an explicit part of our dual search model, but they clearly play a role in scientific discovery. As Feist and Gorman (1998) note, what little research there is on the motivation to do science suggests that "the most creative and eminent scientists are the most persistent, hard working, and driven," and that, moreover, these scientists "tend to be driven more by internal than external reward."(p. 35). Thus far, nearly all laboratory studies of the discovery process—including our own—have simply assumed that participants were motivated to do well on the tasks presented to them. In study 7 (Dancer), we introduced one small manipulation to increase our participants' motivation by designing a microworld that, on the face of it, might be more appealing to young girls. We found that when we compared the performance of girls in grades five through twelve, there were suggestions of increased interest in the Dancer microworld for the youngest group. However, it was only manifested during the initial training period. Once the discovery process began in earnest, both Dancer and BT children performed very much the same way. It is clear that much remains to be done to explore the way that different levels of motivation might affect the discovery process.

Enriching the Background of the Discovery Process
Although science proceeds in a context of a vast literature of existing experimental and theoretical results, the participants in our standard paradigm start out without the benefit of any such earlier work on the discovery problem facing them. This lack of anything corresponding to such a prior body of knowledge weakens the external validity of our approach. Thus, in study 8 we decided to create such a context by providing participants with either prior experiments, prior hypotheses, or both. We had expected that each type of additional information would improve performance, and that their combination would improve it even more. However, that is not what happened. The exact cause of this unexpected result remains to be explored. As I noted in chapter 6, the problem may lie in the justification we gave for presenting "suggested" hypotheses and experiments, so in future work we may provide a more convincing argument for why participants should seriously consider

the implications of such prior results. More generally, one potentially productive extension of our paradigm would be to find other ways in which to situate the discovery process such that our participants engage into a more extended and ongoing process of discovery.

The MilkTruck microworld described in study 9 provided just such a discovery context. The added complexity of the types of hypotheses that participants had to formulate provided an opportunity for us to observe several interesting extensions of our initial theoretical framework. We found a systematic increase in the complexity of experiments, and we found the use of a new heuristic (PUSH) for dealing with unresolved hypotheses. Finally, the data generated by participants' behavior with MilkTruck led us to propose an additional space: the data representation space. This leads us to an important theoretical issue: how to determine the number of spaces involved in scientific discovery. In the next section, I consider this problem.

How Many Spaces in Scientific Discovery?

For most of this book I have characterized discovery processes in terms of the dual space framework. The experiment space and the hypothesis space have served us well in interpreting the results from all of our Big-Trak-like microworlds. In addition, the two-space framework provides a useful way to categorize the many computational models of discovery that have been developed in recent years.[1] Although this categorization might provide a starting point for the integration of these different models into a very rich computational implementation of the dual search framework, I will not explore that possibility any further here. Instead, I want to address an issue that first arose in the context of the MilkTruck data analysis described in the previous chapter: how many spaces are necessary to describe the discovery process?

Adding a New Space: A Case Study
When we analyzed the behavior of MilkTruck participants, we encountered evidence that was difficult to interpret as either experiment-space search or hypothesis-space search. We found that substantial portions of participants' efforts were focused on the problem of what to notice and encode. This analysis—reported in detail in chapter 7—led us to propose an additional space, namely the data representation space. The most compelling behaviors were those in which participants made substantial changes in the features to which they attended and for which they formed representations. These representations included such things as the path of the truck, the movement of the animated driver at the end of the route, individual program steps, and entire program seg-

ments. We argued that this process involved more than just a selective encoding of a complex phenomenon, because even when some items have been encoded they must be assembled into an integrated representation, and the determination of an appropriate and effective representation itself involves search-based problem solving. In this case, the search is not in a space of hypotheses or of experiments, but rather in a space of data representations.

The sense in which we used "data representation" in chapter 7 focused on the participants' search for *which* elements of a phenomenon to encode and analyze. Equally important, and perhaps warranting a space of its own, is the problem of how to *organize* and *display* various external depictions of those data elements: for example, as a table, a graph, and of what type, and at what level of aggregation. There is no question that search for an effective representation can play a crucial role in the discovery process. Peter Cheng and Herbert Simon (1992) compare the relative difficulty of mathematical and diagrammatic representations in Galileo's research, and they conclude: "law induction, and scientific discovery more generally, requires the right representation for success." Finding the right representation is crucial, and finding it requires constrained search in a large space of possibilities.

Beyond Two Spaces
Although the dual space framework has an appealing simplicity and symmetry, the MilkTruck data challenged it and led to the postulation of a third space. This raises an obvious question: just how many spaces are necessary to fully account for the kinds of problem-solving search that go into scientific discovery? The issue of just what the "right" number of spaces is, and what the criteria should be for deciding this issue has generated a small literature focused on the problem. At first, the debate—in which my colleagues and I have played an active role—focused on whether the magic number was two (Klahr and Dunbar, 1988), three (Baker and Dunbar, 1996; Burns and Vollmeyer, 1997), four (Schunn and Klahr, 1995, 1996) or *n* (Wolf and Beskin, 1996). But I have come to the conclusion that there is no "right" number of spaces, because that is entirely dependent on the interaction between the problem solver and the discovery context. A problem that might require problem-space search for a novice might be quickly solved through recognition by an expert.

> Before any search process can be applied, its relevance must be recognized by the detection of appropriate patterns in the situation. Observation of such patterns evokes information about the situation that can help guide the search. As this information usually is

domain specific, the recognition mechanism tends to make it available just where it is potentially relevant. . . .

Although scientific problems are much less well-defined than the puzzles commonly studied in the psychology laboratory, they can be characterized in these terms. In both cases, well-definedness and recognition depend not only on the problem, but also on the knowledge that is available to the problem-solver. For that reason, much of the training of scientists is aimed at increasing the degree of well-definedness of problems in their domain. (Klahr and Simon, 1999, p. 532)

A well-worked scientific domain might, in the face of a new theory, require search in a new space, as described in Thagard's (1998) analysis of the discovery of the bacterial origins of stomach ulcers in which he identified search in at least three major spaces: hypothesis space, experiment space, and a space of instrumentation. More important than the number of spaces is the creation of a set of criteria for justifying the theoretical expansion of spaces. In the next section I will provide an informal example of the conditions under which a new space arises and then, in the following section, I will propose some criteria.

Inducing Search in a New Space: An Example   Consider participants trying to solve simple letter series completion tasks (cf., Simon and Kotovsky, 1963), such as ABMCDM__. Participants will initially select a representation that involves relations on the English alphabet, and they will seek patterns of sames, differents, nexts, double nexts, priors, and so on. In this case, the representation is immediately evoked by the stimulus. Any of several possible measures would likely converge on some sort of associative mechanism, rather than a search process, for evoking the correct representation.

Now consider what happens when participants get a trick problem, such as OTTFFSS_. Here too, they start with the obvious representation in which the letters are simply the letters of the English alphabet. But this representation leads participants to formulate increasingly complex and ad hoc explanations for the O at the beginning of the series. Ultimately, participants using this straightforward representation hit an impasse. Then they start to consider whether the letters stand for something else.

At this point, we argue, they are searching a data representation space. That is, they must consider other ways to characterize the features of the list. In the present instance, they might reason that because the earlier lists are based on the alphabet, and the alphabet is a (and the most) familiar ordered list of symbols, then there might be other ordered lists that are relevant: days of the week, names of the kings of England, presidents of the United States, number names, months, and so forth. Perhaps the letters in the sequence are related to some feature of these other lists (in this case the first letter of the English names of the integers).

Criteria for Proposing Additional Spaces   How does one decide whether to add a new problem space? Schunn and Klahr (1995) proposed three criteria that could be used in making the distinction: logical, empirical and implementational. I will describe each of them briefly.

1. *Logical criteria* ensure that different spaces are mutually exclusive. Both the goals used for searching the space and the entities that are searched should distinguish one space from another. For example, one goal of the MilkTruck data representation space— the identification of meaningful features—does not appear in the hypothesis or experiment spaces for MilkTruck.

2. *Empirical criteria* ensure that search in different spaces involves different search heuristics and is influenced by different factors. Most importantly, there should be activity in each search space. For example, if a MilkTruck participant focused entirely on the truck's path throughout, then consideration of the data representation space would not be a useful characterization of that participant's behavior. This failure to search in a different space might occur in two ways. First, the participant could know so little about a domain that only one state in that space is available to that participant. Second, participants might be so knowledgeable about a domain that they are able to pick a good state immediately and need not search any further. More generally, whether or not there is search in a particular problem space depends, in part, on the problem solver's knowledge. Suppose, for example, that I asked a successful MilkTruck participant to try a second pass through the MilkTruck discovery process, but this time to discover how δ worked after I had made some minor changes in how it functioned. It would make little sense to search the data representation space at the outset. Instead, the participant would start at that point in the space that had led to success on the first session and remain there throughout the discovery process.

3. *Implementational criteria* provide a strong constraint on the proliferation of additional spaces. As one attempts to create a computational model of a discovery, it becomes necessary to create completely unambiguous characterizations of different problem spaces: their goals, operators, and elements. One must also distinguish search in a particular space from coordination among multiple spaces. The creation of computational representations and

processes provides a clear test of the extent to which a possible new space is substantially different from those already adequate to explaining behavior in the domain.

Scientific practice takes place in a wide variety of possible spaces: spaces of hypotheses, experiments, instrumentation, representations, experimental paradigms, publication practices, and so on. These spaces are "possible" rather than certain, because for experienced scientists—as for experts in any domain—problem-solving search only occurs as a last resort, when strong methods, based on recognition, do not yield solutions.

> If we press to the boundaries of creativity, the main difference we see from more mundane examples of problem solving is that the problems become less well structured, recognition becomes less powerful in evoking pre-learned solutions or powerful domain-specific search heuristics, and more, not less, reliance has to be placed on weak methods. The more creative the problem solving, the more primitive the tools. Perhaps this is why childlike characteristics, such as the propensity to wonder, are so often attributed to creative scientists and artists. (Klahr and Simon, 1999, p. 540)

Beyond the Child as Scientist

At several points in this book I have discussed the child-as-scientist issue and presented some of the contradictory claims and evidence surrounding it. Now it is time to consider how the theoretical and empirical contributions in this book bear on the issue.

First, a bit of background. The origins of this child-as-scientist issue, at least as they appear in the psychological literature, can be traced to Jean Piaget's pioneering investigations. In studying what he called "genetic epistemology," he documented the emergence of children's exploration and understanding of such fundamental scientific entities as space, time, quantity, number, life, and probability. Some researchers, noting the striking similarities between the fundamental goals of science and Piaget's analysis of children's efforts to understand the world about them, have concluded that children's thinking in this vein bears many of the hallmarks of scientific thinking. Others, also influenced by Piaget, but more by his stage theory than by his focus on children's emerging knowledge of the world, have concluded that the early stages of cognitive development, as characterized by Piaget, make it impossible for children to think scientifically.

This issue will, I believe, remain unresolvable until it becomes better formulated. When stated at the level of broad characteristics, arguments for or against the child as scientist make about as much sense as arguments for the child as farmer, or lawyer or artist. In essence, the argument is an analogy from a base (scientific thinking) to a target (children's thinking). The problem lies in the total lack of precision of the base of the analogy. Absent a clear specification of just what scientific thinking is, it is impossible to decide the extent to which children do or do not exhibit the "essential" properties of that type of thought. Typically, those engaging in the argument define a particular aspect of science that they deem one of its essences, and then seek to prove or disprove children's ability to exhibit those processes or representations. But such essences are usually (1) described in very coarse grain and (2) only part of the full repertoire of processes involved in the discovery cycle of hypothesis formation and experimentation.

I believe that in order to make a sensible evaluation of the child-as-scientist issue we need both a detailed specification of what scientific thinking is, and equally detailed and well-specified operationalization of the various components of that model. Only then will we be able to chart the developmental course of each of these components as well as their integration into the overall scientific discovery process. That is what my colleagues and I have begun to do in this book, and that is what I hope our work will inspire others to continue.

It is clear that, by third grade at least, children exhibit the global properties of scientific thinking depicted at the higher levels of the SDDS framework: they formulate hypotheses, they design experiments, and they interpret evidence. More importantly, they know that one way to evaluate hypotheses is to gather evidence.[2] For some, that might suffice as evidence supporting the positive view of the child as scientist. However, as soon as one unpacks each of these global processes into their components, as we have begun to do with the SDDS framework and the many studies based on it, then a much more complex, conservative, and particularized characterization of children's ability to think scientifically emerges. The details of this view were presented at the end of chapter 5, where we noted that there were characteristic differences in how children and adults searched both the hypothesis space and the experiment space. Our findings are consistent with a more generally stated summary based on a broad review of children's scientific reasoning abilities (DeLoache, Miller, and Pierroutsakos, 1998):

> Drawing evidence-based conclusions about causal relationships is the essence of scientific reasoning. For both children and adults, Popperian hypothetical-deductive scientific reasoning is a difficult activity, often simplified through heuristic processes (such as focusing on positive evidence) that can lead to erroneous

conclusions. From an early age, children show at least a rudimentary ability to distinguish between theory and evidence and they organize their understanding of the world into models that bear important resemblances to scientific theories. . . . Their ability to systematically organize experiments that will verify their beliefs is quite limited, however, and children are more likely than adults to improperly interpret the results of such experiments (pp. 840–841).

Our work, as well as the broader literature on the development of scientific reasoning skills, suggests that in order for children's discovery skills to approach those of adults' several constraints must be met: (1) hypotheses must be easily accessible or few in number, (2) the experimental alternatives must also be few in number, and (3) the domain must provide feedback relevant to discriminating among plausible hypotheses. Moreover, the SDDS framework enables us to reevaluate other empirical studies of the child-as-scientist issue in terms of the demands they place on various components of dual search. Consider, for example, studies by Koslowski (1996) and by Amsel and Brock (1996) indicating that children's evaluation of covariation evidence is heavily influenced by their ability to generate plausible causal mechanisms that could have produced that evidence. Their results clearly indicate that during the evidence evaluation phase, children do not limit their evaluation to the data at hand, but further constrain their search for hypotheses according to the availability of plausible mechanisms that could have produced those data. We can also use the framework to interpret Sodian, Zaitchik, and Carey's (1991) investigation of first and second graders' ability to choose a discriminating experiment. Recall that they found that children can correctly choose the right experiment from an experiment space consisting of only two elements in order to test a hypothesis from a hypothesis space also consisting of only two elements. This is an important milestone in the development of scientific thinking, but it is hardly sufficient to claim full-blown "scientific thought" in the young child.

Implications for Instruction

A full specification of the detailed developmental trajectory of children's scientific reasoning skills is of more than academic interest. Such a specification could inform the crafting of goals, materials and procedures for science instruction, especially in the elementary school years. As in the case of the child-as-scientist issue, Piaget's legacy is influential. At present, the most common theoretical conceptualizations underlying proposals for science instruction are based primarily on his theory, which is still widely taught in schools of education. Even today, this influence leads to strong claims about adapting the instruction to the Piagetian norms. For example, in a recent book summarizing the history of ideas in science education, George DeBoer (1991) writes:

> Piaget's stages of mental development are closely related to the skills that are needed to think scientifically. The ability to control variables, to consider all possible combinations of events, to think correlationally, to reason probabilistically, and to generate hypotheses are all mental abilities that Piaget places in the formal operational category. The development of formal operational thought is not believed by Piagetian researchers to begin until early to mid-adolescence and for some, at least is not fully developed until late adolescence, if at all. . . . Should fifth-grade students be expected to generate hypotheses or to conduct studies in which variables need to be controlled? What about seventh-graders? . . . If fifth-graders cannot control variables and seem to lack the ability to understand the concept of experimental control, then the teacher can find an explanation for that failure in the work of developmental researchers (pp. 232–233).

This point of view—characteristic of much of the Piagetian thinking in educational circles—is fraught with problems. For one thing, Piaget provided no such guidelines for educational practice, a point made forcefully more than two decades ago by Guy Groen (1978):

> Most "applications" of Piaget's theory to education have been naïve applications of stage theory more or less in isolation. It will be seen that stage theory, when taken out of its proper context, is a very weak theory indeed. It cannot be applied without major embellishments, which are apt to be highly idiosyncratic and frequently lead to practices that are actually inconsistent with Piaget's own theory! From this stems much of the confusion about Piaget (p. 46).
>
> In the meantime, it might lessen the current state of confusion if developers of educational products were more willing to acknowledge that they were filling the gaps with their own ideas, and refrain from the currently fashionable practice of attributing them to Piaget (p. 53).

Even more problematic is the fact that the last twenty years of research on cognitive development provide little support for the Piagetian notion of broad domain-independent stages and a single developmental trajectory through them. Much of the recent research has focused, instead, on highly particularized cognitive processes relevant for specific aspects of scientific thinking, on children's use of multiple strategies at any point in development, and in the highly variable use of such strategies (Siegler, 1996).

For example, the Sodian, Zaitchik, and Carey (1991) study mentioned earlier provides a clear example of first graders' ability to coordinate theory and evidence when given sufficient constraints on search in both the experiment space and the hypothesis space. This performance goes well beyond what Piagetian stage theory would predict, and yet, as I noted earlier in this chapter, it hardly qualifies as evidence to support the child-as-scientist notion. This work does, however, provide a concrete benchmark for those interested in advancing children's understanding of science. This specific capacity revealed by Sodian, Zaitchik, and Carey could be used as the basis for teaching both domain knowledge (e.g., some knowledge about mechanics or plant growth) and process skills (how to choose an effective experimental test in a limited context). The instructional implication would be to carefully limit the number of alternative hypotheses and alternative experiments in engaging young children in their earliest scientific investigations.

Similarly, young children's understanding of the difference between determinate and indeterminate evidence is the foundation upon which the idea of unconfounded experimental design rests, so it is important to determine the age at which children have the capacity to reason about such evidence. As Fay and Klahr (1996) demonstrated, the answer depends on the particulars of the pattern of evidence. When evidence is clearly and overwhelmingly determinate or indeterminate, preschoolers have no trouble recognizing it as such, but when presented with positive capture problems, they do very poorly. The point here is not to explore the nuances of that particular pattern, but rather to demonstrate that even with respect to a seemingly simple question about whether preschoolers can distinguish determinate from indeterminate evidence, the answer depends on the details, and those details can be used to guide instructional practice.

Rather than approach science education from a theoretical position that views science instruction through the lens of a theory proposing a series of overarching developmental stages, each with characteristic limitations, it might be more productive to use a different kind of theoretical framework, one that elucidates the major components of what we see as the goal of scientific thinking—a set of cognitive objectives (Greeno, 1976). Once such a set has been formulated, we can then propose a sequence of instructional practices to reach that goal. We have already done this in highly circumscribed domains, such as teaching children how to debug computer programs (Klahr and Carver, 1988), and I believe that the framework described in this book provides a set of targets for the much more ambitious goal of teaching children how to think scientifically. There are many steps to such a program, each one requiring an extensive series of elaborations of each of the SDDS components. However, our success in one small corner of this framework provides grounds for optimism about the feasibility of the approach.

For example, one of the most common objectives in elementary science instruction is to teach children what is called the "control of variables strategy"—a procedure in which children learn how to set up experimental contrasts such that only one thing is varied at a time, while all other relevant factors are held constant. Although this procedure—and the understanding of why it leads to determinate rather than indeterminate outcomes—is a central instructional goal, it is typically taught in the context of a lot of domain knowledge rather than as a domain-general method. Thus, when children err in designing or interpreting their experiments, they are easily confused because they are unable to distinguish between their lack of domain knowledge (e.g., plants grow better in warm than in cold temperatures) and a flaw in their experimental designs (e.g., they put one plant in the sun and the other in the dark). The confusion in this example is that children might have failed to search the hypothesis space adequately—not thinking about the possibility that dark rooms are cooler than sunny ones—or failed to constrain their experiment-space search to unconfounded comparisons between dark and light rooms having the same temperature. Chen and Klahr (1999) were able to devise a very brief but direct instructional intervention that gave children this powerful constraint on experiment-space search, and they demonstrated that, by 4th grade at least, children could transfer the skill to remote domains and contexts over a long period of time.

Conclusion

The primary aim of this volume has been to contribute to both the hypothesis space and the experiment space associated with the psychological study of the scientific discovery process. With respect to the hypothesis space, we have proposed a model of scientific thinking as a type of search in multiple, interacting, problem spaces. With respect to the experiment space, we have developed a paradigm that uses discovery microworlds to evoke scientific thinking in our participants. And throughout we have explored the developmental aspects of this multiple search.

The approach taken here is but one of several ways to study science. Others include historical and sociological analyses; computational modeling; and on-site, real-time observations of science as it is being conducted. As described in chapter 1, each of these approaches has its own strengths and limitations, and a complete account of the discovery process will include findings from all of them. Fortunately, the strengths of one approach tend to offset the weaknesses of another, and some important convergent findings are emerging from the full set (Klahr and Simon, 1999). In this volume I have tried to demonstrate the strengths and contributions of the discovery microworld approach.

This book will have achieved its aims if it convinces the reader that, rather than being an impenetrable mystery, the psychology of scientific discovery can be studied by using the same methods that apply to the study of any other natural or behavioral phenomena. It will have been even more successful if the particular findings reported here are taken as acceptable explanations for certain behaviors associated with the discovery process and if the methods used here are extended to explore further the many remaining questions. For example, one aspect of scientific practice that I have not dealt with at all in this book is collaboration. Obviously, this is an important factor in scientific discovery, as well as many other forms of problem solving, and it has generated an extensive literature in cognitive and developmental psychology (e.g., Azmitia, 1988; Castellan, 1993; Resnick, Levine, and Teasley, 1991). The microworld studies described in this volume have proven to be easily extended to investigations of collaborative discovery (e.g., Teasley, 1995; Okada and Simon, 1997). Given the important role of collaboration in science, I hope that others interested in the problems addressed here will join my colleagues and me in an extended collaboration as we continue to search for ways to advance our knowledge of the discovery process.

Notes

1. Some computational models focus mainly on search in the hypothesis space: for example, the BACON models and variants (Langley et al., 1987), IDS (Nordhausen and Langley, 1993), PHINEAS (Falkenhainer, 1990), COPER (Kokar, 1986), MECHEM (Valdés-Pérez, 1994), HYPGENE (Karp, 1990, 1993), AbE (O'Rorke, Morris, and Schulenburg, 1990), OCCAM (Pizzani, 1990), and ECHO (Thagard, 1988). Other models focus mainly on the process of experiment generation and evaluation: for example, DEED (Rajamoney, 1993) and DIDO (Scott and Markovitch, 1993). A few deal with both processes: for example, KEKADA (Kulkarni and Simon, 1988), STERN (Cheng, 1990), HDD (Reimann, 1990), IE (Shrager, 1985), and LIVE (Shen, 1993).

2. Indeed, some studies (Sloutsky, Rader, and Morris, 1998) demonstrate that children prefer to seek evidence even when it is unnecessary, such as when they are asked to evaluate the truth or falsity of tautologies or contradictions.

References

Amsel, E., and S. Brock. (1996). The development of evidence evaluation skills. *Cognitive Development* 11: 523–550.

Azmitia, M. (1988). Peer interaction and problem solving: when are two heads better than one? *Child Development* 59: 87–96.

Baker, L. M., and K. Dunbar. (1996). Problem spaces in real-world science: what are they and how do scientists search them? In G. W. Cottrell, ed., *Proceedings of the Eighteenth Annual Conference of the Cognitive Science Society*, pp. 21–22. Mahwah, N.J.: Erlbaum.

Bartlett, Frederic C. (1958). *Thinking: An Experimental and Social Study.* New York: Basic Books.

Bazerman, C. (1988). *Shaping Written Knowledge: The Genre and Activity of the Experimental Article in Science.* Madison: University of Wisconsin Press.

Bijker, W. E., T. P. Hughes, and T. Pinch. (1987). *The Social Construction of Technological Systems: New Directions in the Sociology and History of Technology.* Cambridge, Mass.: MIT Press.

Bloor, D. (1981). *Knowledge and Social Imagery.* London: Routledge and Kegan Paul.

Boden, M. A. (1990). *The Creative Mind: Myths and Mechanisms.* London: Basic Books.

Boden, M. A. (1994). Précis of the creative mind: myths and mechanisms. *Behavioral and Brain Sciences* 17: 519–570.

Bower, G. H., and T. R. Trabasso. (1964). Concept identification. In R. C. Atkinson, ed., *Studies in Mathematical Psychology*, pp. 32–94. Stanford, Calif.: Stanford University Press.

Brewer, W. F., and C. A. Chinn. (1994). The theory-ladeness of data: an experimental demonstration. In A. Ram and K. Eiselt, eds., *Proceedings of the Sixteenth Annual Conference of the Cognitive Science Society*, pp. 61–65. Hillsdale, N.J.: Erlbaum.

Brewer, W. F., and A. Samarapungavan. (1991). Child theories versus scientific theories: differences in reasoning or differences in knowledge? In R. R. Hoffman and D. S. Palermo, eds., *Cognition and the Symbolic Processes: Applied and Ecological Perspectives*, pp. 209–232. Hillsdale, N.J.: Erlbaum.

Brown, A. L., J. D. Bransford, R. A. Ferrara, and J. C. Campione. (1983). Learning, remembering, and understanding. In P. H. Mussen, ed., *Handbook of Child Psychology: Cognitive Development* (4th ed.) Vol. 3, pp. 77–166. New York: Wiley.

Bruner, J. S., J. J. Goodnow, and G. A. Austin. (1956). *A Study of Thinking.* New York: NY Science Editions.

Bullock, M., A. Ziegler, and S. Martin. (1993). Scientific thinking. In F. E. Weinert and W. Schneider, eds., *LOGIC Report 9: Assessment Procedures and Results of Wave 6*, pp. 66–110. Munich: Max Plank Institute for Psychological Research.

Bullock, M., and A. Ziegler. (1999). Scientific reasoning: developmental and individual differences. In F. E. Weinert and W. Schneider, eds., *Individual Development from 3 to 12:*

Findings from the Munich Longitudinal Study, pp. 38–54. New York: Cambridge University Press.

Burns, B. D., and R. Vollmeyer. (1997). A three-space theory of problem solving. In M. G. Shafto and P. Langley, eds., *Proceedings of the Nineteenth Annual Meeting of the Cognitive Science Society*, p. 879. Mahwah, N.J.: Erlbaum.

Callahan, J. D., and S. W. Sorensen. (1992). Using TETRAD II as an automated exploratory tool. *Social Science Computer Review* 10(3): 329–336.

Carey, S. (1985). *Conceptual Change in Childhood*. Cambridge, Mass.: Bradford Books/MIT Press.

Case, R. (1974). Structures and strictures: some functional limitations on the course of cognitive growth. *Cognitive Psychology* 6: 544–573.

Castellan, J. J., ed. (1993). *Current Issues in Individual and Group Decision Making*. Hillsdale, N.J.: Erlbaum.

Chase, W. G., and H. A. Simon. (1973). The mind's eye in chess. In W. G. Chase, ed., *Visual Information Processing*, pp. 215–281. New York: Academic Press.

Chen, Z., and D. Klahr. (1999). All other things being equal: children's acquisition of the control of variables strategy. *Child Development* 70(5): 1098–1120.

Cheng, P. C.-H. (1990). *Modeling Scientific Discovery*. Ph.D. dissertation, The Open University.

Cheng, P. C.-H., and H. A. Simon. (1992). The right representation for discovery: finding the conservation of momentum. In D. Sleeman and P. Edwards, eds., *Machine Learning: Proceedings of the Ninth International Conference* (ML92), pp. 62–77. San Mateo, CA: Morgan Kaufmann.

Chinn, C. A., and W. F. Brewer. (1992). Psychological responses to anomalous data. In J. K. Kruschke, ed., *Proceedings of the Fourteenth Annual Conference of the Cognitive Science Society*, pp. 165–170. Hillsdale, N.J.: Erlbaum.

Chinn, C. A., and W. F. Brewer. (1998). An empirical test of a taxonomy of responses to anomalous data in science. *Journal of Research in Science Teaching* 35(6): 623–654.

Crick, F. (1988). *What Mad Pursuit: A Personal View of Scientific Discovery*. New York: Basic Books.

Darden, L. (1992). Strategies for anomaly resolution. In R. N. Giere, ed., *Cognitive Models of Science*, pp. 251–273. Minneapolis: University of Minnesota Press.

Darden, L. (1997). Recent work in computational scientific discovery. In M. G. Shafto and P. Langley, eds., *Proceedings of the Nineteenth Annual Meeting of the Cognitive Science Society*, pp. 161–166. Mahwah, N.J.: Erlbaum.

DeBoer, G. E. (1991). *A History of Ideas in Science Education: Implications for Practice*. New York: Teachers College Press.

DeLoache, J. S., K. F. Miller, and S. L. Pierroutsakos. (1998). Reasoning and problem solving. In D. Kuhn and R. S. Siegler, eds., *Handbook of Child Psychology* (5th ed.), Vol. 2, *Cognition, Perception, and Language*, pp. 801–850. New York: Wiley.

Dunbar, K. (1993). Concept discovery in a scientific domain. *Cognitive Science* 17: 397–434.

Dunbar, K. (1995). How scientists really reason: scientific reasoning in real-world laboratories. In R. J. Sternberg and J. Davidson, eds., *The Nature of Insight*, pp. 365–395. Cambridge, Mass.: MIT Press.

Dunbar, K. (1997). How scientists think: on-line creativity and conceptual change in science. In T. Ward, S. Smith, and S. Vaid, eds., *Conceptual Structures and Processes: Emergence, Discovery, and Change*, pp. 461–492. Washington, D.C.: APA Press.

Dunbar, K., and L. A. Baker. (1994). Goals, analogy, and the social constraints of scientific discovery. *Behavioral and Brain Sciences* 17: 538–539.

Dunbar, K., and D. Klahr. (1989). Developmental differences in scientific discovery strategies. In D. Klahr and K. Kotovsky, eds., *Complete Information Processing: The Impact of Herbert A. Simon*. Hillsdale, N.J.: Erlbaum.

Dunbar, K., and C. D. Schunn. (1990). The temporal nature of scientific discovery: the roles of priming and analogy. In M. Piattelli-Palmarini, ed., *Proceedings of the Twelfth Annual Conference of the Cognitive Science Society*, pp. 93–100. Hillsdale, N.J.: Erlbaum.

Duncan, S. C., and R. D. Tweney. (1997). The problem-behavior map as cognitive-historical analysis: the example of Michael Faraday. In M. G. Shafto and P. Langley, eds., *Proceedings of the Nineteenth Annual Conference of the Cognitive Science Society*, p. 901. Hillsdale, N.J.: Erlbaum.

Dunker, K. (1945). On problem solving. *Psychological Monographs* 58(5): 270.

Einhorn, H. J., and R. M. Hogarth. (1986). Judging probable cause. *Psychological Bulletin* 99: 3–19.

Einstein, A. (1936). Physics and reality. Reprinted in A. Einstein (1950), *Out of My Later Years*. New York: Philosophical Library.

Elder, J. (1990). Hands on. *Education Life*, supplement to the *New York Times*, January 7.

Erdos, P., S. Fajtlowicz, and W. Staton. (1991). Degree sequences in the triangle-free graphs. *Discrete Mathematics* 92(1): 85–88.

Ericsson, K. A., and H. A. Simon. (1993). *Protocol Analysis: Verbal Reports as Data*. Cambridge, Mass.: MIT Press.

Falkenhainer, B. C. (1990). A unified approach to explanation and theory formation. In J. Shrager and P. Langley, eds., *Computational Models of Scientific Discovery and Theory Formation*, pp. 157–196. San Mateo, Calif.: Morgan Kaufmann.

Fay, A. L., and D. Klahr. (1996). Knowing about guessing and guessing about knowing: preschoolers' understanding of indeterminacy. *Child Development* 67: 689–716.

Feist, G. J. (1991). *The Psychology of Science: Personality, Cognitive, Motivational and Working Styles of Eminent and Less Eminent Scientists*. Ph.D. dissertation, University of California at Berkeley.

Feist, G. J. (1994). Personality and working style predictors of integrative complexity: a study of scientists' thinking about research and teaching. *Journal of Personality and Social Psychology* 67: 474–484.

Feist, G. J., and M. E. Gorman. (1998). The psychology of science: review and integration of a nascent discipline. *Review of General Psychology* 2(1): 3–47.

Flavell, J. H. (1977). *Cognitive Development*. Englewood Cliffs, N.J.: Prentice-Hall.

Forbus, K. D., and D. Gentner. (1991). MAC/FAC: a model of similarity-based access and mapping. In K. J. Hammond and D. Gentner, eds., *Proceedings of the Thirteenth Annual Conference of the Cognitive Science Society*, pp. 504–509. Hillsdale, N.J.: Erlbaum.

Fromm, E. (1998). Lost and found half a century later: letters by Freud and Einstein. *American Psychologist* 53(11): 1195–1198.

Galison, P. (1987). *How Experiments End*. Chicago: University of Chicago Press.

Gentner, D. (1983). Structure-mapping: a theoretical framework for analogy. *Cognitive Science* 7: 155–170.

Gentner, D., and M. Jeziorski. (1989). Historical shifts in the use of analogy in science. In B. Gholson, W. Shadish, R. Beimeyer, and A. Houts, eds., *The Psychology of Science: Contributions to Metascience*, pp. 296–325. Cambridge: Cambridge University Press.

Gholson, B., M. Levine, and S. Phillips. (1972). Hypotheses, strategies, and stereotypes in discrimination learning. *Journal of Experimental Child Psychology* 13: 423–446.

Gick, M. L., and K. J. Holyoak. (1983). Schema induction and analogic transfer. *Cognitive Psychology* 15: 138.

Giere, R. N. (1988). *Explaining Science: A Cognitive Approach*. Chicago: University of Chicago Press.

Giere, R. N. (1993). Précis of cognitive models of science. *Psycoloquy* 4(56): <www.princeton.edu/~harnad/psyc.html>.

Gooding, D. (1990). *Experiment and the Making of Meaning*. Dordrecht: Nijhoff/Kluwer.

Gopnik, A. (1996). The scientist as child. *Philosophy of Science* 63(4):485–514.

Gorman, M. E. (1989). Error, falsification and scientific inference: An experimental investigation. *Quarterly Journal of Experimental Psychology* 41A(2): 385–412.

Gorman, M. E. (1992). *Simulating Science: Heuristics, Mental Models, and Technoscientific Thinking.* Bloomington: Indiana University Press.

Goswami, U. (1996). Analogical reasoning and cognitive development. *Advances in Child Development and Behavior* 26: 91–139.

Greeno, J. G. (1976). Cognitive objectives of instruction: theory of knowledge for solving problems and answering questions. In D. Klahr, ed., *Cognition and Instruction,* pp. 123–159. Hillsdale, N.J.: Erlbaum.

Groen, G. J. (1978). The theoretical ideas of Piaget and educational practice. In P. Suppes, ed., *Impact of Research in Education: Some Case Studies.* Washington, D.C.: National Academy of Education.

Gross, P. R., and N. Levitt. (1994). *Higher Superstition: The Academic Left and Its Quarrels with Science.* Baltimore: Johns Hopkins University Press.

Gruber, H. E. (1974). *Darwin on Man: A Psychological Study of Scientific Creativity.* New York: E. P. Dutton.

Hadamard, J. (1945). *The Psychology of Invention in the Mathematical Field.* New York: Dover.

Halford, G. S. (1992). Analogical reasoning and conceptual complexity in cognitive development. *Human Development* 35: 193–217.

Hayes-Roth, B., and F. Hayes-Roth. (1979). A cognitive model of planning. *Cognitive Science* 3: 275–310.

Hendrickson, J. B., and T. Sander. (1995). COGNOS: A Beilstein-type system for organizing organic reactions. *Journal of Chemical Information and Computer Sciences* 35(2): 251.

Holmes, F. L. (1985). *Lavoisier and the Chemistry of Life: An Exploration of Scientific Creativity.* Madison: University of Wisconsin Press.

Holyoak, K. J., and P. Thagard. (1995). *Mental Leaps: Analogy in Creative Thought.* Cambridge, Mass.: MIT Press.

Hovland, C., and E. Hunt. (1960). The computer simulation of concept attainment. *Behavioral Science* 5: 265–267.

Inhelder, B., and J. Piaget. (1958). *The Growth of Logical Thinking from Childhood to Adolescence.* New York: Basic Books.

Ippolito, M. F., and R. D. Tweney. (1995). The inception of insight. In R. J. Sternberg and J. E. Davidson, eds., *The Nature of Insight,* pp. 433–462. Cambridge, Mass.: MIT Press.

John-Steiner, V. (1997). *Notebooks of the Mind.* New York: Oxford University Press.

Judson, H. F. (1979). *The Eighth Day of Creation.* New York: Simon and Schuster.

Kaplan, C. A., and H. A. Simon. (1990). In search of insight. *Cognitive Psychology* 22: 374–419.

Karmiloff-Smith, A. (1988). A child is a theoretician, not an inductivist. *Mind and Language* 3: 183–195.

Karp, P. (1990). Hypothesis formation as design. In J. Shrager and P. Langley, eds., *Computational Models of Scientific Discovery and Theory Formation,* pp. 275–317. San Mateo, Calif.: Morgan Kaufmann.

Keil, F. C. (1981). Constraints on knowledge and cognitive development. *Psychological Review* 88: 197–227.

Kern, L. H., H. L. Mirels, and V. G. Hinshaw. (1983). Scientists' understanding of propositional logic: an experimental investigation. *Social Studies of Science* 13: 131–146.

King, M. L., Jr. (1963). *Strength to Love.* New York: Harper & Row.

Klahr, D. (1985). Solving problems with ambiguous subgoal ordering: preschoolers' performance. *Child Development* 56: 940–952.

Klahr, D. (1994). Searching for cognition in cognitive models of science. Psycoloquy 5(94): <www.princeton.edu/~harnad/psyc.html>.

Klahr, D., and S. M. Carver. (1988). Cognitive objectives in a LOGO debugging curriculum: instruction, learning, and transfer. *Cognitive Psychology* 20: 362–404.

Klahr, D., and S. M. Carver. (1995). Scientific thinking about scientific thinking. *Monographs of the Society for Research in Child Development* 245, Vol. 60, no. 3.

Klahr, D., and K. Dunbar. (1988). Dual space search during scientific reasoning. *Cognitive Science* 12: 1–55.

Klahr, D., K. Dunbar, and A. L. Fay. (1990). Designing good experiments to test bad hypotheses. In J. Shrager and P. Langley, eds., *Computational Models of Discovery and Theory Formation*, pp. 355–402. San Mateo, Calif.: Morgan Kaufmann.

Klahr, D., A. L. Fay, and K. Dunbar. (1993). Heuristics for scientific experimentation: a developmental study. *Cognitive Psychology* 24(1): 111–146.

Klahr, D., and M. Robinson. (1981). Formal assessment of problem solving and planning processes in preschool children. *Cognitive Psychology* 13: 113–148.

Klahr, D., and H. A. Simon. (1999). Studies of scientific discovery: complementary approaches and convergent findings. *Psychological Bulletin* 125: 524–543.

Klayman, J., and Y. Ha. (1987). Confirmation, disconfirmation and information in hypothesis testing. *Psychological Review* 94: 211–228.

Klayman, J., and Y. Ha. (1989). Hypothesis testing in rule discovery: strategy, structure, and content. *Journal of Experimental Psychology: Learning, Memory, and Cognition* 15(4): 596–604.

Kokar, M. M. (1986). Determining arguments of invariant functional descriptions. *Machine Learning* 1(4): 403–422.

Koslowski, B. (1996). *Theory and Evidence: The Development of Scientific Reasoning*. Cambridge, Mass.: MIT Press.

Koslowski, B., and L. Okagaki. (1986). Non-Humean indices of causation in problem-solving situations: causal mechanisms, analogous effects, and the status of rival alternative accounts. *Child Development* 57: 1100–1108.

Koslowski, B., L. Okagaki, C. Lorenz, and D. Umbach. (1989). When covariation is not enough: the role of causal mechanism, sampling method, and sample size in causal reasoning. *Child Development* 60: 1316–1327.

Krems, J., and T. R. Johnson. (1995). Integration of anomalous data in multicausal explanations. In J. D. Moore and J. F. Lehman, eds., *Proceedings of the Seventeenth Annual Conference of the Cognitive Science Society*, pp. 277–282. Mahwah, N.J.: Erlbaum.

Kuhn, D. (1989). Children and adults as intuitive scientists. *Psychological Review* 96: 674–689.

Kuhn, D. (1992). Piaget's child as scientist. In H. Beilin and P. Pufall, eds., *Piaget's Theory: Prospects and Possibilities*, pp. 185–208. Hillsdale, N.J.: Erlbaum.

Kuhn, D., E. Amsel, and M. O'Loughlin. (1988). *The Development of Scientific Reasoning Skills*. Orlando, Fla.: Academic Press.

Kuhn, D., and J. Angelev. (1976). An experimental study of the development of formal operational thought. *Child Development* 47: 697–706.

Kuhn, D., M. Garcia-Mila, A. Zohar, and C. Andersen. (1995). Strategies of knowledge acquisition. *Monographs of the Society for Research in Child Development* 60(4): pp. 1–128.

Kuhn, D., and E. Phelps. (1982). The development of problem-solving strategies. In H. Reese, ed., *Advances in Child Development and Behavior* Vol. 17, pp. 1–44. New York: Academic Press.

Kuhn, T. (1962). *The Structure of Scientific Revolutions*. Chicago: University of Chicago Press.

Kulkarni, D., and H. A. Simon. (1990). Experimentation in machine discovery. In J. Shrager and P. Langley, eds., *Computational Models of Scientific Discovery and Theory Formation*, pp. 255–273. San Mateo, Calif.: Morgan Kaufmann.

Lakatos, I., and A. Musgrave, eds. (1970). *Criticism and the Growth of Knowledge.* New York: Cambridge University Press.

Langley, P., H. A. Simon, G. L. Bradshaw, and J. M. Zytkow. (1987). *Scientific Discovery: Computational Explorations of the Creative Processes.* Cambridge, Mass.: MIT Press.

Larkin, J. H., J. McDermott, D. P. Simon, and H. A. Simon. (1980). Expert and novice performance in solving physics problems. *Science* 208: 1335–1342.

Latour, B., and S. Woolgar. (1986). *Laboratory Life: The Construction of Scientific Facts.* Princeton, N.J.: Princeton University Press.

Laudan, L. (1977). *Progress and Its Problems.* Berkeley: University of California Press.

Lovett, M. C., and J. R. Anderson. (1995). Making heads or tails out of selecting problem solving strategies. In J. D. Moore and J. F. Lehman, eds., *Proceedings of the Seventeenth Annual Conference of the Cognitive Science Society,* pp. 265–270. Hillsdale, N.J.: Erlbaum.

Lovett, M. C., and J. R. Anderson. (1996). History of success and current context in problem solving: combined influences on operator selection. *Cognitive Psychology* 31: 168–217.

Mahoney, M. J. (1979). Psychology of the scientist: an evaluative review. *Social Studies of Science* 9: 349–375.

Mahoney, M. J., and B. G. DeMonbreun. (1978). Psychology of the scientist: an analysis of problem-solving bias. *Cognitive Therapy and Research* 1(3): 229–238.

McCloskey, M. (1983). Naive theories of motion. In D. Gentner and A. L. Stevens, eds., *Mental Models,* pp. 299–324. Hillsdale, N.J.: Erlbaum.

Miller, G. A., E. Galanter, and K. Pribram. (1960). *Plans and the Structure of Behavior.* New York: Holt, Rinehart & Winston.

Minsky, M. (1975). *A Framework for Representing Knowledge: The Psychology of Computer Vision.* New York: McGraw-Hill.

Mitroff, L. L. (1974). *The Subjective Side of Science.* New York: Elsevier.

Mynatt, C. R., M. E. Doherty, and R. D. Tweney. (1977). Confirmation bias in a simulated research environment: an experimental study of scientific inference. *Quarterly Journal of Experimental Psychology* 29: 85–95.

Mynatt, C. R., M. E. Doherty, and R. D. Tweney. (1978). Consequences of confirmation and disconfirmation in a simulated research environment. *Quarterly Journal of Experimental Psychology* 30: 395–406.

Nersessian, N. J. (1992). How do scientists think? Capturing the dynamics of conceptual change in science. In R. N. Giere, ed., *Cognitive Models of Science,* pp. 3–44. Minneapolis: University of Minnesota Press.

Newell, A. (1973). You can't play 20 questions with nature and win: projective comments on the papers of this symposium. In W. G. Chase, ed., *Visual Information Processing,* pp. 283–308. New York: Academic Press.

Newell, A. (1990). *Unified Theories of Cognition.* Cambridge, Mass.: Harvard University Press.

Newell, A., J. C. Shaw, and H. A. Simon. (1958). Elements of a theory of human problem solving. *Psychological Review* 65: 151–166.

Newell, A., and H. A. Simon. (1972). *Human Problem Solving.* Englewood Cliffs, N.J.: Prentice-Hall.

Nordhausen, B., and P. Langley. (1993). An integrated framework for empirical discovery. *Machine Learning* 12: 17–47.

O'Brien, D. P., G. Costa, and W. F. Overton. (1986). Evaluations of causal and conditional hypotheses. *Quarterly Journal of Experimental Psychology* 38: 493–512.

Okada, T. (1994). *Collaborative Scientific Discovery Processes.* Ph.D. dissertation, Carnegie Mellon University.

Okada, T., and H. A. Simon. (1997). Collaborative discovery in a scientific domain. *Cognitive Science* 21: 109–146.

O'Rorke, P., S. Morris, and D. Schulenburg. (1990). Theory formation by abduction: a case study based on the chemical revolution. In J. Shrager and P. Langley, eds., *Computational Models of Scientific Discovery and Theory Formation*, pp. 197–224. San Mateo, Calif.: Morgan Kaufmann.

Papert, S. (1980). *Mindstorms: Children, Computers, and Powerful Ideas*. New York: Basic Books.

Penner, D., and D. Klahr. (1996a). The interaction of domain-specific knowledge and domain-general discovery strategies: a study with sinking objects. *Child Development* 67: 2709–2727.

Penner, D., and D. Klahr. (1996b). When to trust the evidence: further investigations of the effects of system error on the Wason 2-4-6 task. *Memory & Cognition* 24(5): 655–668.

Perkins, D. N. (1981). *The Mind's Best Work*. Cambridge, Mass.: Harvard University Press.

Piaget, J. (1952). *The Origins of Intelligence in Children*. New York: International University Press.

Pickering, A., ed. (1992). *Science as Practice and Culture*. Chicago: University of Chicago Press.

Pizzani, M. J. (1990). *Creating a Memory of Causal Relationships*. Hillsdale, N.J.: Erlbaum.

Poincaré, H. (1929). *The Foundation of Science*. New York: The Science Press.

Popper, K. R. (1959). *The Logic of Scientific Discovery*. London: Hutchinson.

Rajamoney, S. A. (1993). The design of discrimination experiments. *Machine Learning* 12: 185–203.

Rasmussen, J. (1981). Models of mental strategies in process plant diagnosis. In W. B. Rouse and J. Rasmussen, eds., *Human Detection and Diagnosis of System Failures*, pp. 241–258. New York: Plenum Press.

Reimann, P. (1990). *Problem Solving Models of Scientific Discovery Learning Processes*. Frankfurt am Main: Peter Lang.

Resnick, L. B., J. M. Levine, and S. D. Teasley. (1991). *Perspectives on Socially Shared Cognition*. Washington, D.C.: American Psychological Association.

Ross, B. H. (1984). Remindings and their effects in learning a cognitive skill. *Cognitive Psychology* 16: 371–416.

Rowe, A. (1953). *The Making of a Scientist*. New York: Dodd, Mead.

Ruffman, T., J. Perner, D. R. Olson, and M. Doherty. (1993). Reflecting on scientific thinking: children's understanding of the hypothesis-evidence relation. *Child Development* 64: 1617–1636.

Sadish, W. R., and S. Fuller, eds. (1994). *Social Psychology of Science*. New York: Guilford Press.

Samarapungavan, A. (1992). Children's judgments in theory-choice tasks: scientific rationality in childhood. *Cognition* 45: 1–32.

Schauble, L. (1990). Belief revision in children: the role of prior knowledge and strategies for generating evidence. *Journal of Experimental Child Psychology* 49: 31–57.

Schauble, L. (1996). The development of scientific reasoning in knowledge-rich contexts. *Developmental Psychology* 32(1): 102–119.

Schauble, L., and R. Glaser. (1990). Scientific thinking in children and adults. In D. Kuhn, ed., *Developmental Perspectives on Teaching and Learning Thinking Skills*, pp. 9–26. Basel and New York: Karger.

Schauble, L., R. Glaser, K. Raghavan, and M. Reiner. (1991). Causal models and experimentation strategies in scientific reasoning. *Journal of the Learning Sciences* 1: 201–238.

Schauble, L., L. E. Klopfer, and K. Raghavan. (1991). Students' transition from an engineering model to a science model of experimentation. *Journal of Research in Science Teaching* 28: 859–882.

Scholnick, E. K., and S. L. Friedman. (1987). The planning construct in the psychological literature. In S. L. Friedman, E. K. Scholnick, and R. R. Cocking, eds., *Blueprints for Thinking*, pp. 3–38. Cambridge: Cambridge University Press.

Schunn, C. D., and K. Dunbar. (1996). Priming, analogy, and awareness in complex reasoning. *Memory & Cognition* 24(3): 271–284.

Schunn, C. D., and D. Klahr. (1992). Complexity management in a discovery task. In J. K. Kruschke, ed., *Proceedings of the Fourteenth Annual Conference of the Cognitive Science Society*, pp. 177–182. Mahwah, N.J.: Erlbaum.

Schunn, C. D., and D. Klahr. (1993). Other vs. self-generated hypotheses in scientific discovery. In W. Kintsch, ed., *Proceedings of the Fifteenth Annual Meeting of the Cognitive Science Society*, p. 900. Mahwah, N.J.: Erlbaum.

Schunn, C. D., and D. Klahr. (1995). A 4-space model of scientific discovery. In J. D. Moore and J. F. Lehman, eds., *Proceedings of the Seventeenth Annual Conference of the Cognitive Science Society*, pp. 106–111. Mahwah, N.J.: Erlbaum.

Schunn, C. D., and D. Klahr. (1996). Integrated yet different: logical, empirical, and implementational arguments for a 4-space model of inductive problem solving. In G. Cottrell, ed., *Proceedings of the Eighteenth Annual Meeting of the Cognitive Science Society*, pp. 25–26. Mahwah, N.J.: Erlbaum.

Schuster, M. L. (1940). *A Treasury of the World's Great Letters from Ancient Days to Our Own Time*. New York: Simon and Schuster.

Scott, P. D., and S. Markovitch. (1993). Experience selection and problem choice in an exploratory learning system. *Machine Learning* 12: 49–67.

Shaklee, H., and D. Paszek. (1985). Covariation judgment: systematic rule use in middle childhood. *Child Development* 56: 1229–1240.

Shen, W. M. (1993). Discovery as autonomous learning from the environment. *Machine Learning* 12: 143–165.

Shrager, J. (1985). *Instructionless Learning: Discovery of the Mental Model of a Complex Device*. Ph.D. dissertation, Carnegie Mellon University.

Shrager, J. (1987). Theory change via view application in instructionless learning. *Machine Learning* 2: 247–276.

Shrager, J., and P. Langley, eds. (1990). *Computational Models of Scientific Discovery and Theory Formation*. San Mateo, Calif.: Morgan Kaufmann.

Siegler, R. S. (1976). Three aspects of cognitive development. *Cognitive Psychology* 8: 481–520.

Siegler, R. S. (1987). The perils of averaging data over strategies: an example from children's addition. *Journal of Experimental Psychology* 116: 250–264.

Siegler, R. S. (1996). *Emerging Minds: The Process of Change in Children's Thinking*. New York: Oxford University Press.

Siegler, R. S., and E. Jenkins. (1989). *How Children Discover New Strategies*. Hillsdale, N.J.: Erlbaum.

Siegler, R. S., and R. M. Liebert. (1975). Acquisition of formal scientific reasoning by 10- and 13-year-olds: designing a factorial experiment. *Developmental Psychology* 10: 401–402.

Simon, H. A. (1966). Scientific discovery and the psychology of problem solving. In R. Colony, ed., *Mind and Cosmos*, pp. 22–40. Pittsburgh: University of Pittsburgh Press.

Simon, H. A. (1975). The functional equivalence of problem-solving skills. *Cognitive Psychology* 7: 268–288.

Simon, H. A. (1977). *Models of Discovery*. Dordrecht: Reidel.

Simon, H. A. (1983). Understanding the processes of science: the psychology of scientific discovery. In T. Gamelius, ed., *Progress in Science and its Social Conditions*, pp. 159–170. Oxford: Pergamon.

Simon, H. A., and K. Kotovsky. (1963). Human acquisition of concepts for sequential patterns. *Psychological Review* 70(6): 534–546.

Simon, H. A., P. Langley, and G. L. Bradshaw. (1981). Scientific discovery as problem solving. *Synthese* 47: 1–27.

Simon, H. A., and G. Lea. (1974). Problem solving and rule induction: a unified view. In L. Gregg, ed., *Knowledge and Cognition*, pp. 105–128. Hillsdale, N.J.: Lawrence Erlbaum Associates.

Skinner, B. F. (1956). A case history in scientific method. *The American Psychologist* 11: 221–233.

Sloutsky, V. M., A. W. Rader, and B. J. Morris. (1998). Increasing informativeness and reducing ambiguities: adaptive strategies in human information processing. In M. A. Gernsbacher and S. J. Derry, eds., *Proceedings of the Twentieth Annual Conference of the Cognitive Science Society*, pp. 997–1002. Mahwah, N.J.: Erlbaum.

Sodian, B., D. Zaitchik, and S. Carey. (1991). Young children's differentiation of hypothetical beliefs from evidence. *Child Development* 62: 753–766.

Sokal, A. (1996). Transgressing the boundaries: towards a transformative hermeneutics of quantum gravity. *Social Text* 46/47: 217–252.

Teasley, S. D. (1995). The role of talk in children's peer collaborations. *Developmental Psychology* 31: 207–220.

Terman, L. M. (1954). Scientists and nonscientists in a group of 800 men. *Psychological Monographs* 68, no. 378.

Thagard, P. (1989). Explanatory coherence. *Behavioral and Brain Sciences* 12: 435–502.

Thagard, P. (1992). *Conceptual Revolutions*. Princeton, N.J.: Princeton University Press.

Thagard, P. (1997). Medical analogies: why and how. In M. G. Shafto and P. Langley, eds., *Proceedings of the Nineteenth Annual Meeting of the Cognitive Science Society*, pp. 739–763. Mahwah, N.J.: Erlbaum.

Thagard, P. (1998). Ulcers and bacteria I: discovery and acceptance. *Studies in the History and Philosophy of Biology and Biomedical Sciences* 29: 107–136.

Tschirgi, J. E. (1980). Sensible reasoning: a hypothesis about hypotheses. *Child Development* 51: 1–10.

Tumblin, A., and B. Gholson. (1981). Hypothesis theory and the development of conceptual learning. *Psychological Bulletin* 90: 102–124.

Tweney, R. D. (1990). Five questions for computationalists. In J. Shrager and P. Langley, eds., *Computational Models of Discovery and Theory Formation*, pp. 471–484. San Mateo, Calif.: Morgan Kaufmann.

Tweney, R. D., M. E. Doherty, and C. R. Mynatt, eds. (1981). *On Scientific Thinking*. New York: Columbia University Press.

Udea, K. (1997). Actual use of analogies in remarkable scientific discoveries. In M. G. Shafto and P. Langley, eds., *Proceedings of the Nineteenth Annual Meeting of the Cognitive Science Society*, pp. 763–768. Mahwah, N.J.: Erlbaum.

Valdés-Pérez, R. E. (1994a). Conjecturing hidden entities via simplicity and conservation laws: machine discovery in chemistry. *Artificial Intelligence* 65(2): 247–280.

Valdés-Pérez, R. E. (1994b). Algebraic reasoning about reactions: discovery of conserved properties in particle physics. *Machine Learning* 17(1): 47–68.

Valdés-Pérez, R. E. (1994c). Human/computer interactive elucidation of reaction mechanisms: application to catalyzed hydrogenolysis of ethane. *Catalysis Letters* 28(1): 79–87.

Valdés-Pérez, R. E. (1995). Some recent human/computer discoveries in science and what accounts for them. *Artificial Intelligence* 16(3): 37–44.

Vosniadou, S., and W. F. Brewer. (1992). Mental models of the earth: a study of conceptual change in childhood. *Cognitive Psychology* 24: 535–585.

Vosniadou, S., and W. F. Brewer. (1994). Mental models of the day/night cycle. *Cognitive Science* 18: 123–183.

Ward, S. L., and W. F. Overton. (1990). Semantic familiarity, relevance, and the development of deductive reasoning. *Developmental Psychology* 26(3): 488–493.

Wason, P. C. (1960). On the failure to eliminate hypotheses in a conceptual task. *Quarterly Journal of Experimental Psychology* 12: 129–140.

Wason, P. C. (1968). Reasoning about a rule. *Quarterly Journal of Experimental Psychology* 20: 273–281.

Weisberg, R. W. (1993). *Creativity: Beyond the Myth of Genius*. New York: W. H. Freeman.

Wellman, H. M. (1983). Metamemory revisited. In M. T. H. Chi, ed., *Trends in Memory Development Research*, pp. 31–51. New York: Karger.

Wellman, H. M., and S. Gelman. (1992). Cognitive development: foundational theories of core domains. *Annual Review of Psychology* 43: 337–375.

Wertheimer, M. (1945). *Productive Thinking.* (Reprint, 1959.) New York: Harper & Row.

Wickelgren, W. A. (1974). *How to Solve Problems: Elements of a Theory of Problems and Problem Solving*. San Francisco: W. H. Freeman.

Wiser, M. (1989). Does learning science involve theory change? Paper presented at the biannual meeting of the Society for Research in Child Development, Kansas City.

Wolf, D. F., and J. R. Beskin. (1996). Task domains in N-space models: giving explanation its due. In G. Cottrell, ed., *Proceedings of the Eighteenth Annual Meeting of the Cognitive Science Society*, pp. 27–28. Mahwah, N.J.: Erlbaum.

Author Index

Subject Index